NEW APPROACHES TO JESUS AND THE GOSPELS

NEW APPROACHES TO JESUS AND THE GOSPELS

A PHENOMENOLOGICAL AND EXEGETICAL STUDY OF SYNOPTIC CHRISTOLOGY

ROYCE GORDON GRUENLER

BAKER BOOK HOUSE
Grand Rapids, Michigan 49506

Contents

Preface

In their recent festschrift, *Christological Perspectives: Essays in Honor of Harvey K. McArthur*,[1] Robert Berkey and Sarah Edwards, the editors, have drawn together some challenging essays from contemporary biblical scholars on an issue of central importance to New Testament exegesis and to the vitality of Christian faith today. There is wide theological diversity among the contributors to the volume, but one point Berkey makes well is that interest in Christology is stronger than ever, due perhaps among biblical scholars to the fact that the basic question "Where did it all begin?" is the most important unresolved issue in the christological debate. Did Christology have its birth in Jesus' historic self-awareness, or is it essentially a product of the post-resurrection Christian community? Much present-day research is governed by the Bultmannian emphasis on the christological creativity of the early church, and an attitude of skepticism hangs over the possibility of confronting the intentionality of Jesus. On the other hand, important studies by C. F. D. Moule, I. H. Marshall, and Martin Hengel are representative of a more positive approach and are indicative of a renewed appreciation of the traditional view that Christology began with Jesus himself. Critical methodology alone does not seem able to resolve the issue, however.

Recent interests in some quarters have returned to a modified turn-of-the-century sociological approach to Jewish and Hellenistic backgrounds to New Testament christological titles. But the situation is very open, with opinion tending toward Judaic and Jewish-Christian settings as prelude to a proper understanding of the historical Jesus. Berkey makes a perceptive observation that "if those earliest layers encompass even the possibility of a 'divine nature' Christology, then it is simply not possible to dismiss summarily those higher christological affirma-

1. (New York: Pilgrim Press, 1982).

tions from the historical Jesus himself."[2] Very cautiously he advances his modest hope that with new discoveries and new methods we will continue to be forced back to the christological drawing board, though he is more confident that the once-for-all claim of faith in Christ will never be wholly supported or proved by any historical consensus of critical scholarship.

I could mention other recent works that signal "a little cloud like a man's hand . . . rising out of the sea" (I Kings 18:44) to end the drought that Bultmannian exegesis has inflicted upon gospel research in the last two generations, but one more title will do in this brief preface, though I will name dozens more in the main body of the text. John Riches, in *Jesus and the Transformation of Judaism*,[3] cautiously allows the hitherto forbidden subject of Jesus' intentionality to be mentioned again in scholarly circles. While the results of his fascinating study are much too tentative (New Testament scholars have a habit of looking over their shoulders at other New Testament scholars when running), Riches is on the right track when he writes of Jesus' consciousness "that the judgement and forgiveness which is mediated through his words and actions is not simply an announcement of what is to come but *is* already the reality and power of God";[4] and, "moreover, Jesus in thus embodying or symbolizing the way of forgiving love, pointed to himself not simply as an example for men to follow, or as a source of inspiration for them, but as the very point where God's love meets them: Whoever is ashamed of me and of my words. . . ."[5]

Suffice it to say that I have myself been forced back in recent years to the drawing board, to the Gospels themselves, and to a re-examination of Jesus' words and works with the tools of language analysis I know best. I feel more assured than ever that what we have in the gospel accounts are authentic portraits of Jesus the founder of Christianity, whose spoken and acted language discloses a high christological consciousness that firmly establishes the foundation of New Testament Christology. It remains for the reader to follow my analysis and make up his or her own mind about its validity. Much is at stake in the outcome of our christological convictions, less indeed for the sake of biblical scholarship than for Christian faith itself.

2. *Christological Perspectives*, p. 18.
3. (London: Darton, Longman & Todd, 1980).
4. *Jesus and the Transformation of Judaism*, p. 184. His italics.
5. *Ibid.*, p. 188.

In any undertaking of this kind many persons make important contributions along the way. I am most grateful to my wife and children for their supportive compassion for a scholarly husband and father. A happy and peaceful home makes research and writing a deep satisfaction indeed. Faculty colleagues and administration at Gordon-Conwell Theological Seminary were generous in encouraging me to take a sabbatical in 1981 to bring the manuscript to completion, and for that I am grateful. Secretarial help has been invaluable, and I want to pay tribute to Kathleen Horak and Shari Hobby, my typists, and to my Byington Fellows Wendy Zoba (who transcribed much of my handwritten copy) and David Aune (who gave valuable aid in proofreading).

I express my gratitude to Linda Triemstra, project editor for Baker Book House, for her wise suggestions and expert help in bringing the book to completion.

Royce Gordon Gruenler
Gordon-Conwell Theological Seminary

Introduction

The present study offers my modest, though I hope imaginative, reflections on several new and promising approaches to Jesus and the Gospels that have meant a great deal to me over the past few years — since in fact I had a change of personal commitment from a former liberalism which had run dry to the rediscovery of the vitality of my earlier evangelical heritage. This rediscovery of "a happy dwelling place of the human mind," to borrow Michael Polanyi's apt expression, prompts me to offer to the reader seven creative thinkers of modern times who saw many things correctly and who may serve as helpful guides to understanding Jesus and the Gospels in a new way.

If I were to place each of the seven on a scale of personal commitment to biblical faith, Ludwig Wittgenstein would not appear very far up the graph. Yet his hermeneutical insights, when applied to Jesus and the Gospels "from the outside and obliquely," as it were, offer a valuable corrective to a good deal of modern critical thought that is so taken up with the (I think mistaken) notion of impersonal analysis that it can no longer "look and see" who the Jesus of the Gospels really is. Wittgenstein says we must once again focus on the person who stands back of his spoken and acted language, that is, on the one who personally indwells his words and acts. I am pleased to see that Anthony C. Thiselton's recent study, *The Two Horizons* (Grand Rapids: Eerdmans, 1980), also holds the later Wittgenstein in considerable esteem as a valuable tool for biblical studies, though his application is different from mine and does not concentrate on the person of Jesus. I find Thiselton's work confirmatory, though I am less happy with his adoption of Hans-Georg Gadamer's notion of the two horizons, which seems to me to place more weight on the right of the interpreter than on the prerogative of Jesus and the evangelists to establish the canonical tradition of revelation and redemption. Yet Thiselton's study begs careful

11

reading for its compendious research on Martin Heidegger, Rudolf Bultmann, and Gadamer, as well as Wittgenstein.

Several other recent studies have substantially confirmed the direction of my thinking since my return to evangelical theology. Ben F.
Meyer's *The Aims of Jesus* (London: SCM, 1979) not only speaks boldly
once again of the intention of Jesus who generates a tradition and establishes a normative horizon for posterity, but it also challenges two
doctrines of modernity which I take to be the most problematic in
present-day gospel criticism. The first is the unimaginative and unbiblical notion that the world is closed to the miraculous and supernatural,
while the second is equally characteristic of our "chronological snobbery," namely, that the past must be interpreted largely in terms of the
present.

As an antidote to these modern doctrines, I. T. Ramsey's disquisition
on the validity of the "logically odd" in the Scriptures is healthy and
even entertaining. Unlike Wittgenstein, Ramsey writes "from within"
the gospel story, as do C. S. Lewis and J. R. R. Tolkien, who are among
my favorites because they have such a deep appreciation of the archetypal world transposed upon our own in which marvelous things occur,
foremost of course the grand miracle of Jesus and his story. Lewis also
serves to remind the gospel interpreter that the first question of criticism ought not to be, "How did it *really* happen?" or "Is it a good work
of art?" but "What kind of reader are you?" His reply is that the really
good reader or interpreter of the work of art is attentive and obedient
to the story, gets inside it, and sees it from within. I am convinced that
this is especially true of gospel interpretation and that few scholars
achieve this goal. Much gospel criticism simply lacks imagination and
belief; and for that reason the modern-day hermeneut could hardly do
better than immerse himself in the imaginative theology of Lewis to see
what a truly germinal mind can do with old themes.

Polanyi, though too Tillichian for my tastes when he touches on
theology, is Augustinian in epistemology and serves up the final coup
de grâce to the modern doctrine of impersonal objectivism, making, I
think, an incontrovertible case that words by themselves mean nothing,
but convey meaning only as they are used and accredited by persons
in commitment situations. All knowledge is personal knowledge in the
Augustinian sense of "I believe in order that I may understand" (so also
Cornelius Van Til). All persons speak and act in some setting of conviviality and trust, working from tacit beliefs toward focal projects. The
proposition is much like Wittgenstein's description of personal lan-

guage-games and forms of life, though more systematically developed, and is such an obvious truth that one ought to be embarrassed to mention it, except that our post-Enlightenment period has fallen into forgetfulness about the priority of persons in human discourse.

All these novel ways of speaking old truths have an important bearing on the rediscovery of Jesus in the Gospels and on opening up his words and works, indeed his person, to a direct phenomenological meeting — for in a person's language we meet the intentional person himself. As to how much of the language of the Gospels is Jesus' own and not created by the enthusiastic but unhistorical visions of early Christian prophets, another quiet revolution is occuring in perceptive quarters of gospel scholarship. David Hill's study on *New Testament Prophecy* (Atlanta: John Knox, 1980) has laid to rest the convenient doctrine of radical gospel criticism, required by the presuppositions of Bultmann and his school, that such activity on the part of early Christian prophets was widespread. Surprisingly that is not the case, and there is hardly any evidence to support the theory. Hill draws attention "to the immense difficulties that belong to the attempt to decide which sayings derive from prophets," as well as to the questionable presuppositions that underlie the decision. I will have occasion to refer extensively to Hill's thesis in part 1 of my study.

The way is now open to re-examine the Gospels again with a more open hermeneutic, attentive in true phenomenological fashion to the text, bracketing unbiblical presuppositions, and allowing Jesus to speak and act as creative person in the gospel story. It all anticipates an exciting era in gospel studies to which I hope this volume makes some contribution as a primer for promising approaches to Jesus and the Gospels. A word concerning important names not included in my list might be in order, in the event, as is likely, the reader may miss his favorite author. If the book were longer, I would have included Edmund Husserl, E. D. Hirsch, Gadamer, Thiselton, and probably Morton Kelsey, who does fascinating things with the third dimension of the supernatural. I have omitted mentioning process hermeneutics, mainly because I have a separate critique of the school prepared, which explains my reasons for rejecting this initially attractive but ultimately unbiblical naturalism which is more neo-Buddhist than neo-Christian. For the present, the seven hermeneuts I have offered in this volume constitute a good main course with a bit of dessert, a hearty meal for a beginning. Other courses may be presented later if the appetite of the guest has been sufficiently whetted.

Above all, I want the reader to know that my primary concern in this study is exegetical, for I write as a New Testament interpreter with the conviction that the Gospels come alive when we approach them openly and expectantly and with the simple intention of sharing the faith of the evangelists who wrote them and who bear witness to their real author, Jesus, the central figure of the story.

In part 1 I employ a phenomenology of persons to highlight the fundamental claims of Jesus, working with an agreed-upon core of authentic sayings that gives radical and conservative critics a starting point for debate. The methodology employed in this section is admittedly a surface phenomenology, since it can only take us as far as the claims that Jesus makes for himself through his speech and acts. The direction of exegesis here is from the outside in. Part 2 engages the text from the inside out, introducing hermeneutical approaches which, though varied, agree that a deep phenomenology can be achieved only when the phenomenon being described (in this case the person of Jesus and his claims) is confronted with belief and commitment on the part of the interpreter. Reluctance or failure to move beyond surface grammar to depth grammar will force the critic of the Gospels to misconstrue their intent, while the interpreter who is genuinely open to Jesus as person through faith and commitment will discover the inner truth of the story and its deeper dimensions. This is the posture Polanyi describes as fiduciary and heuristic and is, I am convinced, the only truly scientific access we have to Jesus and the Christian story he embodies in his words and acts. This approach is utterly and genuinely phenomenological because it allows Jesus to be who he is, and the evangelists to be who they are as they present their portraits of Jesus in the context of belief.

The principal result of this study is its discovery that the external application of radical critical methods to the Gospels, when combined with a rigorous phenomenology of persons, yields convincing evidence that Jesus' concept of himself is so incredible on any human level that it becomes academic to insist on separating his implicit from his explicit christological claims. Hence the use of redaction criticism to distinguish the two sets of sayings I take to be misguided because of an improper methodology and a faulty phenomenology of persons. If my argument is sound, redaction analysis should be limited to describing the nuances of portraiture that are evidenced in the four Gospels, as the evangelists describe from their complementary angles of vision the many-sided meaning of Jesus, who discloses himself in variegated patterns of speech and behavior. A basic unity of Jesus as person pervades the four Gospels, while their diversity evidences the inexhaustible richness of his complexity — like a jewel of many facets that reflects its beauty in multiple planes and may be viewed from as many perspectives.

I hope this study will generate some dialogue among New Testament scholars regarding methodology and the widely recognized failure of biblical criticism as generally practiced to produce assured results and to serve the church constructively. I anticipate a good deal of protest from the radical side, and even from some evangelical quarters, over my reformulation of the scope and limitations of redaction criticism; but on the basis of the investigation in part 1, which I hope represents a new application of a phenomenology of persons to exegesis, I honestly cannot say that I find a single explicit christological utterance of Jesus in the Gospels, including the Gospel of John, that is generically inappropriate to his implicit claims arrived at by the criterion of dissimilarity. "What sort of person would make such claims and act in such a manner?" has been the guiding question of my research. The answer, following Wittgenstein's invitation to "look and see," has emerged from the phenomena of Jesus' form of life and language-game and has shaken my former liberal assumptions about Jesus and the Gospels and how biblical criticism ought to function.

I anticipate the rejoinder, "What else would we expect from an evangelical Neutestamentler but a conservative appraisal of the data?" But I hasten to assure the reader that it was the investigation of the data themselves that led me to adopt an evangelical posture (having long before forsaken it) as the natural outcome of my inquiry. My hope, then, extends beyond the initial opening of dialogue over New Testament hermeneutics and exegesis to a desire that the reader might rediscover, as I have, something of the vitality of New Testament faith that centers upon that Person who consciously intended what he, with the Father and the Spirit, accomplished — the gracious forgiveness of sins and the reconciliation of sinners at open table-fellowship in the inaugurated kingdom of God.

List of Abbreviations

BS	Bibliotheca Sacra
CBQ	Catholic Biblical Quarterly
JBL	Journal of Biblical Literature
JBR	Journal of Bible and Religion
JETS	Journal of the Evangelical Theological Society
JR	Journal of Religion
IDB	The Interpreter's Dictionary of the Bible
NTS	New Testament Studies
SJT	Scottish Journal of Theology
Theol.	Theology
ThT	Theology Today
ThZ	Theologische Zeitschrift
WTJ	Westminster Theological Journal
ZNW	Zeitschrift für die neutestamentliche Wissenschaft und die Kunde der älteren Kirche

Part One

A Phenomenology
from the Outside In

1

Implied Christological Claims in the Core Sayings of Jesus
An Application of Ludwig Wittgenstein's Phenomenology

Since the phenomenology of Martin Heidegger has gained such wide influence in New Testament hermeneutics, principally through the influence of the word-event school (Rudolf Bultmann and his followers), there has been a noticeable loss of interest in the intention and horizon of Jesus as person. The focus of gospel studies seems to have shifted away from the creative words and acts of Jesus (except for studies in the parables) to language that is claimed to have independent and anonymous status within the early church. Redactional research has shifted its interest to the intention of the gospel writers, but even those writers seem to be shrouded in relative ambiguity in view of their traditions, sociological settings, and audiences.

In this study I will offer a promising methodology that may help us to recover Jesus' intention to generate a new tradition. This analysis examines the ordinary discourse of spoken and acted language and describes how persons do in fact stand in back of their words and acts, and how these words and acts disclose the intention of the persons who indwell them. The implications of a phenomenology of persons to Jesus' self-concept are considerable for gospel research, and especially for determining the extent of pre-Easter Christology.

The Method

This largely unexplored hermeneutical approach to Jesus as person is available to New Testament scholarship in Ludwig Wittgenstein's gnomic descriptions of our use of language. For him, personal words and acts are not ostensive references to an inaccessible third-person fact or thing that lies hidden behind them, but disclosures of the person himself who is speaking and acting with the backing of his own first-

19

person personal pronoun *I*. Against a third-person paradigm that encourages the assimilation of a person to thing-language, Wittgenstein explores the persistence of the first-person personal pronoun *I* as an important clue to the intentionality and uniqueness of the person who indwells his linguistic "form of life." My application of this hermeneutic to Jesus' form of life will focus upon his use of the first-person personal pronoun *I* and its verbal equivalents as a significant clue to his unique intentionality, as he gives personal backing and signature to his spoken and acted language.

Wittgenstein's primary concern in his later stage of thought in the *Philosophical Investigations* is to investigate ordinary discourse where persons as subjects preside. He wants to guard against the modern tendency to treat the knower either as a thing or as a passive recipient, or as both, which brackets out the function of the knower himself. A modern fascination with speech has mesmerized scholarship to such an extent that it tends to apotheosize language by focusing on speech apart from persons speaking. Hence the personal dimension of language disappears and things begin to be separated from their names. Wittgenstein is concerned about this reductionism and the skepticism with which the modern specialist tends to reduce everything to impersonal abstractions, forsaking the word for the sign and the person for the notation.

As my former colleague Dallas High has remarked of the later Wittgenstein, all the form-making activity of language is a reality in which persons define and extend themselves. Language is inseparable from the person who uses it. It is not a closed system independent of selves as speakers and hearers:

> When, for example, I use a form of words, I am dwelling in that form of words, and giving my personal signature to them. Insofar as you hear what I am saying and understand what I mean, you may be said to be dwelling in that form of words, too. Without personal, human indwelling, language is no longer living and concrete speech. . . .[1]

The later Wittgenstein has reminded us that language, like all form-making activity, is grounded in its civil status, in personal subscription,

---

1. Dallas High, *Language, Persons, and Belief: Studies in Wittgenstein's "Philosophical Investigations" and Religious Uses of Language* (New York: Oxford University Press, 1967), p. 22.

because it is as human beings that we participate in the activity of speaking and hearing. It is a simple and obvious truth that persons indwell their language, but the fact is often overlooked.

> What we are supplying are really remarks on the natural history of human beings: we are not contributing curiosities however, but observations which no one has doubted, but which has escaped remark only because they are always before our eyes.[2]

Wittgenstein reminds us with penetrating perception that the meaning of language is closely tied together with the use a person makes of that language. Without assuming that everything is exhausted by the formula that meaning equals use, we may allow that Wittgenstein has hold of an important truth that can lend considerable help in the search to understand Jesus' intention and meaning through his use of language:

> Every sign *by itself* seems dead. What gives it life? — In use it is *alive.*
> Is life breathed into it there? — Or is the *use* its life?[3]

How, then, does Jesus *use* language? This question will be uppermost as I explore Wittgenstein's descriptive phenomenology of a person speaking and acting out his language-game and form of life. First, he says, we must rid ourselves of the misleading notion that meanings are things, that words refer to objects, that language is an object in that it asserts or denies impersonal *facts*. This referential theory of meaning is lifeless. It is rather a person's act of intending meaning by speaking in words and gestures that lies at the center of the forms of life. A person indwells his words when he speaks and acts, and without that indwelling no meaning or understanding is possible. Wittgenstein gives a homely example:

> There is a gulf between an order and its execution. It has to be filled by the act of understanding.
>
> Only in the act of understanding is it meant that we are to do THIS. The *order* — why, that is nothing but sounds, inkmarks.[4]

2. Ludwig Wittgenstein, *Philosophical Investigations*, trans. G. E. M. Anscombe (New York: Macmillan, 1953), para. 415.

3. *Ibid.*, para. 432. His italics.

4. *Ibid.*, para. 431. His italics.

That is to say, language is not simply a matter of learning to name *things*, as though there were a one-to-one correspondence between *words* and *things* without reference to persons who give them meaning. Rather, language is learning and indicating how I as a person disclose my form of life to other persons when I speak and act, and how another person's form of life is revealed when he speaks and acts before me. Hence, "to imagine a language means to imagine a form of life."[5]

All of this assumes the inadequacy of a referential word-object theory of language, though this theory is widely employed in current New Testament studies, for the theory pretends that proper historical research consists in lining up historical data that correspond to certain impersonal "facts" — for example, the *language* of Jesus, with little concern for Jesus as author of that language. The verifiability theory of language also comes under the scrutiny of Wittgenstein's critical eye, since it makes scientific discourse normative and assumes that language functions primarily objectively and can be tested without reference to personal intentionality. In fact, Wittgenstein is saying, no single theory suffices to account for the forms of personal language in all their complexity. But what *is* always present is the person, thinking and speaking and acting in discourse with other persons within the richly variegated forms of life: ". . . the lesson to be borne in mind is that no one form of speech is fundamental or primary and that no one form in itself has any priority over another."[6]

This falls hard against the modern penchant for abstract analysis, which prejudices us against the personal components in our language-games. Wittgenstein illustrates this by referring to a pointing arrow, observing that "the arrow points only in the application that a living being makes of it."[7] Accordingly, he is saying, words have significant meaning only as they are used and appropriated by *persons.* This is not to identify meaning exhaustively with use, but to underscore that meaning inevitably points to the bearer of meaning, to the first-person personal pronoun *I*, to the one who is intending, saying, doing something. Language is personally accredited action:

> One cannot guess how a word functions. One has to *look at* its use and learn from that.[8]

5. *Ibid.*, para. 19.
6. High, *Language, Persons, and Belief*, p. 54.
7. *Philosophical Investigations*, para. 454.
8. *Ibid.*, para. 340. His italics.

Yes: meaning something is like going up to someone.[9]

It is the user of language who is primary, for he indwells his words with personal intentionality and meaning.

The following excerpts provide additional insight into Wittgenstein's description of the phenomenon "I," which is disclosed in personal speech and behavior. There is need, he says, for a protophenomenology of the language-game:

> Our mistake is to look for an explanation where we ought to look at what happens as a "proto-phenomenon". That is, where we ought to have said: *this language-game is played*.[10]

Personal intentionality is revealed in saying and doing:

> Why do I want to tell him about an intention too, as well as telling him what I did? — Not because the intention was also something which was going on at that time. But because I want to tell him something about *myself*, which goes beyond what happened at that time.[11]

> I reveal to him something of myself when I tell him what I was going to do. — Not, however, on grounds of self-observation, but by way of a response (it might also be called an intuition).[12]

Revealing oneself and observing another occurs in the context of story or language-game; when entered, the story discloses the meaning of what a person is saying and doing:

> If I say "I meant *him*" very likely a picture comes to my mind, perhaps of how I looked at him, etc.; but the picture is only like an illustration to a story. From it alone it would mostly be impossible to conclude anything at all; only when one knows the story does one know the significance of the picture.[13]

In the telling of a story Wittgenstein distinguishes between the surface grammar of syntax and the depth grammar of meaning:

9. *Ibid.*, para. 457.
10. *Ibid.*, para. 654. His italics.
11. *Ibid.*, para. 656. His italics.
12. *Ibid.*, para. 659. His italics.
13. *Ibid.*, para. 663. His italics.

In the use of words one might distinguish "surface grammar" from "depth grammar". What immediately impresses itself upon us about the use of a word is the way it is used in the construction of the sentence, the part of its use — one might say — that can be taken in by the ear. — And now compare the depth grammar, say of the word "to mean", and what its surface grammar would lead us to suspect. No wonder we find it difficult to know our way about.[14]

If too much of our scholarly activity seems to take place on the level of surface grammar, the role of teaching by example of master with disciple becomes the key to the meaning of depth grammar:

Is it correct for someone to say: "When I gave you this rule, I meant you to . . . in this case"? Even if he did not think of this case at all as he gave the rule? Of course it is correct. For "to mean it" did not mean: to think of it. But now the problem is: how are we to judge whether someone meant such-and-such? — The fact that he has, for example, mastered a particular technique in arithmetic and algebra, and that he taught someone else the expansion of a series in the usual way, is such a criterion.[15]

This leads Wittgenstein to comment that what is presupposed in tacit commitment, namely, personal intention, is what makes sense of our language-game.

"But then they make a tacit presupposition." Then what we do in our language-game always rests on a tacit presupposition.[16]

This is similar to Michael Polanyi's description of the tacit component.[17]

Moreover, for the language-game to work and personal discourse to be possible, it is important that persons speak and act consistently "in character." This is a very important point to remember when we seek to establish the underlying characteristics of Jesus' form of life and compare the continuity of his tacit and explicit christological utterances:

14. *Ibid.*, para. 664.
15. *Ibid.*, para. 692.
16. *Ibid.*, 2.5, p. 179.
17. *Personal Knowledge: Towards a Post-Critical Philosophy* (New York: Harper & Row, 1964), pp. 69–245; *The Tacit Dimension* (New York: Doubleday, 1966), pp. 1–25.

Closely associated things, things which we *have* associated, seem to fit one another. But what is this seeming to fit? How is their seeming to fit manifested? Perhaps like this: We cannot imagine the man who had this name, this face, this handwriting, not to have produced *these* works, but perhaps quite different ones instead (those of another great man).

We cannot imagine it? Do we try? —

Here is a possibility: I hear that someone is painting a picture "Beethoven writing the ninth symphony". I could easily imagine the kind of thing such a picture would shew us. But suppose someone wanted to represent what Goethe would have looked like writing the ninth symphony? Here I could imagine nothing that would not be embarrassing and ridiculous.[18]

Accordingly, if we can establish a characteristic self-understanding of Jesus through his form of life or language-game, as disclosed in undisputed sayings and acts, we should be able to test disputed material against the undisputed. This is what I will attempt to do presently.

Wittgenstein also parallels Polanyi's phenomenology of persons in yet another sense: To say "I . . ." is to say "I believe, I am committed to this . . . ," thus revealing my own intentionality, *myself*:

One can mistrust one's own sense, but not one's own belief.

If there were a verb meaning "to believe falsely", it would not have any significant first person present indicative.

The language of reporting can be given such a turn that a report is not meant to inform the hearer about its subject matter but about the person making the report.[19]

"I believe . . ." throws light on my state. Conclusions about my conduct can be drawn from this expression. So there is a *similarity* here to expressions of emotion, of mood, etc.[20]

To say "I believe" is to say "I intend this statement to be true":

If, however, "I believe it is so" throws light on my state, then so does the assertion "It is so". For the sign "I believe" can't do it, can at the most hint at it.[21]

18. Wittgenstein, *Philosophical Investigations*, 2.6, p. 183.
19. *Ibid.*, 2.10, p. 190.
20. *Ibid.*, 2.10, p. 191. His italics.
21. *Ibid.*

I don't say of myself "I seem to believe"; I use the word *seem* only of someone else. I do not infer my own conviction; I feel conviction; I feel conviction within myself:

> This is how I think of it: Believing is a state of mind. . . . So it is a kind of disposition of the believing person.[22]

To say "I believe falsely" would be as nonsensical as to say "It may be raining, but it isn't." Thus Wittgenstein and Polanyi agree that the intentional, personal subject is at heart fiduciary and stands in a situation of tacit commitment when he or she uses the personal pronoun *I* in speech and behavior.

When Wittgenstein next asks how language conveys our inner intentionality and becomes an actual likeness of our meaning, he answers, "By the way we choose and value words . . . ; it is *the field of force* of a word that is decisive."[23] It is we as persons who invest our public speech and acts with intention, so that to look and see what we are saying and doing is to look and see what we are intending:

> The close relationship between "saying to oneself" and "saying" is manifested in the possibility of telling out loud what one said to oneself, and of an outward action's *accompanying* inward speech.
>
> Let the use of words teach you their meaning.[24]

The observation that one's inner intention indwells his behavior and is discerned in that behavior is succinctly expressed in the following statement.

> Ask not: "What goes on in us, when we are certain that . . . ?" — but: How is "the certainty that this is the case" manifested in human action?[25]

To sum up, Wittgenstein asks us to look and see if we want to know who a person is, because our language-games or forms of life are revelatory of personal intention: "What has to be accepted, the given, is — so one could say — *forms of life*."[26] This very ordinary description

22. *Ibid.* See Polanyi, *Personal Knowledge*, especially pp. 264–268.
23. *Philosophical Investigations*, 2.11, pp. 218–219. My italics.
24. *Ibid.*, 2.11, p. 220. His italics.
25. *Ibid.*, 2.11, p. 225.
26. *Ibid.*, 2.11, p. 226. His italics.

of how we commonly convey personal intention to others through the forms of words and acts is especially helpful in establishing Jesus' claims about himself.

The Application

I will now attempt to apply Wittgenstein's phenomenology of persons to Jesus' form of life, particularly his use of the personal pronoun *I* and its verbal equivalents, and try to discern what he is intending through what he is saying and doing. It is widely agreed, even among more extreme critics such as Norman Perrin, that Jesus made claims about himself and his mission that appeared outlandish in the eyes of formal contemporary Judaism. I will examine several of these authentic sayings that are supported by Jesus' implicit claims to radical, even divine, authority. Perrin's remarks on the sayings are often very informative and will indirectly serve to make my point that Jesus' intention to make christological claims is expressed in his use of language. A characteristic pattern of authority emerges when one applies Wittgenstein's analysis of the forms of life, language-games, and fields of force.

"The Finger of God" (Luke 11:20; parallel, Matt. 12:28)

"But if it is by the finger of God [Matt.: Spirit of God] that I cast out demons, then the kingdom of God has come upon you." [Luke 11:20]

Of this pivotal text Perrin remarks that it is unparalleled in Judaism to find the presence of the kingdom related to the experience of one individual human being; there is a consensus among critics that Jesus was an exorcist; Qumran studies lead us to assume a background of holy-war theology with its eschatological conflict between good and evil. In sum, the emphasis of the pericope on the restoration of a single disordered individual rather than the whole land of Israel is a striking feature of Jesus' claim that he is authoritatively invading the demonic realm.[27]

If Wittgenstein's analysis is applied to this saying of Jesus, which is widely accepted as authentic, it becomes clear that to "look and see" what Jesus is doing and saying is to intuit his intention to proclaim with astounding authority the presence of the kingdom of God in his

27. Norman Perrin, *Rediscovering the Teaching of Jesus* (London: SCM Press; New York: Harper & Row, 1967), pp. 64–67.

own personal speech and behavior. We can only conclude that his form of life discloses his intention to proclaim the presence of the kingdom in terms of his personal pronoun *I*. His field of force is a claim of correlativity with God's reign and Spirit.

The Bridegroom (Mark 2:19)

"Can the wedding guests fast while the bridegroom is with them?"

Jesus' personal claim is implied in this and other eschatological similes, since it is in the nature of simile, metaphor, analogy, and parable to imply "I say to you. . . ." Perrin observes that the eschatological pronouncements in Mark 2:18-22 "proclaim the presence of God manifesting himself as king in aspects of the ministry of Jesus. Jesus understood the kingdom of God as being manifest in his ministry; all else in his teaching takes its point of departure from this central, awe-inspiring — or ridicule-inspiring, according to one's perspective — conviction."[28]

Perrin's summary catches the sense of the saying well. Jesus' announcement that the bridegroom is present and that the promised eschatological wedding is underway could invite awe or ridicule, and did. He was ridiculed as blasphemous by some, considered mad by others, welcomed with awe and gratitude by the receptive. It is important to note that in every case the intentional claim of Jesus was clearly understood. He announced himself as the eschatological bridegroom with more than messianic — with divine — pretensions. Perrin remarks, "It is here that the clear vision of one mind, the depth comprehension of one individual's vision and understanding is most apparent."[29]

Yet, having acknowledged what amounts to Jesus' messianic self-consciousness, Perrin takes a strange turn away from the evidence and refuses to ascribe a definite christological intentionality to Jesus:

Nowhere else is the change from Jesus to the early Church more apparent. Having the tradition of similes and analogies of Jesus, but lacking the vision to maintain or understand them, she transformed them into allegories expressive of a post-Easter faith and reflecting a post-Easter reflection.[30]

28. *Ibid.*, pp. 77–78.
29. *Ibid.*, p. 78.
30. *Ibid.*

This uncertainty as to what to do with Jesus' radical claims is enlightened by Wittgenstein's commonsensical analysis of the use of language. If Jesus evinces an understanding and conviction that is intrinsically messianic, if he speaks in an awe-inspiring and authoritative manner about the arrival of the redeeming reign of God in terms of his own person, and about himself as the bridegroom, is it then so easy to say that "the pedestrian nature of the allegorizing, and the clear reflections of the post-Easter faith or situation, are easy to recognize and to remove"?[31] That is, that it is easy to remove explicit christological claims from implicit claims and ascribe the former to the church?

Surely Perrin's confidence is greater than mine at this point. Far better to allow that Jesus generates a tradition, as Ben F. Meyer cogently argues in his recent study of Jesus' intentionality.[32] For once one allows, in accord with Wittgenstein's analysis of words, acts, and intention, that Jesus' intention resides in his speech and behavior, and that his language is implicitly christological, one is hard pressed to make many facile distinctions between Jesus' Christology and what is assumed to be the Christology of the early church. Surely the latter is not "easy to remove" from the tradition, not when it has already been tacitly admitted that Jesus' images of the finger of God and the bridegroom are radical and messianic in character. Once one establishes this genre as characteristic of Jesus' tacit language-game, it is altogether coherent to accord him the creativity to play an explicit language-game. Generally speaking, both reflect an identical christological intentionality.

Similarly, the similes about new and old wine and a patch and cloth may be described as "something quite startling about Jesus' understanding of his ministry: they tell us that Jesus regarded his ministry as marking a new point of departure quite incompatible with the existing categories of Judaism . . . : something new and different in the ministry of Jesus marks that ministry as bursting the bounds of late Judaism . . . : the Kingdom of God is here!"[33] Jesus dramatically declares the inauguration of the eschatological age in terms of himself, and in so doing makes extraordinary claims which suggest a tacit christological self-understanding.

31. *Ibid.*
32. *The Aims of Jesus* (London: SCM Press, 1979), pp. 252–253.
33. Perrin, *Rediscovering the Teaching of Jesus*, p. 81.

The Parable of the Prodigal Son (Luke 15:11–32)

The intention of Jesus is strongly in evidence in this parable. It is as though he were saying with authority, "*I* say to you. . . ." As Perrin attests,

> the parable clearly reflects the situation of the ministry of Jesus and is equally clearly designed to open men's eyes to the reality of that situation, *as Jesus himself saw it.* It expresses Jesus' understanding and reflects his vision.[34]

This parable, with others, captures the most dramatic of all the words and acts of Jesus, namely, his radical invitation to outcasts and sinners to join with him in open table-fellowship. Wittgenstein's phenomenology of persons helps us focus on the radical form of life that Jesus presents to a mixed audience, including a recalcitrant Judaism. Perrin writes,

> There must have been a factor in the situation which drove both the authorities themselves to desperate measures and also gave them a defence against popular accusation. We suggest that a regular table-fellowship, in the name of the Kingdom of God, between Jesus and his followers, when those followers included "Jews who had made themselves as Gentiles," would have been just such a factor.[35]

Perrin continues with a powerful description of the discontinuity between Jesus' words and acts and the cherished doctrines of contemporary Judaism. The criterion of dissimilarity provides weighty evidence that the creative intention of Jesus assumes unheard-of prerogatives. His behavior is outrageous:

> Then came Jesus, claiming that they were wrong in their understanding of God and his attitude to these outcasts and so striking a blow at the fundamental convictions which upheld the Jewish people. But more than that, Jesus welcomes these outcasts into table-fellowship with himself in the name of the Kingdom of God, in the name of the Jews' ultimate hope, and so both prostituted that hope and also shattered the closed ranks of the community against their enemy. It is hard to imagine anything more offensive to Jewish sensibilities. To have become such an outcast himself would have been much less of an outrage than to

34. *Ibid.*, p. 98. His italics. Compare p. 102.
35. *Ibid.*, p. 103.

welcome those people back into the community in the name of the ultimate hope of that community. Intense conviction, indeed, is necessary to explain such an act on the part of Jesus, and such an act on the part of Jesus is necessary, we would claim, to make sense of the fact of the cross.[36]

Reading such a statement in light of Wittgenstein, one can only conclude that Jesus is consciously assuming a divinely authoritative form of life; hence there must be no reluctance to assign Jesus a christological self-understanding. A simply descriptive phenomenology, quite apart from the christological preferences of the New Testament interpreter, provides compelling evidence that Jesus thought of himself in christological terms; indeed, in divine terms as correlative with God and as standing in the place of God. Following Wittgenstein, we "look and see," and what we see when we look is one who is making outlandish claims for himself. Of course an initial analysis of this kind cannot offer any judgment as to whether that claim to divine authority is true or false, whether it arises from madness, blasphemy, or genuine credentials. That must be left to the response of belief or doubt on a deeper level as one is personally confronted by the intentional claims of Jesus. My deeper commitment is to the genuineness of Jesus' personal claims. But I want to make the point that an initial description of the data in phenomenological terms does not rest upon a particular position theologically. The data speak for themselves: Jesus does intend his form of life to be divinely oracular. He seems clearly to be playing the language-game of God. The field of force of his language is astounding.

The Children in the Marketplace (Matt. 11:16–19)

But to what shall I compare this generation?" [Matt. 11:16]

Jesus' use of the personal pronoun *I* in this offensive saying is enlightened by the foregoing exposition. What offended Jesus' opponents was his joyous conviviality in table-fellowship with sinners, thus announcing in his own acted and spoken parable the inauguration of the saving reign of God.[37] *This* language-game is being played, Wittgenstein would say. "That is the primary thing, the proto-phenomenon."

36. *Ibid.*, p. 103; compare pp. 105–106.
37. *Ibid.*, pp. 105–106.

The Pharisee and the Tax Collector (Luke 18:9-14)

The amount of material that can be added to the few sample citations I have presented is quite impressive, even limiting oneself to the core of sayings arrived at by the criterion of dissimilarity.[38] The overall effect is quite convincing that Jesus was conscious of a divine authority in claiming the power to forgive sins and inviting sinners and outcasts to the messianic banquet table. In the conclusion to the parable of the Pharisee and the tax collector Jesus says with authority tantamount to God's authority, "I tell you, this man went down to his house justified rather than the other."

The clue to Jesus' intention lies accordingly in his language-game or form of life that characterizes the style of his ministry. His personal vision, horizon, and intention can be understood in terms of his use of language. Perrin is on the verge of saying something truly impressive about the intention of Jesus when he observes, "We should note that 'I tell you . . .' with its direct challenge to dearly held preconceptions of the period is an indirect personal claim of great magnitude."[39] Precisely here, at the critical hinge where radical redaction cannot quite make the turn with the evidence to concede the christological consciousness of Jesus, Wittgenstein's phenomenology of persons helps us confront the intentional Jesus, and forces us to ask the question, "What kind of person would speak and act like that?"

Accordingly, I would go further than Perrin and the critical school he represents and say that, quite apart from any theological biases one might have, Perrin's authentic core of sayings provides impressive data for an objective phenomenological analysis of Jesus' christological intention. Using Wittgenstein's ordinary yet profound insights into the disclosure of personal intention through language-games and forms of life, I conclude that the form of Jesus' language evinces a unified pattern of remarkable authority.

Once one moves with the turning of the hinge, however, one discovers that the door has now opened to a wider christological horizon. Once one has stepped through the open door by acknowledging that Jesus' intentionality is at least implicitly christological, the language-games of gospel criticism by which the post-Easter theology of the early

---

38. For a representative list with exegetical notes, see Perrin, *ibid.*, pp. 54-164.
39. *Ibid.*, p. 122.

church is facilely separated from the language of Jesus will have to be rethought. How can we be certain that Jesus himself did not utter the explicit christological sayings that are assigned to his lips by the evangelists? Implicit and explicit christological sayings in the Gospels exhibit a form of life and language-game that is coherent and generically appropriate. In light of David Hill's recent discovery that there is no substantial evidence for the theory that early Christian prophets uttered sayings of the risen Lord and placed them on the lips of the historical Jesus,[40] it is far more likely that sayings ascribed to Jesus in the Gospels actually originated from him, and that variations in wording are due to the paraphrastic and adaptive activity of the evangelists, not to their creation of sayings *de novo*. In the longer study I will consider the gospel materials exegetically and hermeneutically and conclude that the evidence, examined through a phenomenology of persons, points to Jesus himself as the originative source of high Christology. The implications of this for defining the uses and limits of redaction criticism are, of course, substantial. The implications as to the validity and value of an evolutionary model for New Testament Christology, such as James D. Dunn's *Christology in the Making: A New Testament Inquiry into the Origins of the Doctrine of the Incarnation*[41] are, it goes without saying, equally substantial.

40. *New Testament Prophecy* (Atlanta: John Knox, 1980), especially chapter 2, "Jesus: 'A Prophet Mighty in Deed and Word,' " and chapter 7, "Christian Prophets and the Sayings of Jesus."
41. (Philadelphia: Westminster, 1980).

2

Jesus' Proclamation
and Self-understanding
Exegeting the Core Sayings of Radical Criticism

In the preceding chapter I presented fresh methodological approaches to New Testament interpretation, especially to the Gospels and to research about Jesus. Now we need to apply these methodologies technically to specific texts and put them, as it were, to the test. I have already hinted at the direction of my approach in the opening chapter about Ludwig Wittgenstein.

Because Norman Perrin's work has been in the forefront of radical gospel criticism and represents an influential meld of Continental Bultmannian, post-Bultmannian, and Anglo-American redaction criticism, and since his standard work, *Rediscovering the Teaching of Jesus*,[1] is still the best compendium of "authentic" sayings of Jesus arrived at by the most radical application of the criterion of dissimilarity, I propose that we examine his core sayings carefully with a view to what they may tell us about the self-understanding of Jesus, using principally Wittgenstein's phenomenological analysis of personal intentionality as revealed in one's words and acts.

While my own approach to gospel interpretation does not begin with the radical doubt that has compelled the Bultmannian school to its skeptical conclusions, it is salutary as an exercise in methodology to see where such a radical approach leads if it is informed by truly phenomenological insights regarding the inseparability of persons from their language. The thorough application of a phenomenology of persons to the core sayings of radical criticism will be seen to yield surprising and fruitful results, as we have already observed in the first chapter. On the basis of the core sayings, Jesus proves to be a person who makes astounding — even outrageous — claims about himself and his ministry, and with these clues to his self-understanding we will

1. (London: SCM Press; New York: Harper & Row, 1967). See also his later studies, which essentially repeat the same conclusions regarding authentic core material.

34

have to deal directly and honestly in the next several chapters. The evidence cannot be by-passed, as it is so consistently in the radical school because of a faulty phenomenology.

While the excessive use of the criterion of dissimilarity has come under considerable fire by New Testament critics,[2] and also will be thoroughly scrutinized and critiqued later in this study as its deficiencies are brought to light, for my present purposes it plays a useful role because it provides a core of sayings that nearly every biblical critic, from most conservative to most radical, would agree have come from the mouth of the historical Jesus himself. I shall examine each of the sayings to which Perrin accords authentic status with an eye to what sort of person would make such claims, and attempt to imagine what Jesus' self-understanding would have been for him to have spoken and acted as he did. This methodology assumes the validity of ordinary personal discourse through words and acts that reveal one's personal intentionality and self-understanding. Such a phenomenology of persons does not, of course, fully disclose one's own intimate and intricate psychological stream of consciousness to which he alone has privileged access, although currents of that complex stream are perforce disclosed in his self-revelation of himself so that the other whom he confronts has genuine clues of his personal horizon, intention, and understanding. This is, after all, how we come to know one another. The description of Jesus' self-understanding (*Selbstverständnis*) that I will try to draw from his words and works will not be concerned primarily with his developing self-consciousness (*Selbstbewusstsein*), which was essentially the old liberal quest, except as the self-understanding of his mission touches necessarily upon his more complex self-consciousness. It is not my intention to attempt a biography of Jesus, but to describe phenomenologically the characteristic intentionality and horizon, the form of life and language-game that is implied in the minimal core of the authentic sayings of Jesus.

2. See, for example, D. G. A. Calvert, "An Examination of the Criteria for Distinguishing the Authentic Word of Jesus," *NTS* 18 (1971–72): 209–218; M. D. Hooker, "On Using the Wrong Tool," *Theol.* 75 (1972): 570–581, and her incisive essay, "In His Own Image," in *What About the New Testament: Essays in Honour of Christopher Evans*, ed. Morna Hooker and Calvin Hickling (London: SCM Press, 1975), pp. 28–44; David Mealand, "The Dissimilarity Test," *SJT* 31 (1978): 41–50; E. L. Mascall, *Theology and the Gospel of Christ* (London: S.P.C.K., 1977), pp. 87–101; R. S. Barbour, *Traditio-historical Criticism of the Gospels: Some Comments on Current Models* (London: S.P.C.K., 1972).

The word *implied* is significant in my analysis, for in the nature of the case I am working only with sayings that at best *imply* indirectly Jesus' self-understanding of his mission. In that sense I have one hand tied behind my back, since all explicit statements regarding his self-understanding have been temporarily removed by the criterion of dissimilarity and are suspect of having arisen either from Jewish motifs or from doctrines of the later Christian community.[3] Later, if I have done my work well, I will be able to move from the bare core of sayings back to the larger canon of the tradition regarding Jesus and reinstate the discarded material. For now let the agreed-upon core lend its material for analysis. One striking advantage of beginning with Perrin's core, which carries on radical Bultmannian criticism, is not only that it provides a general consensus as a starting point in New Testament scholarship, but also, equally important, discloses startlingly new elements in the teaching of Jesus which are quite original with him and not derived from Judaism or ascribed to him by the church, and which are highlighted by the criterion of dissimilarity.

Let us then begin with the exegesis of the authentic core sayings and ask in each case, "What sort of person would say something like this? What does this claim disclose about his self-concept of mission, his view of personal authority, his intentionality and horizon of vision?" In short, just as countless times during any given day we analyze the phenomena of others' words and acts as clues to the persons who indwell them, and thus come to know these persons, we may come to know Jesus on the phenomenal level by the clues he evinces in his spoken and acted language.

But one word of warning. We must not do what Continental interpreters have done consistently from Bultmann to the present, and that is to stop with the language of Jesus as though it had some independent status of its own apart from the person who speaks, indwells, and personally accredits his words by standing behind them with his signature of intentionality. Thus Perrin speaks of rediscovering the *teaching* of Jesus, but not of rediscovering *Jesus*; Ernst Fuchs and Gerhard Ebeling write extensively about the "word-event" or "speech-event" (*Wortgeschehen*, or *Sprachereignis*) that has some independent status in and of its own, where language is apotheosized apart from the person who speaks. In this vein Ernst Käsemann allows that Jesus makes all

---

3. See Perrin, *Rediscovering the Teaching of Jesus*, pp. 39–43, for a definition of the criterion and his view of its vital importance in gospel criticism.

sorts of astounding claims about himself and his mission — he assumes the prerogatives of the new Moses by placing his own words in antithesis to the Torah ("But I say"), therefore proving himself to be more than a rabbi. He shatters the letter of the law by calling into question the attitude toward the commandment about the Sabbath. He breaks down the classical distinction between the sacred and the secular by stressing the purity and the freedom of the heart. He announces that the reign of God has come to combat the threat of demonic powers. He proclaims that the time must be lived without anxiety. He announces that the kingdom of God is present and already suffering abuse from its opponents since the days of John. And he believes himself full of the Spirit of God when he uses the remarkable word *Amen* at the beginning of important sayings and dispels the demonic in the Spirit's name.

All these evidences are adduced by Käsemann to reveal Jesus' attitude toward his mission. He is ready to speak of Jesus' belief: "It was the belief of Jesus that, in his word, the *basileia* was coming to his hearers." Yet he cannot bring himself to admit Jesus' messianic self-understanding or horizon:

> Does this mean that he understood himself to be the Messiah? The only way of dealing briefly with this question is simply to express at this point one's personal opinion. I personally am convinced that there can be no possible grounds for answering this question in the affirmative. I consider all passages in which any kind of Messianic prediction occurs to be kerygma shaped by the community.[4]

Käsemann's recourse to personal opinion at a crucial moment in analyzing the implication of Jesus' language is a covert admission that factors other than the phenomenological evidence are compelling him away from that evidence, namely, a prior hermeneutical commitment to the notion that faith and self-understanding are not open to historical inquiry and are inaccessible from the clues of spoken and acted language. He is assuming, with others in the Bultmannian school, that a person's word can be separated from his intention and self-understanding, when the most rudimentary observation of everyday discourse should compel us to acknowledge the intimate relationship of personal

---

4. *Essays on New Testament Themes*, trans. W. J. Montague, Studies in Biblical Theology, no. 41 (London: SCM Press, 1964; distributed in the U.S. by Alec R. Allenson), p. 43. Compare pp. 37–42.

language, personal intentionality, and personal self-disclosure. Otherwise we could never know one another and would be locked into windowless privacy without civil status. But as a matter of fact we do
disclose ourselves to one another in terms of our ordinary spoken and
acted language, and only prejudice and faulty methodology prevent
Käsemann and others in the radical school from following the trail of
the evidence to its conclusion. With Wittgenstein I reject the Cartesian
dualism that epistemologically and linguistically bifurcates a person
and a person's public activity. Käsemann knows where the evidence is
leading, but he resists its inexorable logic on other grounds, having
already entered the hermeneutical circle with a disposition weighted
against the possibility that Jesus could ever have thought of himself in
messianic or christological terms. The question that must be relentlessly, even ruthlessly, asked when we assess the core sayings is, "What
sort of intention and self-understanding would Jesus have had to have
spoken and acted out such language?" This is the principal question of
my phenomenological analysis.

The Heideggerian system that lies behind radical gospel criticism
needs to be challenged by a better methodology that views language as
the expression of the person who indwells it and who is disclosed in
terms of its use. This is the descriptive phenomenology I will apply to
the core sayings and that I hope will successfully take up Perrin's challenge that the work of the radical Bultmannian school "could only be
denied by offering an alternative and more convincing explanation of
the actual phenomena in the New Testament texts to which these scholars are calling attention and with which they are dealing."[5] My approach will be to replace the faulty phenomenology of the Bultmannian
school with a more adequate phenomenology based upon an analysis
of personal intentionality as disclosed in ordinary discourse between
persons. The Heideggerian notion that language has independent status
apart from persons not only is bad phenomenology because it contracts
persons out their priority in the function of language-games, but also
has had a devastating effect on gospel criticism. The assumption of the
"new quest" of the historical Jesus has been that it is the *word* of Jesus
and Jesus' understanding of existence, not Jesus' self-understanding and
intentional use of words and acts, that is the proper object of critical

5. *Rediscovering the Teaching of Jesus*, p. 27.

research.[6] As we examine and exegete specific core passages we shall want to go beyond this halfway house which apotheosizes language and contracts the intentional Jesus out of his own speech, and rediscover Jesus the intentional person in and through the language he indwells.

I turn now to the exegetical analysis.

Kingdom Sayings (Luke 11:20; parallel, Matt. 12:28; Luke 17:20-21; Matt. 11:12)

"But if it is by the finger of God that I cast out demons, then the kingdom of God has come upon you." [Luke 11:20; parallel, Matt. 12:28]

Perrin argues that the original saying was very close to the form of Luke 11:20 and approvingly quotes Bultmann on its claim to authenticity: ". . . it is full of that feeling of eschatological power which must have characterized the activity of Jesus."[7] Applying this astute observation on the saying with the further insights of person analysis, we observe that Jesus in his extraordinary use of the personal pronoun *I* evinces a characteristic "eschatological power" that discloses his self-understanding. He is actually intending to speak and act in this form, claiming that in casting out demons he is exhibiting the power of the finger of God. This is an imaginative allusion to the figure .in Exodus 8:19a where the Egyptian magicians, unable to duplicate the third plague of gnats, confess to Pharaoh that "this is the finger of God."[8] Perrin allows that this passage is evidence of realized eschatology because of its holy-war theology, where the kingdom of God is invading the kingdom of darkness; God is acting in Jesus in this situ-

6. See James M. Robinson, "The Recent Debate on the 'New Quest,' " *JBR* 30 (July 1962): 202, where the author is careful to distinguish between the understanding of existence that emerges from Jesus' activity, and Jesus' self-understanding of that activity. Robinson pursues the former and abandons the latter. But it is this very self-understanding by Jesus of his horizon and mission to which the evidence points and that gives the gospel story its authority and credibility.

7. Perrin, *Rediscovering the Teaching of Jesus*, p. 64; Rudolf Bultmann, *History of the Synoptic Tradition*, trans. John Marsh (New York: Harper & Row, 1976), p. 162.

8. Perrin, *Rediscovering the Teaching of Jesus*, pp. 66f. See also T. W. Manson, *Teaching of Jesus*, second ed. (New York: Cambridge University Press, 1951), pp. 82ff. Compare also Exodus 31:18.

ation of conflict. Accordingly, "the claim of the saying is that certain events in the ministry of Jesus are nothing less than *an experience* of the Kingdom of God."⁹ But that is tantamount to saying that Jesus intends to exercise this unusual authority because he understands that he is acting as the mediating agent in realizing the powerful invasion of the reign of God. He is virtually claiming divine prerogatives. He is manifesting the power of God in a new exodus and is exhibiting that power in terms of his personal pronoun *I*. His conscious vision and horizon could not be made much clearer than in this extraordinary claim to authority.

Moreover, Jesus' authoritative originality is strikingly visible in the fact that by this exorcism he deals not with the deliverance of the people as a whole but focuses the eschatological conflict on the deliverance of a single individual. Of this Perrin says, "As we shall see, his concentration upon the individual and his experience is a striking feature of the teaching of Jesus, historically considered, and full justice must be done to it in any interpretation of that meaning."¹⁰ But why say, "a striking feature of the *teaching* of Jesus"? Why not say that it is a "striking feature" of Jesus *himself*, since his teaching discloses who he is and what he intends?

This pivotal saying sets the tone for all the others that point impressively to one who claims exceptional power and authority.

". . . for behold, the kingdom of God is in the midst of you." [Luke 17:21]

The intention of Jesus in this saying (Perrin properly renders *entos hymōn*, "in the midst of you") is signaled not onl ʳ by his inattention to signs in the apocalyptic mode, but also by his prophetic declaration that the kingdom of God is here where God is working in the experience of individuals who have faith.¹¹ Implicitly Jesus is making the claim that he is describing the state of things accurately. How does he come by this knowledge? However he comes by it, he is categorically denying any fascination with apocalyptic details and is virtually claiming that it is in terms of himself that the kingdom of God "is in your midst." Certainly his claim to be authoritative on matters eschatological is impressive and reveals his self-understanding and vision.

9. Perrin, *Rediscovering the Teaching of Jesus*, p. 67.
10. *Ibid.*
11. *Ibid.*, p. 74.

"From the days of John the Baptist until now the kingdom of heaven has suffered violence [*biazetai*], and men of violence [*biastai*] take it by force" (*harpazousin*). [Matt. 11:12]

While Perrin avoids another possible reading, "the kingdom of God has been coming violently" (middle voice), because that would be too Lukan (cf. Luke 16:16) and would play down the role of the Baptist,[12] his translation nonetheless allows an alternative insight into the self-understanding of Jesus. Agreeing with Käsemann,[13] he argues "that in this saying, Jesus is looking back over the completed Old Testament epoch of salvation and is drawing the Baptist to his own side in presenting him 'as the initiator of the new aeon.' "[14] This would afford an important confirmatory insight into the horizon of Jesus, who clearly sees his ministry as a radical and urgent inauguration of the new-kingdom age of conflict with the demonic powers of violence. If my preferred translation of *biazetai* as "has been coming violently" is correct, then Jesus is saying what is consonant with Luke 11:20, namely, that he is now exercising the forceful power of the reign of God in conflict with satanic strongholds. If Perrin is correct in rendering *biazetai* as a passive, then Jesus is feeling the power of diabolic opposition. In either case, the saying reveals Jesus' understanding that in terms of his own ministry the reign of God is *here* as he engages in a war of invasion in which losses are a real possibility. Hence the need for utter discipline and devotion.

Eschatological Similes (Mark 2:19, 21–22)

Perrin remarks that the sayings about the kingdom of God

proclaim the presence of God manifesting himself as king in aspects of the ministry of Jesus. They are the very heart of the message of Jesus. Jesus understood the kingdom of God as being manifest in his ministry; all else in his teaching takes its departure from this central, awe-inspiring — or ridicule-inspiring, according to one's perspective — conviction.[15]

---

12. *Ibid.*, pp. 74f.
13. In "The Problem of the Historical Jesus," *Essays on New Testament Themes*, pp. 15–47, especially pp. 42f.
14. Perrin, *Rediscovering the Teaching of Jesus*, p. 76.
15. *Ibid.*, pp. 77f.

He adds that the following eschatological similes manifest the same conviction. Perrin's language is appropriate, but it should be noted that he is unwittingly referring to Jesus' self-understanding of his mission when he uses the phrase "Jesus understood," and refers to Jesus' "conviction." What sort of person would have a conviction that the reign of God was manifesting itself in his own activity except one who was assuming divine prerogatives? Here I detect strong evidence for pre-Easter Christology in the gospel accounts, as Jesus assumes the role not only of proclaimer but also of executor of divine power in the new age which is breaking in in terms of his own person. In Jesus' incomparable use of simile and analogy, Perrin observes, "the clear vision of one mind, the depth comprehension of one individual's vision and understanding, is most apparent."[16] Surely here as well we have a description in superlative terms of the phenomenon of Jesus' language that prompts Perrin to speak obliquely of Jesus' self-understanding — clear vision, depth comprehension, vision and understanding.

It is Jesus' claim in Mark 2:19 that is most striking (Perrin accepts only verse 19a as authentic — verses 19b and 18–20 are church-created).

And Jesus said to them, "Can the wedding guests fast while the bridegroom is with them?" [Mark 2:19a]

Jesus is saying (as Joachim Jeremias translates it), "Can the wedding guests fast during the wedding?"[17] Perrin interprets the saying to mean that Jesus regarded his ministry as a time of joyous table-fellowship, as a release from normal religious obligations, and an enjoyment of God's wedding which is the symbol of the day of salvation.[18] Perrin sidesteps the tremendous authoritative implication of the saying, however. He argues against Jesus' identification of himself with the bridegroom, though that is the clear intent of the saying, contending that verse 20 is the church's christological reflection about Jesus' death (bridegroom = Jesus). Yet if Jesus is only an announcer, by what authority does he announce in word and deed that the wedding is in progress? What sort of person would claim such outrageous authority, which flies in the face of religious ritual and fasting, except one who is claiming the prerogatives of God?

16. *Ibid.*, p. 78.
17. *The Parables of Jesus*, trans. S. H. Hooke, rev. ed. (New York: Scribner, 1963), p. 52, n. 14.
18. *Rediscovering the Teaching of Jesus*, p. 80.

It is in terms of the new-age prophecy of Hosea 2:16–20, where God will betroth himself as husband to his people, that Jesus speaks implicitly of himself as bridegroom. In Mark 2:19a the wedding guests are clearly the disciples who have been told authoritatively by Jesus, who assumes the role of the bridegroom, not to fast. Only prejudice on the part of the critic who reads churchly christological activity into the sayings could miss this evidence for pre-Easter Christology. It is circular reasoning to argue that verse 20 is church reflection because it makes the equation "Jesus = bridegroom," when Jesus has already made the identification implicitly in verse 19a. Jesus must be allowed to play out his language-game. This is more than the simple announcement that the fast is ended and wedding festivities are in progress. The wedding is in progress because Jesus appears to be consciously acting as God's surrogate bridegroom and therefore has the authority to announce that it is in progress. Once the phenomenon of verse 19a is seen in that light, verse 20 cannot so easily be dismissed as a prophecy after the fact. But such prophetic pronouncements are another dimension of Jesus' horizon and will be considered later in the reconstruction section of my exegesis.

"No one sews a piece of unshrunk cloth on an old garment; if he does, the patch tears away from it, the new from the old, and a worse tear is made. And no one puts new wine into old wineskins; if he does, the wine will burst the skins, and the wine is lost, and so are the skins; but new wine is for fresh skins." [Mark 2:21–22]

These similes, Perrin observes, "tell us something quite startling about Jesus' understanding of his ministry: they tell us that Jesus regarded his ministry as marking a new point of departure quite incompatible with the existing categories of Judaism . . . ; something new and different in the ministry of Jesus marks that ministry as bursting the bounds of late Judaism . . . : the Kingdom of God is here!"[19]

Now the phrases "Jesus' understanding of his ministry" and "[he] regarded his ministry" unavoidably suggest Jesus' self-understanding of his person and mission; and since Perrin correctly describes the evidence as "startling" and radical one can only conclude on the basis of the phenomenological evidence that Jesus had an extraordinarily high opinion of himself, to the point of assuming divine prerogatives and

19. *Ibid.*, p. 81.

launching such an offensive attack on his own Judaism. This radical understanding of his person and mission can only be described as christological and messianic — in his own creative terms, of course, since he was not meeting the messianic expectations of late Judaism. There can be no doubt, however, that Jesus intends to say that "the decisive activity of God as king is now to be experienced by men confronted by [my] ministry in word and deed."[20]

The Parables of the Kingdom

In this exegetical section Perrin approvingly quotes Amos Wilder that "true metaphor or symbol is more than a sign; it is a bearer of the reality to which it refers"; hence the parables are to the disciples ". . . Jesus' interpretation to them of his own vision by the powers of metaphor."[21] This is on target and is what Wittgenstein means when he speaks of the forms of life and language-games: a person discloses himself, his vision, horizon, and self-understanding in terms of his language and form of activity. In the following sayings we are able to describe Jesus' vision clearly as he sees the power of God at work in his own ministry and its reflection in the experience of those who confront the reality of his person and proclamation.

> "But to what shall I compare this generation? It is like children sitting in the market places and calling to their playmates, 'We piped to you, and you did not dance; we wailed, and you did not mourn.' For John came neither eating nor drinking, and they say, 'He has a demon'; the Son of man came eating and drinking, and they say, 'Behold, a glutton and a drunkard, a friend of tax collectors and sinners!' Yet wisdom is justified by her deeds." [Matt. 11:16–19]

The crucial point in this parabolic analogy is that Jesus is calling finis to the lazy and petulant childish language-games of his religious critics and is declaring with unprecedented authority the invitation of outcasts to table-fellowship.[22] Jesus' use of the personal pronoun I ("to what shall I compare") evinces his authoritative status as accurate judge of the situation and of his critics.

20. *Ibid.*, p. 82.
21. Amos Wilder, *The Language of the Gospel: Early Christian Rhetoric* (New York: Harper & Row, 1964), pp. 92f.; see Perrin, *Rediscovering the Teaching of Jesus*, p. 82.
22. See Perrin, *Rediscovering the Teaching of Jesus*, pp. 85–87; 105f.; 119f.

The Joy of Experiencing God's Kingly Activity

"The kingdom of heaven is like a treasure hidden in a field, which a man found and covered up; then in his joy he goes and sells all that he has and buys that field. Again, the kingdom of heaven is like a merchant in search of fine pearls, who, on finding one pearl of great value, went and sold all that he had and bought it." [Matt. 13:44–46]

The central theme of these two parables is surprise and joy at the discovery of great treasure, by which Jesus intends to say that the reign of God is present to be discovered. With what self-understanding and personal estimate of his authority must Jesus have announced that "the secret dream" is "suddenly and surprisingly fulfilled"?[23] Only one supremely self-confident that he speaks with divine authority could make such a radical announcement.

The Challenge of the Forgiveness of Sins

But more astounding is Jesus' announcement that forgiveness of sins is present in terms of his ministry, and still more startling is that the lost and "Gentile sinners" (including Jews who have made themselves as Gentiles) are forgiven and welcomed into table-fellowship.

The Prodigal Son (Luke 15:11–32)

In this parable the Jew who became a swineherd became a Gentile and would be considered dead in his father's eyes. Yet the astounding announcement by Jesus is that this renegade is forgiven and invited to the father's table-fellowship, in total reversal of the theology of Judaism that the son was "dead" (v. 24, ". . . was dead, and is alive . . . was lost, and is found"). Perrin's description of Jesus' vision here is apt, but we need to press his phenomenology with the question, "What opinion must Jesus have had of himself to speak against the viewpoint of the religious authorities as he did?" Perrin observes that

Jesus goes out of his way to contradict this viewpoint. . . . Every touch of which a creative mind could conceive, and still stay within the limits of a realistic story, has been used to depict the free and absolute nature of the father's forgiveness; all in deliberate contrast to the expectation

23. *Ibid.*, p. 89.

of those to whom the parable was addressed. But their viewpoint is not ignored. Far from it! It is introduced on the lips of the elder son.[24]

By what authority does Jesus reverse ordinary Jewish expectations and offer a world completely contrary, where the unforgivable is forgiven? Only one who is conscious of exercising divine privileges (or is mad) could assume the right to proclaim the eschatological presence of the forgiveness of sins with such authority. Yet Jesus precipitates a crisis by announcing precisely that fact, and discloses his self-understanding of the situation, his vision of the salvation that has arrived in terms of his own person and ministry. Whether one calls the twin parables of the younger son and the elder son allegory or analogy (Perrin's brief for the latter against the former doesn't quite carry),[25] the case is clear, and Perrin expresses it well; but notice how much he is unconsciously conceding about the vision and intention of Jesus:

> Here was a situation in which the reality of God and his love was being revealed in a new and decisive way, and in which, therefore, the joys of the salvation time were suddenly available to those who had longed for them so long and so earnestly. The tragedy was that the new situation demanded a willingness to sacrifice principles and attitudes previously regarded as essential to the life of the community and its relationship with God, and for this many were unprepared. The new wine was bursting the old wineskins.[26]

How does Jesus play that language-game without knowing what he is doing? But of course he does know what he is doing — he is consciously speaking as the voice of God on matters that belong only to God, and accordingly is creating a new and decisive Christology which far exceeds in claim to authority the messianic models of Judaism. Jesus is consciously intending to speak as the voice of God in announcing the inauguration of the eschatological time when the unforgivable sinner is forgiven. No other explanation can account for the phenomenon except

24. *Ibid.*, p. 96.

25. *Ibid.*, p. 97, where Perrin claims that the father is not God, the elder son is not a Pharisee, and the story is simply a real family in a family situation; but he immediately thereafter says that "the point that makes it a parable is the analogy between the situation of the family and that of Palestinian Judaism at the time of Jesus' ministry"! One observes here the equivocation of radical criticism regarding allegory and analogy in the parables.

26. *Ibid.*, p. 97.

the alternative of the Pharisees, who see Jesus as demonically possessed and mad with heresy.

But Perrin (and one would assume all other radical critics who are writing from within the church) does not accept the latter alternative. To the contrary, he approvingly quotes Fuchs, who remarks of the parable that the real framework of Jesus' proclamation was his *conduct*.[27] This certainly is correct when we consider the extraordinary phenomenon of Jesus' open table-fellowship with sinners to whom he has extended divine forgiveness. Perrin concludes his discussion of this parable with an observation which, on Wittgensteinian terms, unquestionably discloses Jesus' conscious form of life and language-game:

> The parable clearly reflects the situation of the ministry of Jesus, and is equally clearly designed to open men's eyes to the reality of that situation, as *Jesus himself saw it*. It expresses Jesus' understanding and reflects his vision. It challenges men to join him in joyous celebration of the new relationship with God and one another which the realization that the time of the eschatological forgiveness of sins is *now* made possible.[28]

Accordingly, Perrin's disclaimer in the preface that he has not undertaken any discussion of Jesus' "messianic consciousness" or of the Christology implicit in the teaching, other than occasional allusions to personal claims implicit in a parable or saying,[29] shows a serious sidestepping of the discipline of phenomenological description. It is absolutely essential that one draw honest conclusions from the evidence, and if the objective evidence repeatedly affirms (implicitly, as does the

27. "The Quest of the Historical Jesus," in his *Studies of the Historical Jesus*, Studies in Biblical Theology, no. 42 (London: SCM Press, 1964), English translation by Andrew Scobie of *Zur Frage nach dem historischen Jesus* (Gesammelte Aufsatze II. 1960). Fuchs unfortunately suffers from the same faulty phenomenology of the Bultmannian school that separates Jesus' language and activity from his own personal intentionality. Fuchs is more interested in Jesus' understanding of time, which is an abstraction, than in what Jesus is saying about himself when he announces the new time. A trenchant critique of this deficiency in Fuchs's interpretation can be found in Amos Wilder's "The Word as Address and the Word as Meaning," *New Frontiers in Theology*, vol. 2, *The New Hermeneutic*, ed. James M. Robinson and John B. Cobb, Jr. (New York: Harper & Row, 1964), p. 213.

28. *Rediscovering the Teaching of Jesus*, p. 98. His italics.

29. *Ibid.*, p. 12. Perrin says he hopes to turn to the subject in a future study, but never did substantially. See his essays in *A Modern Pilgrimage in New Testament Christology* (Philadelphia: Fortress, 1974), especially pp. 41–56.

radically reduced evidence we are working with) that Jesus makes stu-
pendous claims about himself and his ministry which far exceed the
messianic expectations of Judaism, and which accord with the explicit
christological claims of the early church, then the whole approach of
radical gospel criticism is itself open to radical criticism. We cannot
assume that Jesus, who makes implicit christological claims about himself, does not also make analogous *explicit* christological claims about
himself. If what I am saying is true, then radical gospel criticism rests
on a false methodology when it assumes that all explicit christological
sayings are put on the lips of Jesus by the early church.[30] Playing the
language-game of radical criticism does not itself lead to that negative
conclusion, but quite the contrary, repeatedly affirms the startling, implicit christological claims of Jesus, as Perrin's exegesis obliquely avers.

The same case can be made with the twin parables of the lost sheep
and the lost coin that, together with the parable of the prodigal son,
complete the triptych of lost, found, and rejoicing.

The Lost Sheep

"What do you think? If a man has a hundred sheep, and one of them
has gone astray, does he not leave the ninety-nine on the hills and go
in search of the one that went astray? And if he finds it, truly, I say to
you, he rejoices over it more than over the ninety-nine that never went
astray." [Matt. 18:12–13]

Perrin prefers the Matthaean version (cf. Luke 15:3–5) because it is
less developed than Luke's; he also objects to Luke's seeing the shepherd
as Jesus' "image of God's activity of love,"[31] since the shepherd in late
Judaism was one who had made himself like a Gentile. Rather, says
Perrin, "the whole situation of the story is analogous to the situation
of the ministry of Jesus . . . : for those who would accept the challenge
and realize the need for 'new wineskins' the possibility of a wholly new
kind of joy was very real."[32]

What Perrin does not see, however, is that in his conscious Christology Jesus not only is presenting himself implicitly as the "image of

---

30. See Perrin's unchanged opinion that all explicit christological sayings are put
in the mouth of Jesus by the early church in *Jesus and the Language of the Kingdom:
Symbol and Metaphor in New Testament Interpretation* (Philadelphia: Fortress, 1976),
for example, pp. 1–12, 40–54.

31. Which is the preference of Jeremias, *The Parables of Jesus*, p. 133.

32. *Rediscovering the Teaching of Jesus*, p. 101.

God's activity and love" (what else could his astounding claims mean?), but also is identifying himself as a shepherd who has made himself a Gentile. The implications are far more profound than radical criticism could imagine, making Luke's "paraphrastic" version (if indeed it is paraphrastic) as legitimate as Matthew's in reflecting the messianic facets of Jesus' intentionality.

The Lost Coin (Luke 15:8–10)

"Or what woman, having ten silver coins, if she loses one coin, does not light a lamp and sweep the house diligently until she finds it? And when she has found it, she calls together her friends and neighbors, saying, 'Rejoice with me, for I have found the coin which I had lost.' " [Luke 15:8–9]

Perrin discards verse 10 as editorial but sees verses 8–9 as integral to the remarkable proclamation of inaugurated eschatology that is present in all of the sayings examined so far. Again I pose the question, "What sort of self-understanding on Jesus' part does the parable suggest?" And what does the critic's comment imply about that self-understanding?

Jesus challenges his hearers to recognize the crisis of the Now of the proclamation, the proclamation of God reaching out to men in the challenge of the forgiveness of sins and offering them thereby the real possibility of a new kind of relationship with himself and with one another.[33]

Perrin now launches into a noteworthy disquisition on the table-fellowship of the kingdom of God, one of the best sections of his study and most revealing of the form of life that Jesus embodied in earnest. As I have already had occasion to mention, the language-game that Jesus was intentionally acting out was of such radical character that the religious authorities correctly understood his claim to possess divine authority to forgive sinners, but they interpreted his claims as blasphemous and sought his execution. My analysis aims to show that Jesus intended to convey to sinners his authority to forgive sins by his invitation to open table-fellowship. A correct description of the phenomenon itself leads inexorably to that conclusion and explains why Jesus' min-

33. *Ibid.*, p. 102.

istry ended on the cross — it gave grave offense to his contemporaries.[34] Jesus' intentionality is clearly read in the language-game of open table-fellowship: "Intense conviction, indeed, is necessary to explain such an act on the part of Jesus, and such an act on the part of Jesus is necessary, we would claim, to make sense of the fact of the cross."[35] One would draw the inescapable conclusion from the phenomenon of regular table-fellowship that Jesus is expressing an implicit Christology which calls forth the practice of early Christian communal meals and the theology of the Lord's Supper which is associated with it.[36]

The Children in the Marketplace (Matt. 11:16–19)

I have already alluded briefly to this parable and its closure on the hypocritical language-game of the religious authorities, but a further word needs to be said of their criticism of Jesus' eating habits and his friendship with tax collectors and sinners. What self-understanding on Jesus' part would compel him to such practice, and his opponents to their drastic hostility? It can only have been Jesus' virtual overturning of contemporary Jewish authority regarding salvation, and his announcement that in terms of his person and practice, joyous reconciliation of outcasts is now going on around the banquet table.

"I tell you, many will come from east and west and sit at table with Abraham, Isaac, and Jacob in the kingdom of heaven." [Matt. 8:11]

The table-fellowship that Jesus is practicing already anticipates the universality that is characteristic of the kingdom of God. All kinds of people who represent the outcast and who have made themselves as Gentiles are invited to the table of joyous reconciliation. This symbol of the forgiveness of sins and a new life of joyous relationship with God and others is the "central feature" of the ministry of Jesus.[37] It also affords an important clue to the self-understanding of Jesus and to a pre-Easter Christology which is implicit in that self-understanding. What sort of person must Jesus have been to have acted in this way and spoken this language? We can only infer from the phenomena that Jesus

---

34. See Perrin's discussion, pp. 102f., and N. A. Dahl, "The Problem of the Historical Jesus," in *Kerygma and History*, ed. Carl E. Braaten and Roy A. Harrisville (New York: Abingdon, 1962), pp. 158f.

35. Perrin, *Rediscovering the Teaching of Jesus*, p. 103.

36. *Ibid.*, pp. 104f.

37. *Ibid.*, p. 107.

held a deep conviction that through his person and form of life the kingdom of God was present, bringing forgiveness of sins (a divine prerogative) and a consequent joyous celebration of the wedding of heaven and earth. The evidence is formidable, even on the level of the core sayings arrived at by the criterion of dissimilarity.

But there are more core sayings, these having to do with the proper human response to Jesus' proclamation of the kingdom of God, and to these I turn in the next chapter.

3

Jesus' Self-understanding Disclosed in Response to His Person

An Exegesis of Jesus' Claims to Authority

I continue the phenomenological analysis of core sayings that center upon Jesus' urgent call to respond to him and his proclamation. These are listed by Norman Perrin in the following categories.

The Importance of Immediate Decision

The Great Supper (Matt. 22:1–14; Luke 14:16–24)

Perrin rejects the allegorical touches of the two versions but allows that the point of the story is about the relationship of guests and host, which is analogous to that between the Jews and God. There is no automatic sitting at table by dint of being a Jew — "he must also respond to the challenge of the hour, the Now of the ministry of Jesus and his proclamation. If he fails to respond to this challenge, then he may find that others have taken the place he had assumed was his."[1]

By what authority in his self-understanding does Jesus have the audacity to distinguish inauthentic from authentic response in terms of himself? The incisive evidence compels us to view Jesus as one who intends to assert that he is possessed of divine authority to demand such decisions of others. The conclusion is inescapable and points again to pre-Easter Christology, with Jesus as focal figure in the eschatological table-fellowship.

The Unjust Steward (Luke 16:1–9)

This story of a disreputable steward is a portrait of a man in crisis who acts decisively[2] and takes advantage of the occasion to extricate himself from condemnation. The point of the parable is the decisiveness of the steward, which is analogous to the decision that is required of

---

1. Norman Perrin, *Rediscovering the Teaching of Jesus* (London: SCM Press; New York: Harper & Row, 1967), p. 114.
2. *Ibid.*, p. 115.

the hearer in regard to Jesus and his proclamation. Here again the urgency of the eschatological moment points to Jesus' self-understanding and his vision of himself as the one in terms of whom the messianic hour is breaking in. His form of life is embodied in the crisis situation of the now.

Preconceived Ideas May Blind One to the Challenge

The Laborers in the Vineyard (Matt. 20:1–6)

This parable reflects an intolerable situation from the worker's point of view because the employer is treating some of his workers according to the law of contractual compensation and others by an arbitrary generosity. One would naturally find offense in the story and respond with a call for consistency: either deal with all legalistically or with all generously. The point of the analogy is precisely this, however — that in the present eschatological activity of God in the person of Jesus a new situation prevails in which it is intolerable for Judaism to insist on binding God to preconceived legalisms. That a worker should receive fair wages for his labors is all right in the worldly sphere, but the presence of God in the now entails the forgiveness of sins by the sheer generosity of grace. Perrin agrees with Ernst Fuchs and his students Eta Linnemann and Eberhard Jüngel that Jesus here implies "a tremendous personal claim" in answering an attack upon his conduct toward outcasts and sinners.[3]

It is phenomenologically correct to say that the evidence of the parable implies "a tremendous personal claim" on the part of Jesus; indeed, it discloses the radical character and authority of Jesus' self-understanding — he indwells his very language with a vision of the forgiveness of sinners and outcasts and of their fellowship in the messianic banquet. Jesus gives personal backing to his behavior; hence, a description of that behavior perforce implies his personal understanding of himself and the disclosure of his personal pronoun *I* in public. His form of life is embodied in the language-using situation, where the receptive hearer understands what he says and perceives his position as speaker. In perceiving Jesus' position as speaker, each hearer will acknowledge that

3. Perrin, *Rediscovering the Teaching of Jesus*, p. 118; Eta Linnemann, *Parables of Jesus: Introduction and Exposition*, trans. John Sturdy (Naperville, IL: Alec R. Allenson, 1966), p. 87. Compare Ernst Fuchs, *Studies of the Historical Jesus*, Studies in Biblical Theology, no. 42 (London: SCM Press, 1964), p. 36; Eberhard Jüngel, *Paulus und Jesus* (Hermeneutische Untersuchungen zur Theologie 2 [Tübingen: J.C.B. Mohr (Paul Siebeck), 1964²]), pp. 168ff.

Jesus is making tremendous claims about himself, but it is also true
that perceiving his exact position will ultimately require a decision as
to whether Jesus is standing back of his language in good faith or in
bad faith, whether he is playing the language-game of fidelity or the
language-game of deception. As Ludwig Wittgenstein observes, "Lying
is a language-game that needs to be learned like any other one."[4] That
is why, ultimately speaking, the final proof of the pudding is in the
eating, and entering the kingdom of God an acceptance in good faith
of the good faith of Jesus as he offers forgiving grace in terms of his
spoken language and the acted language of open table-fellowship. Outcasts and sinners, like the recipients of the employer's unanticipated
generosity in the parable, understand his claim and believe in the good
faith of the one who makes the claim; the religious authorities, like the
earlier workers in the parable, understand the claim but are tied to a
legalistic language-game and misconstrue his claim as arising from bad
faith. Jesus' invitation to all his hearers is that they decisively enter the
realm of grace by faith and participate in the fellowship of open table-
fellowship in the eschatological now. Those who do experience a con-
firmation of his personal claims. But even those who do not accept the
invitation understand the implications of those personal claims.

As long as Perrin and other radical critics do not question Jesus'
genuineness in making extraordinary claims for himself, it is clear that
they are accepting his claims at face value and are assuming his good
faith in making those claims. Since that is the case, my descriptive
phenomenology is all the more effective, for it can be assumed that
Jesus is playing an honest language-game, not a deceptive language-
game. Accordingly, the phenomenology of his person can be carried to
the deeper level of his genuine intentionality and conscious vision. What
he does and says honestly reflects his personal aims. From within the
early Christian community itself, most importantly from those who
were witnesses of his person and ministry, there is strong supportive
evidence that Jesus stood back of his words and works in good faith;
otherwise, as happens with those who practice deceptive language-
games, his followers would have found him out and not continued to
bear witness to their conviction that he faithfully stood back of his
words.[5]

4. *Philosophical Investigations*, trans. G. E. M. Anscombe (New York: Macmillan,
1953), para. 249.

5. On the language-game of the liar, see Dallas High, *Language, Persons, and
Belief: Studies in Wittgenstein's "Philosophical Investigations" and Religious Uses of
Language* (New York: Oxford University Press, 1967), pp. 108–110.

The Two Sons (Matt. 21:28–31)

Jesus is making the point in this parable that to refuse and then to repent is better than to accept and then to refuse. Perrin remarks that "the allusion again is to a situation in which outcasts are accepting forgiveness and other Jews are finding offense in this, and thereby blinding themselves to the reality of their own situation."[6]

What kind of person would make such an incredible comparison, implying by analogy that formal Judaism has said yes but hasn't fulfilled this promise to God, while sinners and outcasts who formerly said no have latterly repented and gone obediently to work in God's vineyard? Only one who understands that he is in a position of authority to make such claims and who envisions the reality of that form of life could make such a claim.

Children in the Marketplace (Matt. 11:16–19; Luke 7:31–35)

I will not discuss this parable beyond my previous exegesis except to note that Perrin again makes a good deal of the epithet "friend of tax collectors and sinners" as equivalent to "holder of table-fellowship with tax collectors and other Jews who have made themselves as Gentiles." This, when coupled with the first epithet, "a glutton and a drunkard," comprises "an unmistakable reference to [a] major aspect of the ministry of Jesus . . . : the table-fellowship 'of the Kingdom of God.' "[7] This well-known form of life in Jesus' ministry is also keynoted by a joyousness that anticipates the happiness of the age to come.[8] My observation about this phenomenon is that only one who is consciously functioning with a sense of messianic fulfillment would have the audacity to give civil status to such proclamation and practice.

The Pharisee and the Tax Collector (Luke 18:9–14a)

While rejecting verse 14b as editorial, Perrin finds the main body of the parable an impressive expression of Jesus' challenge. His use of "I tell you," with its direct challenge to the preconceptions of his hostile contemporaries, "is an indirect personal claim of great magnitude."[9]

Certainly a personal claim of such magnitude, prefaced by the authoritative use of "I tell you" (legō hymin) is persuasive evidence that

6. Rediscovering the Teaching of Jesus, p. 119.
7. Ibid., p. 121.
8. Ibid.
9. Ibid., p. 122.

Jesus possesses an authoritative sense of discernment regarding the forgiveness of sins in this eschatological age.

The Necessary Response to the Challenge

The Good Samaritan (Luke 10:29–37)

The vividness and power of this story are sufficient evidence of its authenticity, Perrin avers, and adds that Jesus "leaves no stone unturned" to make the point: Be prepared to abandon presuppositions. Jesus uses the parable not only to teach a radically new ethic of neighborliness, but more importantly to present "an imitation of God's response to one's own need" in terms of the eschatological forgiveness of sins. Showing mercy is the proper response to being shown mercy. The full force of the parable

> is felt only when it is realized that this lesson is being taught by one who proclaimed a radically new concept of the forgiveness of God: it extended even to the 'Jew who had made himself a Gentile.'[10]

Forgiveness of sins is the proper domain of God, but Jesus' extraordinary illustration of grace and its consequence in terms of an outcast Samaritan exhibits his self-understanding that in terms of his own person this radical forgiveness is present as a challenge and requires an appropriate response. Only one who has a high opinion of his authority could challenge cherished presuppositions and assert new concepts of divine forgiveness, and only this is sufficient to account for the phenomenon of this parable. Implicit in the story itself is a new Christology that far exceeds the old messianism. Jesus' creativity and vision are clearly disclosed to the receptive eye.

The Unmerciful Servant (Matt. 18:23–33)

Perrin omits verses 34–35 as editorial but views the parable as an exemplary story that makes the same points, although in reverse, as the parable of the good Samaritan: As you have been forgiven, so must you forgive. Again the horizon of Jesus' self-understanding is implicit in the principle of the parable: "the experience of God demands a re-

10. *Ibid.*, p. 124.

sponse in terms of imitation of that experience in relationship to one's fellow men."[11]

The Tower Builder and the King Going to War (Luke 14:28-32)

The central theme in both these parables challenges one to sober judgment and earnest self-preparedness.[12] Who but one possessed of an unusual sense of authority would require such a response to his proclamation?

Confidence in God

The Friend at Midnight (The Importuned Friend; Luke 11:5-8)

The sense of the parable hinges on the translation of *anaideian* in verse 8, and Perrin, following Joachim Jeremias, persuasively interprets it "yet *not to lose face* he will rise and give him whatever he needs."[13] The point is that the shame of refusing one in need gives the neighbor confidence to ask. Arguing from the lesser to the greater, Jesus is implying how much more God must hear you. Accordingly, the needy sinner may have complete confidence in God's gracious forgiveness.

What this implies about Jesus' understanding of his ministry is profound—he is claiming nothing less than the authority to speak about a matter that does not legitimately lie within human province, namely, a radically new attitude to the traditionally outcast sinner.

The Unjust Judge (The Importuned Judge; Luke 18:1-8)

Perrin accepts verses 2-5 as authentic, with verse 1 as a Lukan introduction and verses 6-8 as later tradition. Working with the core saying of verses 2-5, he remarks that again we have an argument by Jesus from the lesser to the greater and that the appeal is to faith on the part of the hearer: "If an unjust judge can be importuned into responding to a poor widow, how much more can you trust the God who reaches out to you in the word of forgiveness."[14] Perrin offers a disclaimer to the word *faith*, fearing an overly evangelical application of what he considers a later churchly doctrine of faith in Jesus. Nonetheless he is compelled by the evidence as a whole to allow that Jesus

---

11. *Ibid.*, p. 126.
12. *Ibid.*, p. 128.
13. See Perrin, *ibid.* My italics. See also Jeremias, *The Parables of Jesus*, trans. S. H. Hooke, rev. ed. (New York: Scribners, 1963), p. 158.
14. *Rediscovering the Teaching of Jesus*, p. 130.

is challenging his hearers to faith and prayer in a radical way. Jesus is not inviting them to share *his* faith, as earlier and more recent liberal theology has suggested (for example, Fuchs), but is calling men and women to faith in the present miraculous presence of the kingdom of God, such that it can be said by Jesus, "Your faith has saved you." There is nothing in Hellenistic or Jewish literature that is anything like this importuning of God's present power to exorcise and to heal by faith.[15] Faith is never demanded of the patient in those miracle stories. On the other hand, Perrin argues, the evidence of Jesus' exorcisms is strong in the synoptic tradition and his call for faith remarkable and strikingly different.[16] Jesus' use of the unusual formula "your faith has saved you" or its equivalent (Mark 2:5, the paralytic; Mark 5:34, the woman with the flow of blood; Mark 10:52, blind Bartimaeus; Luke 7:50, the woman who was a sinner; Luke 17:19, the Samaritan leper) is convincing evidence of his remarkable authority. (Two additional passages are cited and discussed by Perrin to underscore Jesus' proclamation of the power of importuning faith: Matthew 17:20 on "moving mountains" [cf. Mark 11:23], and Luke 17:6 on "uprooting trees." Both have to do with the inconceivable power of faith.)

Healing and the forgiveness of sins are linked together as evidence of the presence of the kingdom of God (cf. Mark 2:7; 3:22–27). Now it is precisely here that Perrin unwittingly serves to support my phenomenological analysis of the evidence that points to Jesus' understanding of himself as one who exercises divine prerogatives. In the context of these passages faith begins as recognition:

> . . . recognition that Jesus does, in fact, have the authority to forgive sins, and recognition that the exorcisms are, indeed, a manifestation of the Kingdom of God, all possible arguments to the contrary notwithstanding. . . . Jesus *could* have been blaspheming, his exorcisms *could* be collusion with evil forces . . . , but for faith both are a manifestation of the kingly activity of God.[17]

Faith is therefore recognition and trust that God is active in the ministry of Jesus and "that Jesus is what he implicitly claims to be."[18]

15. See Perrin's lengthy discussion, *ibid.*, pp. 132–142.

16. This is tendered against more skeptical form critics by the criterion of dissimilarity, though Perrin continues to be very skeptical himself about recovering accuracy of detail in the synoptic stories.

17. Perrin, *Rediscovering the Teaching of Jesus*, p. 140.

18. *Ibid.*

Perrin is unconvincing when he attempts to qualify the obvious christological implications of this admission by insisting that nevertheless
faith is used absolutely here and is not directly faith in God or in Jesus.
But I would reply that absolute trust and obedience on the part of one
who believes is not trust in an abstraction such as the "kingdom," as
though faith could float free, but is trust in the believability and fidelity
of the one who stands behind such offers. In other words, I am arguing
that if Perrin has gone this far he should go all the way with the
evidence, for the evidence clearly leads us to affirm that Jesus implicitly
claims to do what only God can do, to forgive sins, and that those who
have faith in his verbal offer and see evidence of healing in his works
do not have faith in his words and acts but in *him*, because he indwells
his words and acts and is inseparable from them. Perrin has sufficient
evidence for a satisfactory phenomenology of Jesus and makes a correct
initial description but does not follow through with a proper phenomenology of persons. Accordingly, his summary of the section on faith
says a great deal about Jesus but skirts the question of Jesus' self-
understanding because of a curious notion that a language-game can
be apotheosized and abstracted from the person who plays it, indwells
it, stands back of it, and affixes his signature to it. Note the depersonalized language:

> Involved in faith is absolute trust and complete obedience. We may
> summarize: Jesus challenged men to faith as recognition and response
> to the challenge of his proclamation — recognition that God was, indeed,
> active as king in his ministry, and in a specific event, occasion or in-
> cident for the individual concerned, and response in terms of absolute
> trust and complete obedience.[19]

But that will not do, because it is essentially propositional faith —
faith in Jesus' proclamation, or more mysteriously, "absolute trust and
complete obedience" without any reference at all to what or to whom
one is to be in complete obedience, and in what or in whom one is to
have absolute trust. The real disclosure point in Perrin's sentence is,
"Recognition that God was, indeed, active as king in his ministry,"
which is to be construed not as mere assent to that bare proposition
but as confidence and belief in Jesus that the kingly rule of God is
actually incarnate in his person, and confidence that Jesus is con-

19. *Ibid.*, pp. 141f.

sciously aware of his authority and stands back of his propositional claims with intentional fidelity and that he authenticates those claims with appropriate miracles and exorcisms which give civil status to his sense of mission. That is where a proper phenomenology should finally bring us.

Only one who believes that he embodies divine authority could extend such radical challenges to discipleship. The passages that follow convinced Rudolf Bultmann of their genuineness because they are so dissimilar to anything contemporary to Jesus, are new and characteristic of his preaching.[20]

Challenge to Discipleship (Luke 9:62; Mark 10:23b, 25; Luke 14:11, cf. 16:15)

Luke 9:62

"No one who puts his hand to the plow and looks back is fit for the kingdom of God."

The "vivid naturalness of imagery" impresses Perrin that this saying is authentic, but even more impressive is "the radical nature of the demand."[21] But what sort of person could make such a demand except one utterly convinced of the divine nature of his calling and of the presence of the kingdom in his own form of life?

Mark 10:23b, 25

"How hard it will be [v. 24: is] . . . to enter the kingdom of God. . . . It is easier for a camel to go through the eye of a needle than for a rich man to enter the kingdom of God."

Although the idiom of entering the kingdom of God is found in both Judaism and the early church, Perrin overrides the criterion of dissimilarity because the saying is widespread in the tradition and meets the requirements of the criterion of multiple attestation. Moreover, Jesus' attitude toward riches is more radical than that of the rabbis, who sought to strike a balance on the subject. My question is, what sort of understanding must Jesus have had of himself if Perrin can describe

20. *History of the Synoptic Tradition*, trans. John Marsh (New York: Harper & Row, 1976), p. 105; Perrin, *Rediscovering the Teaching of Jesus*, p. 142.
21. *Rediscovering the Teaching of Jesus*, p. 142.

him in the following manner: "Jesus, on the other hand, sees in riches a great danger. The reason is probably that he saw in riches a hindrance to the absolute nature of the self-surrender necessary as response to the challenge of the proclamation."[22] The logic of person analysis would lead us to conclude that the absolute challenge of the proclamation is really the absolute challenge of the *proclaimer*, since a proclamation does nothing by itself and has no independent status apart from the person who proclaims it and stands back of it with authority. It is curious language Perrin insists on using. Why not say that Jesus "saw in riches a hindrance to the absolute self-surrender necessary in response to him," since the response to discipleship is always to follow *him*? The response is not to an abstract challenge or proclamation but to the one who issues the challenge, that is, to Jesus himself. The empirical evidence of the Gospels is that people followed Jesus, not a challenge or proclamation. They gathered in table-fellowship with *him*, followed *his* bidding, and proclaimed his message in response to *him*. Anything less would be to commit the fallacy of misplaced concreteness. And what this Markan passage says of Jesus' self-understanding is astounding: in making an absolute demand of his hearers he is evincing a self-concept that implies that he considers himself absolutely worth following. Who could make such a demand and have so high an estimate of his authority but one who is either mad or the divinely authoritative person he claims to be? Phenomenologically the evidence leads to one or to the other.

This is even more true of the next saying.

Luke 9:60a

"Leave the dead to bury their own dead."

Surely this, "possibly the most radical of the sayings of Jesus on response to the challenge," is going too far! Who could possibly make such an offensive and insensitive statement except one who is absolutely convinced that following him is worth more than anything else in the world? According to the criterion of dissimilarity, the radical nature of the saying is the guarantee of its authenticity and affords us a valuable insight into the astonishing originality of Jesus' concept of self and mission. What must Jesus be thinking of himself if, in Perrin's words, the all-demanding challenge of the kingdom "must transcend all

22. *Ibid.*, p. 144.

other responsibilities and duties, however naturally and normally important those might be"?[23]

Matthew 7:13a (cf. Luke 13:24)

"Enter by the narrow gate. . . ." [Matt. 7:13a]

The same is true of this saying about entering the kingdom, which stresses "the radical nature of Jesus' demand."[24] If Jesus' demand is radical, then he himself is radical. The phenomenological evidence inexorably points to Jesus as a radical person with a radical understanding of himself and his mission.

Luke 14:11 (cf. 16:15)

"For everyone who exalts himself will be humbled, and he who humbles himself will be exalted." [Luke 14:11]

The same point is made in reverse in this saying. But who can possibly turn all human values upside down and imply that "all must be, and will be, in accordance with the values of God"?[25] Only one who is conscious of speaking with the authority of God.

The New Attitude (Mark 10:15; Matt. 5:39b–41; Matt. 5:44–48)

Mark 10:15

"Truly, I say to you, whoever does not receive the kingdom of God like a child shall not enter it."

This saying is described as perhaps "the most memorable and pregnant" of all Jesus' utterances and as evidencing a remarkable "originality" — "It sums up a whole aspect of the teaching of Jesus in one unforgettable image: a man must bring to his response to the activity of God the ready trust and instinctive obedience of a child."[26] The revolutionary originality of Jesus is implicit in the saying and can come only from one who is absolutely convinced that he has the authority

23. *Ibid.*, p. 144.
24. *Ibid.*, p. 145.
25. *Ibid.*
26. *Ibid.*, p. 146.

to challenge the "adult" theology of Judaism and turn the whole system upside down with a demand for an entirely new attitude toward receiving the kingdom of God. The kingdom is not to be received with the sophisticated attitude of critical thought, but with the joyous and unquestioning sense of discovery that characterizes the little child. Who but a self-conscious authority could lay down the absurd (for worldly eyes) criterion that to enter the kingdom of God one must become a child again (does this not also imply a thoroughgoing rebirth in one's total attitude)?

We should also note that the unusual use of the personal pronoun *I* in the formula "truly, I say to you" (*amēn legō hymin*) gives additional weight of authority not only to the demand itself but also to my argument that Jesus is indwelling the saying with intentional authority. He understands himself to have the right to make demands that only God has the right to make.

Matthew 5:39b–41

"But if any one strikes you on the right cheek, turn to him the other also; and if any one would sue you and take your coat, let him have your cloak as well; and if any one forces you to go one mile, go with him two miles."

While the philosophers of the day (Epictetus and the Stoics, for example) found it in their best interests not to quarrel with the power of Roman arms, Jesus' demand is unexpectedly different. "The teaching of Jesus challenges men to an attitude radically different from the prudential morality of an Epictetus: they are to see in the imposition a challenge to service and to accept it gladly."[27] This "radically different" demand obtains in the other two examples, where one is formally insulted by a backhanded slap on the right cheek, or relinquishes against the rights of Jewish law (Exod. 22:26–27; Deut. 24:12–13) his outer garment. In all three instances the command of Jesus is, "Do not stand on your rights but rather give more than could be demanded of you!"[28] Perrin feels that these are ridiculous if taken literally but illustrate a principle that is deliberately expressed in an extreme manner by Jesus, following "the axiom that Jesus knew what he was talking about."[29]

27. *Ibid.*
28. *Ibid.*, p. 147.
29. *Ibid.*

That, certainly, is a clear admission of Jesus' self-understanding and self-conscious awareness of having a special authority to utter such radical challenges. And what principle is Jesus enunciating? It is "a radically new approach to the business of living . . .":

> Not natural pride, not a standing on one's own rights, not even a prudential acceptance, are the proper response to these crises *now*, however much they might have been so *before*. In light of the challenge of God and of the new relationship with one's fellow man one must respond in a new way, in a way appropriate to the new situation.[30]

The daring that motivates Jesus to contrast the *now* with the *before* and to place himself in authority over Moses indicates clearly that he is intending to speak with divine authority, for the proclamations of Moses that Jesus claims to supersede by the formula, "you have heard that it was said . . . , but I say to you," are not proclamations of Moses but of God.

Matthew 5:44–48

"Love your enemies . . ." [Matt. 5:44]

Yet another in the series of antitheses in Matthew 5 which Perrin accepts as authentic is this radical teaching "directed to those who have experienced the love of God in terms of forgiveness of sins" and have "gathered together in the 'table-fellowship of the Kingdom'."[31] Who could speak so authoritatively about those who have been sinners and enemies of God and are now recipients of divine love, forgiveness, and table-fellowship, except one who consciously mediates that radical love in his spoken word of forgiveness and in his acted word of table-fellowship? Jesus is assuming the prerogatives of God in this form of speech. The language-game is new and radical and supersedes the traditional language-game of his religious contemporaries who consider forgiven and fellowshiping outcasts and sinners as still unforgiven and unworthy of banqueting in the kingdom of God. Not only does it require a sense of divine authority on Jesus' part to forgive and to fellowship with outcasts and sinners, but equally so to challenge them to love *their* enemies as they, the former enemies of God, have been loved by *him*. Jesus' authoritative challenge is a challenge to be imitators of what God

30. *Ibid.*, p. 148. His italics.
31. *Ibid.*

is doing through him: "the challenge is to exceed the normal and natural attitudes of love, affection, kindness, and courtesy. . . . Once these words of Jesus can be seen in their original context, any words of ours become superfluous."[32]

Mark 7:15

"There is nothing outside a man which by going into him can defile him; but the things which come out of a man are what defile him."

Perrin acknowledges the completely original content of this saying of Jesus, because it goes completely against the grain of rabbinic and sectarian Judaism by insisting that only one's own attitudes and behavior, not foods and external practices, defile. It is one of the most remarkable statements of Jesus and is "completely coherent with the most equally radical attitude and behavior of Jesus in connection with 'tax collectors and sinners.' "[33]

When the saying is placed in the context of the kingdom proclamation, "we can see at once that the experience of God acting as king requires a radically new attitude to life in the world,"[34] where there is no longer clean and unclean, Jew and Gentile, but the reality of divine forgiveness which brings inner transformation. We can take Perrin's analysis to its logical conclusion and see that in Jesus' forgiving of sinners and in his fellowshiping with them in joyous feasting he personifies the kingly activity of God. His speech conveys forgiveness from sin, his behavior welcomes the forgiven around the table of the inaugurated kingdom. Jesus is not concerned with external rituals, but rather with inner attitudes. From this saying we gather that he is implying his own purity of intention, his own untrammeled love of the unlovely, and is calling upon his hearers to work from the inside out, not from the outside in. Only if Jesus is conscious that God is working eschatologically in him and that he is the embodied king of the kingdom does it make sense for him to speak in such extraordinary terms.

The Response to the Challenge of the Reality of God (The Lord's Prayer, Matt. 6:12; parallel, Luke 11:4)

"Forgive us our sins, as we ourselves herewith forgive everyone who has sinned against us."[35]

32. *Ibid.*, p. 149.
33. *Ibid.*, p. 150.
34. *Ibid.*
35. Perrin's translation, *ibid.*, p. 151; see p. 152.

This prayer not only satisfies the criterion of dissimilarity "absolutely," but also is, according to Perrin, essential in understanding the teaching of Jesus. It is a disciple's prayer, to be prayed by those who have already experienced the forgiveness of sins and who pray for a continuation of that experience of God as king. Forgiveness of sins is a central aspect of experiencing God's kingship. Forgiveness of others then follows one's being forgiven.[36]

Several compelling conclusions may be drawn from Perrin's exegesis. One is that forgiveness is a present reality in Jesus' ministry and that by his acts and words he is personifying the contemporaneity of radical forgiveness of the outcast. In the larger context of his teaching about the kingdom of God, furthermore, the reign of God is seen to be present: Jesus is claiming that both the kingdom of God and forgiveness are available and is implicitly claiming their presence in terms of response to himself and his demands. Assuming that Jesus knows what he is doing, we properly interpret the whole phenomenon as an implicit testimony to his conscious intention to realize messianic expectations and to embody in his form of life a radically creative Christology. How else could he speak with such authority, assume the reality of forgiveness, and demand that his disciples forgive in the same spirit of love by which they have been forgiven?

Turning next to Jesus' sayings about the future, Perrin undertakes a series of exegetical explorations that confirms the approach I have taken toward the self-understanding of Jesus. An adequate phenomenology of persons will propel the exegesis of authentic passages to its proper conclusion and allow us to see Jesus as a person with an extraordinary self-concept regarding the future as well as the present.

Confidence in God's Future

The Sower (Mark 4:3–9)

The primary point of this parable is the contrast between the small amount of seed and the bountiful harvest. Forgiveness and table-fellowship, like the seed, are planted and taking root, but this is only an anticipation of the richest blessings to come:

With the proclamation of the Kingdom by Jesus on the one hand and this parable on the other, we are justified in arguing that Jesus, for all

36. See Perrin's discussion, *ibid.*, pp. 152ff.

the claims he made and implied about the significance of his ministry and message, none the less looked forward to a consummation to which this was related as seed-time to harvest.[37]

We may have all kinds of difficulties in interpreting this emphasis in Jesus' teaching, in Perrin's opinion, but that cannot circumvent the fact that the emphasis is there. The phenomenon of this particular parable discloses Jesus' awareness that something marvelous has been planted in his ministry, which is moving inexorably on to fulfillment. The only difficulty one could have with the fact of this phenomenon is if one were predisposed to picture Jesus as not so authoritative regarding what is and is to be, and were unwilling to follow the evidence to its logical conclusion in the original mind of Jesus. He is, after all, implying some quite amazing things about himself, the present, and the future.

The contrast between the small beginnings and big endings of the kingdom is also the theme of the next saying.

The Mustard Seed (Mark 4:30–32)

Who but one who is supremely self-confident about what is coming to pass through his words and acts and about what will be brought to fruition in the future could utter such a saying?[38]

The Leaven (Matt. 13:33)

The "point of departure is the activity of God as king," says Perrin,[39] and the activity of God as king is seen in the breaking in of God's power in the leavenlike ministry of Jesus, whose self-understanding of his person and mission is again implicit in this little analogue.

The Seed Growing of Itself (Mark 4:26–29)

The reign of God is at work and affords the believer sure confidence that the divine activity in the ministry of Jesus will come to a triumphant conclusion. This group of parables about small beginnings and big endings certainly implies more than Perrin's overly cautious opinion that "Jesus had confidence in God and sought to inculcate others with this confidence . . . ,"[40] though he allows that with additional data on

37. *Ibid.*, p. 156.
38. See Perrin's discussion, *ibid.*, pp. 157f.
39. *Ibid.*, p. 158.
40. *Ibid.*, p. 159.

the message of Jesus we might be able to go further. But the data I have already analyzed from Perrin's core of authentic sayings is sufficient evidence that Jesus' claims about himself go far beyond anything that might be stereotyped as his personal confidence in God. Had Perrin a better phenomenological method he would have been able to see that in these parables of mysterious growth, as in all of the other sayings, Jesus is claiming implicitly to be exercising divine prerogatives.

The Kingdom of God As a Future Expectation

Luke 11:2 (parallel, Matt. 6:10)

"Thy kingdom come." [Luke 11:2]

This is a disciple's prayer, uttered by those who experience the kingship of God in their lives and who pray for its future consummation:

> This petition is, then, further evidence that Jesus did look forward to a future consummation of that which had begun in his ministry and in the experience of men challenged by that ministry.[41]

The saying exudes Jesus' vision and confidence that what God has done in his present works and words will come to completion inexorably in the future: only a prophetic consciousness of extraordinary depth and authority could claim the presence and coming of the kingship of God as Jesus does in this petition.

Matthew 8:11 (parallel, Luke 13:28–29)

"I tell you, many will come from east and west and sit at table with Abraham, Isaac, and Jacob in the kingdom of heaven." [Matt. 8:11]

Perrin prefers the Lukan version of the story but the Matthaean wording as closer to the originally independent saying. While the symbolism of the messianic feast is typically Jewish (e.g., Isa. 25:6–8), the striking differences in Jesus' use of the figure are uncharacteristic vividness and brevity, an association of the banquet with the end-time state of blessedness in the kingdom, and the implied inclusion of the outcast and Gentile. But what is most impressive when the saying is set in the context of the other kingdom and banquet figures (e.g., the marriage feast in Mark 2:19) is Jesus' implication that the banquet has

41. *Ibid.*, p. 161.

already begun in the regular table-fellowship which is elsewhere characteristic of his ministry and which celebrates the coming of outcasts
and Jews who have made themselves as Gentiles.[42]

The authority of one who can make such a claim for the present and
for a future consummation of that fellowship has to be extraordinary.
The saying finds its inauguration in Jesus' act of table-fellowship and
underscores his awareness of what he is doing, his consciousness of
introducing the messianic age of the feast, and his authority to forgive
and include those who come from east and west.

Discovering Jesus' Intentionality

This completes Perrin's exegesis of what he considers core authentic
sayings arrived at by a critical use of the criterion of dissimilarity. A
long section follows on the sayings about the Son of man, in which
Perrin dismisses virtually all as having any claim to authenticity. I shall
take up that question, as well as other discarded sayings, in the next
chapter. But for the present, suffice it to say that my analysis of a group
of unquestionably authentic sayings arrived at by a "state of the art"
Bultmannian methodology yields impressive results when informed by
a phenomenology of persons that makes the simple notation that one's
self-understanding is embodied ineluctably in his language of speech
and action. Would we want to know who Jesus really is? Then "look
and see" what he says and what he does, as Wittgenstein invites us to
do.[43] Look at the forms of life and language-games Jesus is embodying
in his civil language and we will see that in and through all the mul-
tifarious relationships are "family resemblances," "a complicated network of similarities overlapping and criss-crossing: sometimes overall
similarities, sometimes similarities of detail."[44] There is no one fixed
and unequivocal use of rhetoric in Jesus' language-game, but what does
stand out in examination of the woven strands of his speech and acts
are the threads of forgiveness (speech) and table-fellowship (acts). The
two are complementary and indicate an intentional self who weaves a
complicated pattern around the simple themes of wholeness and reconciliation. These family resemblances furthermore disclose one who
knows what he is doing as he deliberately claims authority to forgive

42. *Ibid.*, p. 163.
43. *Philosophical Investigations*, para. 66.
44. *Ibid.*, para. 66, 67.

sins and welcomes outcasts back into fellowship with God. The whole
intent of his ministry reduces to this simple theme, as he does "battle
against the bewitchment of our intelligence by means of language"[45]
and by his own unusual language-game aims to bring to light what has
become hidden:

> The aspects of things that are most important for us are hidden
> because of their simplicity and familiarity. (One is unable to notice
> something — because it is always before one's eyes.) The real founda-
> tions of his enquiry do not strike a man at all. Unless *that* fact has at
> some time struck him. — And this means: we fail to be struck by what,
> once seen, is most striking and most powerful.[46]

Perhaps the simplest way to express this is to suggest that what
Jesus is doing in his sayings, parables, and table-fellowship is to paint
pictures of the kingship of God and what it means to enter it.

> What really comes to mind when we *understand* a word? — Isn't it
> something like a picture? Can't it *be* a picture?[47]

Exactly. And Jesus means to say that *he* embodies that picture as incarnate king of the kingdom (Luke 11:20) and as bridegroom of the
marriage feast (Mark 2:19). These are "the natural expression of [his]
intention";[48] "*this language-game is played.*"[49] When we read the gospel in its entirety and get all the sayings and acts of Jesus placed in
their proper setting, then we begin to understand that the various pictures by which Jesus models himself are part of a larger story in which
he is the protagonist ("only when one knows the story does one know
the significance of the picture").[50] Jesus is asking his hearers and view-
ers to listen to and look at what he is saying and doing,[51] and accordingly is consciously pointing to himself as the incarnate picture of
forgiveness and fellowship, of incarnate love. Moreover, he is inviting
them to participate in the activity, the form of life, the language-game

---

45. *Ibid.*, para. 109.
46. *Ibid.*, para. 129. His italics.
47. *Ibid.*, para. 139. His italics.
48. *Ibid.*, para. 647.
49. *Ibid.*, para. 654. His italics.
50. *Ibid.*, para. 663.
51. *Ibid.*, para. 669: ". . . one can point to a thing by *looking* or *listening.*" His
italics.

that is most characteristic of the forgiveness and joy that the kingdom of God brings — open table-fellowship. Thus if we want to know what Jesus meant, we look at what he did and what he taught others to do. Wittgenstein remarks, ". . . how are we to judge whether someone meant such-and-such? — The fact that he has, for example, mastered a particular technique . . . and that he taught someone else . . . , is such a criterion."[52] Hence, meaning is *behaving* in a certain way, not simply thinking. Jesus' intended meaning, his self-understanding, his messianic self-consciousness, *is* his behavior and its effects in open table-fellowship with tax collectors and sinners who have found forgiveness through him. Jesus' self-consciousness of being Messiah is not for us an inaccessible feeling he has inside him, but the demonstration of that intention in public through words and bodily activity.[53] The demonstration of this self-understanding in his words and acts builds up an association of patterns which we begin to understand as characteristic of his form of life. We cannot imagine him speaking or acting in a radically different way.[54] The cumulative study of Perrin's radical approach to the authentic sayings and accompanying practice of Jesus has its salutary effect in this at least, that a characteristic pattern of life emerges which is formidable in its implicit claim to represent God personally. Jesus indwells his bodily actions — his "inner process" is disclosed in his behavior, in his surroundings: "What is happening now has significance — in these surroundings. The surroundings give it its importance . . . (A smiling mouth *smiles* only in a human face)."[55] "What is the natural expression of an intention? — Look at a cat when it stalks a bird; or a beast when it wants to escape."[56] What is the "natural expression" of Jesus' intention? Look at his sayings about forgiveness and his practice of celebrating the wedding feast of the kingdom of God in open table-fellowship. These are the two foremost indicators of his intentionality, and because of their radical claim to divine authority can only be deemed creatively messianic and christological by implication. Jesus' intention in these words and acts is not an inaccessible something closeted deep within his private ego; it "does not 'accompany' the action any more than the thought 'accompanies'

52. *Ibid.*, para. 692.
53. *Ibid.*, 2.6.
54. *Ibid.*, 2.6; cf. part 1, para. 153, 154, 580.
55. *Ibid.*, para. 583.
56. *Ibid.*, para. 647.

speech."[57] It is that *with which* he speaks and acts. Intention, speech, and behavior are inseparable; hence, to refer to Jesus' language is necessarily to refer to *him* as intentional person. Since we identify other persons through hearing their speech and observing their behavior, we do in fact identify their intention and therefore their person through their speech and work. Intention is not an obscure and hidden entity that exists apart from speech and action in the civil sphere, as the Cartesian mind is disjoined from body. Rather, intention cannot be expressed in any other way than through the action and language of the person intending. Nothing is added to the description of an action when we say that it was intentional. That is G. E. M. Anscombe's argument in her monograph, *Intention.*[58] It is of central importance in the analysis of persons and is a very important point to grasp. When one *describes* a person's action in a particular situation one *ascribes* a particular intention because the two are inseparable. To describe an action means to ascribe an intentional agent who performs the action, for the agent cannot be described or ascribed without his action. The one leads to the other.

P. F. Strawson makes the same point in his illuminating study, *Individuals: An Essay in Descriptive Metaphysics.*[59] Strawson purposes to remind us that the most logically primitive idea in our description of individuals is the concept of persons as body-mind unities who are interrelated with other persons. If purely private experiences were all we had to work with in our investigation of states of consciousness there would be no way of distinguishing one person's experiences from another's. All would be mine, and therefore no one's:

> To put it briefly. One can ascribe states of consciousness to oneself only if one can ascribe them to others. One can ascribe them to others only if one can identify other objects of experience. And one cannot identify others if one can identify them only as subjects of experience, possessors of states of consciousness.[60]

There are two very important points in this argument that bear upon our interpretation of Jesus' language. The first is that one's self-consciousness as a person is inseparable from one's relationship to others.

57. *Ibid.*, 2.11.
58. (Oxford: Basil Blackwell & Mott, 1957), p. 29.
59. (London: Methuen, 1964).
60. Strawson, *Individuals*, p. 150.

That is, a person is not a purely isolated ego in the Cartesian sense. The second is related to the first and is of considerable importance in understanding the Old and New Testament concern that personal intention, word, and act be viewed in holistic fashion and not as separable and independent items (which is the case in play-acting or hypocrisy). Strawson reminds us that we come into being as persons only because we are able to relate to others and identify them as incarnate persons with their own unique intentionality, speech, and bodily action. The characteristics that identify another person may be material predicates (Strawson calls them M-predicates), such as, "weighs 140 pounds" or "is in the drawing room." Since these descriptions can also be made of material bodies to which states of consciousness are not applied, the more important identifying characteristics of persons are what Strawson calls P-predicates or person predicates, such as, "is smiling," "is going for a walk," "is in pain," "is thinking hard," "believes in God," and so on.

In Jesus' case the P-predicates would be "is forgiving someone's sins," "is healing that person," or "is having table-fellowship with those people." His person, hence his intention, is discovered *in* his speech and acts, as is the intention of any other person: "The primary reference of predicates of intention is *not* consciousness, but the bodily, observable action of the person."[61] This is a very important hermeneutical insight to bring to bear on gospel exegesis. It corrects the abandoned quests of the historical Jesus, which have spent misdirected searches for the pure personal subjectivity of Jesus. But of course *that* search has to be abandoned, as has the Kantian search for the "thing in itself." But the method of descriptive phenomenology I am employing discovers the subjectivity of a person in the objectivity of his behavior:

> What we are saying is that a concept of the person which includes objectivity does not thereby de-subjectify the person in the sense of denying him subjecthood. Rather it credits the subjecthood of the person in a particularly significant way by indicating its presence in a form intrinsically intelligible to others.[62]

In the simpler language of Jesus, "You will know them by their fruits" (Matt. 7:16). Here Jesus expresses his thematic witness to the integral

61. Robert H. King, "The Concept of the Person," *JR* 46 (January 1966): 41.
62. *Ibid.*, p. 42.

self, to the inner and the outer, to consciousness and body, to subjectivity and objectivity, to intention and the language activity that is so characteristic of his own words and works.

It is a striking fact of modern New Testament research that the essential clues for correctly reading the implicit christological self-understanding of Jesus are abundantly clear. Yet the proper methodology by which to interpret these phenomena is curiously missing. In *The Foundations of New Testament Christology*, R. H. Fuller succinctly summarizes the "state of the art" as far as the irreducible findings of modern criticism are concerned:

> An examination of Jesus' words — his proclamation of the reign of God, and his call for decision, his enunciation of God's demand, and his teaching about the nearness of God — and of his conduct — his calling men to follow him and his healings, his eating with publicans and sinners — forces upon us the conclusion that underlying his word and work is an implicit Christology. In Jesus as he understood himself, there is an immediate confrontation with "God's presence and his very self," offering judgment and salvation.[63]

Perrin concurs with this opinion, as we have seen in some detail, and reiterates this confidence in his later study, *A Modern Pilgrimage in New Testament Christology*.[64] He remarks that "each of the major elements of [Jesus'] teaching . . . contains a surprising aspect of uniqueness, of boldness, of audacity. . . . He is acting, and implicitly claiming to act, as I once heard Ernst Fuchs express it in a class at the 'Kirkliche Hochschule' in Berlin, *'Als ob er an die Stelle Gottes stünde'* (as if he stood in the very place of God himself)."[65]

This is an accurate description of the phenomena and is absolutely convincing evidence that Jesus did intend to stand in the very place of God himself. If the phenomenological evidence is followed to its natural conclusion, however, moving with the hinge as the christological door opens, we are introduced to an even wider horizon which visually encompasses not only implicit claims to messiahship but explicit christological claims as well.

But radical criticism appears incapable of making that very natural and rational swing. For immediately after marshaling a convincing case

63. (New York: Scribner, 1965), p. 106.
64. (Philadelphia: Fortress, 1974), especially pp. 51f.
65. *Ibid.*, pp. 51–52.

for Jesus' *implicit* christological claims, Perrin inexplicably abandons the trend of the evidence and reverts to abstract thing-language, the sort of category mistake that I see at the center of contemporary radical gospel research. Instead of saying that Jesus' unique claim to authority implies his conscious identification of his person with the person of God, Perrin argues that the actual authority of Jesus' words and deeds is derived from the kingdom of God.[66] Hence, a follower of Jesus does not come to know God's presence as king in his own experience by seeing Jesus as the personal embodiment of the reign of God, but by experiencing the kingdom. The language has fallen into abstraction, and the author has committed the fallacy of misplaced concreteness. Abstractions do not do anything; even the kingdom of God, misinterpreted as an impersonal "thing," does not do anything for anyone. The kingdom of God is the reign *of God*; it is God's judging and forgiving activity by which God *as person* makes himself known. And it is the language-game and form of life that Jesus indwells as he consciously manifests the forgiving and healing of God in his personal speech and behavior.

Accordingly, Perrin and those who follow his Bultmannian analysis are quite wrong methodologically when they slip off the hinge and close the door on person analysis. The following is a classic example of a serious category mistake in phenomenological analysis, and I quote Perrin at some length to illustrate how the critic can move from person-language to thing-language with hardly a wink of an eye. But the modulation has the gravest consequences for New Testament Christology beyond the egregious category error in analysis:

> What is true of the address of God [*abba*] is true of the totality of the message of Jesus: it implies a claim for his person and it reflects his authority. But if we concentrate our attention upon that implication and build greatly upon that authority then we are doing violence to the message itself. The authority of that message was derived from the reality of the kingdom it proclaimed, not from the person of the proclaimer. However true it may be to say that the person cannot be separated from his words, it is also true that the authority of the historical Jesus was the authority of the proclamation, not that of the proclaimer.[67]

66. *Ibid.*, p. 52.
67. *Ibid.*, p. 53.

To this line of argument I respond with a resounding no. Message, kingdom, proclamation, all are abstractions derived from the concrete person who stands back of them and indwells them with personal accreditation. They are aspects of Jesus' self-revelation and disclose his intention to claim this authority and to act as focal agent in the public arena of salvation. There is a hidden agenda in the radical critical program, which is to charge the early church with responsibility for making Jesus the proclaimer the proclaimed.[68] Not only does that assumption avoid the evidence that Jesus makes no distinction between proclaimer and proclamation, thus originating a tradition that the early church coherently followed, but implies quite the opposite and impugns the reliability of the early church regarding the original message of Jesus.

But the a priori assumption of radical redaction critics that the church widely created sayings of Jesus and put them on his lips receives a fundamental challenge from a thoroughgoing phenomenological analysis of the data. In the next chapter I will adduce further evidence that a facile distinction between Jesus' implicit christological behavior and his explicit christological behavior cannot be sustained, and that there is no evidence of widespread prophetic activity in the early church, as radical critics have claimed in support of the theory that Christian prophets created sayings of Jesus that were placed on his lips after the fact.

68. See *ibid.*

4

Jesus' Explicit Christological Claims
Employing the Criteria of Coherence and Continuity

In this chapter we shall see that an honest analysis of data about the sayings of Jesus and the supposed role of Christian prophets in the early church brings to light an astounding fact about contemporary New Testament criticism. When we bracket the widespread hermeneutical presupposition that the early church created all of the explicitly christological utterances that fall from the lips of Jesus in the Gospels and look at the evidence for such churchly activity from a purely descriptive and phenomenological point of view, free of any particular dogmatic commitment, we discover that there are no empirical data to validate the claim that the church created explicit christological sayings and placed them in the mouth of Jesus. What we do find are indications that the early church reflected upon the implications of Jesus' christological form of life in second-order theology which weaves a coherent and continuous pattern with his dominical originality. But we have no sure methodology by which to distinguish original sayings of Jesus from alleged church-created sayings. As soon as the full force of the phenomenological evidence in the preceding three chapters hits us with its incontrovertible evidence that Jesus' language-game is played out at the high altitude of a claim to divine authority, there is no possible way to distinguish indubitably his implicit christological claims from explicit christological claims that fall from his lips. Critics may bicker about this verse or that in regard to the evangelists' paraphrastic freedom as they shape their materials, but the stakes are higher than individual passages. We are talking about the fundamental assumption of radical redactional exegesis, namely, that the church is responsible for *all* explicit christological utterances assigned to the mouth of Jesus.

Simply on the descriptive level of implicit christological sayings the radical doctrine founders, for the principal insight of the phenomenology of persons makes it abundantly clear that Jesus' intentionality is not something *in addition to* his claims to divine prerogatives, but is disclosed *in* those very forms of language. What he factually discloses about himself is his incredible claim to have authority to speak as the voice of God. Without being forced at this point to make any judgment as to the truth of his claims on the purely descriptive level of phenomenological analysis, there is no inherent reason to doubt (in fact, there is every right to expect by the criterion of coherence) that Jesus also made appropriate explicit christological claims about himself. Hence, in this chapter the question I want to address is, "How does one know that Jesus did not actually make a particular explicit christological claim, if it is coherent with his implicit christological claims arrived at by the criterion of dissimilarity?" Bracketing the Cartesian principle of "when in doubt, discard," which of the explicit christological utterances that fall from Jesus' lips could be deemed inappropriate and incoherent in light of what we know undoubtedly about his implicit messianic self-understanding? What would a purely phenomenological analysis of the data lead us to expect?

Prophetic Activity in the Early Church

Before we proceed to examine the explicit christological utterances of Jesus that are discarded by radical critics as church-created, it is important for us to demolish the linchpin doctrine that has held radical methodology together since the early days of Bultmann. The doctrine in its simplest form is the widespread assumption that early Christian prophets in the church were responsible for explicit christological sayings that found their way in the tradition to the lips of the historical Jesus, but were never actually spoken by him. The demolition of this doctrine will be seen to proceed not along theological lines so much as by the sheer absence of convincing data. There is really no phenomenological evidence to support the hypothesis, and since I am attempting in this first section of my study to work from the outside in and to be as rigorously scientific as possible in simply describing the data, I shall want to let the facts speak for themselves.

In preparing the groundwork for an objective study of data concerning New Testament prophets we shall want to keep in mind an important distinction that David Hill makes in his recent and thoroughly convincing study, *New Testament Prophecy*. Describing the evangelists' freedom in adapting their materials, Hill observes that "there is no evidence that the liberty of adaptation — which, be it noted, is not the same as the creation of sayings *ex nihilo* — was taken casually."[1] The caution of that statement is commendable, but even more so is the warning that the paraphrastic freedom of the evangelists in fashioning the traditions according to their needs and settings is not the same as their creating new traditions and placing new sayings on the lips of Jesus. There is abundant evidence of *adaptive* paraphrasing in the early church, but the evidence does not suggest any substantive alteration and addition of the tradition; quite the contrary, a conscious distinction between the words of the earthly and exalted Jesus is always observed.

At the heart of contemporary radical criticism is the opposite assumption, however, that the gospel tradition is substantially affected by churchly invention. Norman Perrin, as I have noted, makes the assumption at the beginning of his study: "The early Church made no attempt to distinguish between the words the earthly Jesus had spoken and those spoken by the risen Lord through a prophet in the community."[2] That assumption governs Perrin's exegesis to the very last page of his work, as it does Rudolf Bultmann in *The History of the Synoptic Tradition:* "The Church drew no distinction between such utterances by Christian prophets and the sayings of Jesus in the tradition, for the reason that even the dominical sayings in the tradition were not the pronouncements of a past authority, but sayings of the risen Lord, who is always a contemporary for the Church."[3] And again, "The 'I-sayings' were predominantly the work of the *Hellenistic Churches*, though a beginning had already been made in the *Palestinian Church.* Here too Christian prophets filled by the Spirit spoke in the name of the ascended Lord sayings like Rev. 16:15."[4]

Hill's study addresses this hypothesis head on in view of the factual evidence and deals it a "crippling blow," to quote Ben F. Meyer in his

1. *New Testament Prophecy* (Atlanta: John Knox, 1980), p. 185.
2. *Rediscovering the Teaching of Jesus* (London: SCM Press; New York: Harper & Row, 1967), p. 15.
3. Trans. John Marsh (New York: Harper & Row, 1976), pp. 127–128; compare pp. 39–41, 50, 101f., 125f., 145–163. Footnote 1 on page 127 is especially significant.
4. *Ibid.*, p. 163. See Hermann von Sodon, "Das Interesse des apostolischen Zeitalters an der evangelischen Geschichte," *Theologische Abhandlung.* Carl Weizsächer ... gewidmet, ed. A. von Harnack (Freiburg: Mohr, 1892), p. 153, for one of the earliest formulations of the doctrine.

commendable work, *The Aims of Jesus*.[5] After examining the background of prophecy in the Old Testament and intertestamental literature, Jesus' prophetic characteristics, and evidences of Christian prophecy in Revelation, Acts, and Paul, Hill focuses on what is of principal concern in this study, "Christian Prophets and the Sayings of Jesus" (chap. 7). A brief résumé of his arguments will afford the reader some appreciation of how devastating the evidence against the radical hypothesis actually is.

The Distinction Between Jesus' Words and Prophets' Words

The first point to be noted is that since Paul distinguishes between the words of Jesus and his own words in I Corinthians 7:10, 12, and 25, it is likely that there was another wing in the early church characterized by *Enthusiasmus*, who strung their own utterances "in the Spirit" together with the carefully preserved *logia* of Jesus, thus creating a situation of serious doctrinal error.[6] Paul is careful to make the distinction, indicating that in the authoritative apostolic wing of the church the utterances of Jesus and personal opinion are kept separate. This point is also made by F. Neugebauer — that if, as Bultmann supposes, the sayings of anonymous charismatic prophets "gradually" won status as words of Jesus, then the Christian community did actually make a distinction between the two; but if the prophets' words had the same authority as Jesus' own words there would have been no need to retroject these words onto the lips of Jesus.[7]

Hill then adduces the evidence of cautious critics such as Birger Gerhardsson and H. Schürmann, who would remind us of the care with which the followers of Jesus would have transmitted his teaching activity,[8] although one would not need to agree with Gerhardsson in every detail. Schürmann has argued a strong case for the likelihood that pre-

5. (London: SCM Press, 1979), p. 74. Meyer refers to Hill's programmatic article "On the Evidence for the Creative Role of Christian Prophets," *NTS* 20 (1974): 262–274. For an earlier critique of Bultmann's view, see F. Neugebauer, "Geistsprüche und Jesuslogien," *ZNW* 53 (1962): 218–228.

6. See Martin Dibelius, *From Tradition to Gospel*, trans. Bertram L. Woolf (Greenwood, SC: Attic Press, 1971), p. 24; Hill, *New Testament Prophecy*, p. 162.

7. "Geistsprüche und Jesuslogien," pp. 218–228.

8. Birger Gerhardsson, *Memory and Manuscript*, trans. Eric J. Sharpe (Lund: C. W. K. Gleerup, 1961), and *Tradition and Transmission in Early Christianity*, trans. Eric J. Sharpe (Lund: C. W. K. Gleerup, 1964); H. Schürmann, *Traditionsgeschichtliche Untersuchungen zu den synoptischen Evangelien* (Düsseldorf: Patmos-Verlag, 1968).

Easter *logia* of Jesus provide the setting for post-Easter adaptations of those sayings. There is evidence that the early church *adapts* the sayings of Jesus, but not that it *creates* new ones.

Bultmann's evidence for the hypothesis of creative Christian prophecy is seen to be quite flimsy. He refers to the earlier work of Hermann Gunkel and Hermann von Soden, to the Book of Revelation, and to Odes of Solomon 42:6, which supposedly describes the function of Palestinian Christian prophets:

> "For I have risen and stand by them
> And speak through their mouth."[9]

The problem in citing the Odes as evidence of early Christian prophets is that it is probably a second-century Gnostic hymnbook and likely refers to believers in the sense of Luke 21:15, where Jesus promises to give his followers "a mouth and wisdom" in times of persecution that their adversaries will not be able to withstand or contradict. The passage from the Odes has nothing to do with a distinct group of creative Christian prophets.[10] Von Soden's argument, which Bultmann cites, is seen to rest on no empirical evidence, not even in reference to the writing of circular letters in the Book of Revelation, for there the letters are acknowledged to be utterances of the risen Lord and lend no support to the notion of such words being placed on the lips of the historical Jesus.[11] The early church carefully distinguishes between the words of Jesus and the risen Lord, between the Spirit addressing someone (Acts 10:19; 11:12; 13:2; 21:11) and the words of the Lord (Acts 9:4ff.; 10f.; 18:9; 23:11). I Thessalonians 4:15 ("By the word of the Lord") probably refers to Jesus' eschatological method as a whole, but certainly could not be cited to support the theory about Christian prophets. Bultmann's appeal to Gunkel is also without supportive evidence, for Gunkel merely assumes what the text does not say.[12] The Odes of Solomon simply will not support the hypothesis. Nor, as we have seen, will the Book of Revelation, even though Philipp Vielhauer, Joachim Jeremias, and numerous others employ texts such as Revelation 2–3 and 16:15 to support the notion. It is more likely that Revelation 3:20–21, which echoes

9. *The History of the Synoptic Tradition*, pp. 127–128, n. 1.
10. See Hill, *New Testament Prophecy*, p. 164.
11. *Ibid.*, p. 165.
12. *Ibid.*, pp. 166–168.

Luke 22:29–30 and Luke 12:36, and Revelation 16:15, which echoes Luke 12:39 and Matthew 24:43, are precisely that — echoes of genuine utterances of the historical Jesus. In no event do they lend any support to the hypothesis that Christian prophets were uttering sayings of the risen Lord which then could be placed in the mouth of the historical Jesus.

An even more serious question arises in regard to the use of Revelation as typical of the supposed Christian prophet, for the seer of the Apocalypse occupies a unique role as prophet and to him all other members of the community are subordinate, including the prophets.[13] He does not function as a model for other Christian prophets. Nor is there any evidence in the Synoptics or in John that explicit christological utterances originate from enthusiastic prophets. Nor does Acts imply that any Christian prophet spoke in the name of the risen Christ (Agabus is described as speaking by the Spirit, 11:28; 21:11). Nor does Paul offer any evidence that the prophetic gift of I Corinthians 14:3 empowers one to produce utterances of the Lord, and he himself gives no evidence of speaking as Christ himself.

Ernst Käsemann's supposition of widespread prophetic activity, an elaboration of Bultmann's, is also without empirical evidence. His belief that Christian prophets created such chiastic *Sätze heiligen Rechtes* ("Sentences of Holy Law") as Matthew 10:32 and I Corinthians 3:17 (prophets supposedly speaking as the final eschatological judge)[14] is quite without any convincing data. The genre of the chiasms is likely not legal but sapiental, that is, they are wisdom exhortations.[15] Käsemann adduces no sustaining evidence for a supposition assumed to be fact. Hill's critique of Käsemann is devastating and puts to rest an empirically unsupportable doctrine of the Bultmannian school:

> If it is to merit further consideration, the case for the attribution to Christian prophets of a creative role in respect of *logia Iēsou* requires validation by fresh and convincing arguments. Repetition of the evidence so far adduced cannot establish the theory.[16]

13. *Ibid.*, p. 169.

14. See Käsemann's "Sentences of Holy Law in the New Testament," *New Testament Questions of Today* (London: SCM Press, 1969), pp. 66–81.

15. See Hill, *New Testament Prophecy*, p. 171, and Klaus Berger, "Zu den sogenannten Sätzen heiligen Rechts," *NTS* 16 (1979–80): 10–40, and "Die sogenannten 'Sätze heiligen Rechts' im NT: Ihre Funktion und ihr Sitz im Leben," *ThZ* 28 (1972): 305–330.

16. *New Testament Prophecy*, p. 174.

Pursuing the evidence for the existence of New Testament prophets with the rigor of a team effort, a group of American scholars formed a Seminar on Christian Prophecy under the auspices of the Society of Biblical Literature (SBL) and spent half a decade in the 1970s reading and discussing papers on the subject, only to disband with the admission that there is no substantial evidence for the hypothesis and that one's point of entry into the hermeneutical circle determines one's conclusion. Hill criticizes Gerald Hawthorne's arguments that the early church identified Jesus and the risen Lord, expected people to prophesy, waited upon new words from the living Lord (John 16:12–15), respected the prophet's words as the words of Christ, viewed them as contiguous with the words of Jesus; that Paul considered himself a spokesman of the risen Lord (e.g., Gal. 1:11–12), commingled traditions of Jesus with those of the exalted Christ (I Cor. 11:23, 26), and himself spoke as a prophet (I Thess. 4:15); that early Christian prophets employed the freedom of *pesher* in modifying traditional sayings of Jesus or adding new ones (e.g., Mark 10:11–12), or in placing Old Testament texts on the lips of Jesus (Heb. 2:11–13; 10:5–7), in fusing Jesus' words with the prophet's (e.g., John 3:10–21); and that in later tradition the prophet's role is recognized in certain quarters of the early church, for example, the ending(s) of Mark, John 7:53 – 8:11, the *Didache*, and the writings of Justin Martyr and of Melito of Sardis.[17] Hawthorne's hermeneutical principle accordingly is that the authenticity of a saying derives not from the degree of probability that it was really spoken by Jesus, but by the fact that it comes by the authority of the Lord himself. Hence the historical question of authenticity is completely circumvented by using a doctrine of inspiration as a guarantee that whether Jesus really uttered a particular saying or a prophet said it for him, the same Christ is behind each saying and guarantees its objective truth.

Before we examine Hill's critique of Hawthorne it should be noted that there is a widespread tendency among contemporary evangelical scholars to follow something akin to Hawthorne's hermeneutic. Ralph P. Martin assumes the same posture in his study of the Gospels and shows complete abandon as to whether Jesus actually uttered a saying or

---

17. See Hawthorne, "Christian Prophets and the Sayings of Jesus: Evidence of and Criteria for," *SBL Seminar Papers*, 1975, vol. 2 (Missoula, MT: Scholars Press), pp. 174–178. Hawthorne, it should be noted, is very cautious.

whether it derives from the risen Lord speaking through an inspired Christian prophet:

> ... the words of Jesus are now embedded in canonical Scripture and for that reason gain their authority regardless of their origin, just as we read Revelation 3:20 as a true word of Christ today.[18]

In the entire volume of 314 pages Martin rarely deals with the subject of the historical Jesus. The entire study is carried out along redactional lines, such that if the reader did not know that Martin believed in the supernatural inspiration of the text, his study would be indistinguishable from what a member of the Bultmannian school might have written. E. Earle Ellis tends to think in somewhat the same fashion, placing heavy emphasis on the *pesher* tradition to explain the creativity of New Testament prophets and redactors.[19] This "each way free" approach of evangelical New Testament scholars has an initial appeal because it makes dialogue with more radical scholars possible and even profitable, and seems to promise answers to the problem (for traditional evangelicals) of the remarkable freedom on the part of the New Testament writers to paraphrase and adapt both Old Testament texts and the materials of the tradition concerning Jesus. It is precisely on this issue, however, that I think we need to make the most careful distinction between the church's *adapting* the tradition about Jesus, and *adding* new sayings to the tradition. As Hill correctly reminds both liberal and evangelical redactionists, "there is no evidence that the liberty of adaptation — which be it noted, is not the same as the creation of sayings *ex nihilo* — was taken casually" by the early church.[20] As a matter of fact, the creation of new sayings of Jesus is precisely what we find in the noncanonical apocryphal gospels written by Gnostic authors:

> in these works it is not the Jesus of history who teaches by action and word, but the resurrected Lord who conveys truths and revelations to this or that privileged individual disciple. Had the Christian community

---

18. *New Testament Foundations: A Guide for Christian Students*, vol. 1, *The Four Gospels* (Grand Rapids: Eerdmans, 1975), p. 159.

19. *The Gospel of Luke* (London: Oliphants, 1966), p. 172; *Prophecy and Hermeneutic in Early Christianity: New Testament Essays* (Grand Rapids: Eerdmans, 1978).

20. *New Testament Prophecy*, p. 185; also p. 163.

fallen into this dangerous position in the first few decades of its existence?[21]

There is indeed a dangerous tendency in contemporary redactionism of both Bultmannian and evangelical varieties to fall into a neo-Gnostic disregard of the historical Jesus. A certain laziness characterizes this unconcern for the incarnate, embodied presence of forgiveness and fellowship in the person of Jesus. But it is perhaps premature to press any doctrinal issue before we have done our descriptive homework. Once again we move forward vigorously with the phenomenological method and ask, "What is the evidence for the hypothesis about early Christian prophets?"

The Status of Christian Prophets

Hill's response to Hawthorne and others who share his position is that there is no evidence in the New Testament that would suggest the Christian prophet enjoyed dominical status. The prophets mentioned in Corinthians, as much as we know of them, were congregational prophets who themselves needed testing and control and who held nothing like the apostolic authority of Paul. Furthermore, there is not a single prophetic word that can be positively adduced to have become part of the tradition of Jesus' utterances. If the *possibility* is entertained that there was commingling of words of Jesus and words of the exalted Lord, then we have to ask "by what criteria may we decide which sayings belong to the latter category?"[22] That is the question that must be relentlessly pursued, and it must be pressed in light of the substantial phenomenological data of my earlier study where Jesus is already seen to have been in the habit of making implicit christological claims and would be likely, according to the criterion of coherence, to make explicit claims as well. Unless it can be shown that there are factual data to describe the function of prophets in the early church and to substantiate their alleged creation of dominical utterances, we should remain unconvinced. Until proven otherwise, the data would compel us to assume that Jesus himself intended and delivered the utterance.

The attempt to gather data on Christian prophetism and to apply it to Mark 3:28–29 has been made by M. Eugene Boring, who lists six reasons for his view that a Christian prophet is responsible for the

21. *Ibid.*, p. 163.
22. *Ibid.*, p. 180.

redaction: the saying seems not to fit well in its context and thus is an independent saying; it has the forms of prophetic speech, with its *amēn*, chiasmus, and legal genre; it has an eschatological tone characteristic of Christian prophecy; it possesses an authority less appropriate to the Christian scribe than the Christian prophet; it appears to be a *pesher* on Isaiah 63:1–11 (especially v. 10), which is a typical function of the Christian prophet; the presence of the Holy Spirit is characteristic of Christian prophecy.[23]

Hill's relentless pursuit of hard data is again evident as he presses six penetrating questions against Boring's evidence.[24] First, an uncomfortable fit is no sure argument that a saying is not dominical. I would observe further that an exegesis of the larger Markan sense unit (3:20–30) in light of its parallels in Luke 11:14–23 and Matthew 12:22–32 makes clear that Jesus' claim to be casting out demons by the "finger" (Matt.: "Spirit") of God is empirical evidence that the kingdom of God has arrived in Jesus' activity, and anyone who misconstrues that arrival and impugns its power by assigning it to demonic activity is guilty of the ultimate blasphemy against the Spirit. There is nothing uncomfortable about Mark 3:28–30 in its larger sense setting; it can hardly be adduced as evidence of early Christian prophetic activity. Second, the *amēn* formula in Mark 3:28, far from supporting the hypothesis about prophets, is characteristic of Jesus' authoritative use of the first-person pronoun *I* (Matt. 12:28; parallel, Luke 11:20). Third, there is no evidence that Christian prophecy was always eschatological (it was also hortatory) and that it always originated with Christian prophets. Fourth, claim to authority is not exclusive with Christian prophets (data are anyway lacking), but there is abundant evidence that Jesus made authoritative claims; hence, this utterance would pass the coherence test in that respect. Fifth, Jesus could have just as well have made the original *pesher* exegesis of Isaiah 63:1–11 himself (if indeed that is the reference of Mark 3:28–30), and in terms of his own person and mission. Sixth, while the presence of the Holy Spirit is characteristic of Christian prophecy, it is not exclusively so, as Luke 11:20 and Matthew 12:28 attest of Jesus' own use of the Spirit's power.

Hill summarizes his case with the warning that "we have to draw

23. "How may we identify Oracles of Christian Prophets in the Synoptic Tradition? Mark 3:28–29 as a Test Case," *JBL* 91 (1972): 501–521.
24. *New Testament Prophecy*, p. 182.

attention to the immense difficulties that belong to the attempt to decide which sayings derive from prophets, as well as to the numerous pre-suppositions that underlie Boring's decision in the case of Mark 3:28–29." A second case study on Matthew 10:23 by Boring, which was presented at the SBL Seminar on Christian Prophecy in 1976,[25] attempts to show that the *amēn legō hymin* formula indicates a Chris-tian prophetic speech setting, as does the use of the phrase *the Son of man*, to which Hill retorts, "To say that 'the whole tradition of Son of man sayings depends on an early prophetic speech event smacks of irresponsibility: one wonders what next will be claimed for 'Christian prophetic speech'!"[26]

There follows a brief summary by Hill in which he concedes that certain passages such as Luke 11:49–51 and 21:20–24 may reflect the *pesher* applications of a Christian prophet, but he remains unconvinced that any solid data have been adduced to prove the widespread activity of Christian prophets in the early church. We really do not know very much about these prophets, he allows, and cannot go beyond possibil-ities to assured results.[27]

This, I think, on the purely descriptive level of phenomenological analysis of available data, free of dogmatic considerations, spells the end of a hypothesis that has skewed the results of several generations of gospel research. A rigorous exegetical phenomenology has given us solid data regarding Jesus' extraordinary claims to divine authority — ironically by using the most radical tool of radical criticism, the cri-terion of dissimilarity — and has yielded virtually nothing in favor of the hypothesis about early Christian prophecy.

The results are truly astounding, and I want to press them home as we turn the corner on the question of what to do with all the explicit christological utterances that Christian prophets are supposed to have put on Jesus' lips. We can now begin to appreciate how very unscientific is Perrin's claim that the major source (the synoptic Gospels) of our knowledge of Jesus "contains a great deal of teaching material ascribed to Jesus, and it turns out to be precisely that: teaching *ascribed* to Jesus

---

25. "Christian Prophecy and Matthew 10:23: A Test Exegesis," *SBL Seminar Papers*, 1976, vol. 2 (Missoula, MT: Scholars Press), pp. 127–133. See his review of Hill, *JBL* 100 (1981): 300–302, and his longer study, *Sayings of the Risen Jesus: Christian Prophets and the Synoptic Tradition* (Cambridge: Cambridge University Press, 1982).

26. *New Testament Prophecy*, p. 183.

27. *Ibid.*, pp. 184ff.

and yet in fact, stemming from the early Church."[28] But of course that is precisely what the empirical data do *not* support. The phenomenological method has been abused by certain dogmatic considerations that do not bear scientific scrutiny.

Christology As an Evolutionary Development

I am sorry to say that the same deficiency in descriptive methodology characterizes James D. Dunn's recent *Christology in the Making*,[29] which is a large study of 443 pages, including 49 pages of bibliography and 86 pages of endnotes. But the study gets off on the wrong foot immediately with Dunn's decision that "the quest for Jesus' own self-understanding is not made a central endeavor, nor an investigation of the relation between 'the historical Jesus and the Christ of faith'. . . . The object in the following pages is simply and solely to inquire into the origin or origins of the doctrine of the incarnation. . . ."[30] If the reader has followed my study carefully to this point he will know rather precisely where Dunn is going to come out on the other end, for the deliberate bracketing of Jesus' own christological self-understanding means that the church, not Jesus, will be viewed as the chief originator of New Testament Christology. And this is what Dunn assumes to the conclusion of his study. Throughout, his notion is that New Testament Christology is an evolutionary development, "a development from the concept of the word as the word of preaching, where Christ is the sum and substance of the message proclaimed, to the concept of the word as Christ himself, Christ the *incarnation* of God's word uttered from the beginning of time in creative and redemptive power."[31]

There are two interpretative claims here that need to be carefully examined. The first claim is false. New Testament Christology does not develop from the abstraction of "message" to the personalizing of word as Christ himself. In claiming that as a truth Dunn is simply not true to the facts. At the very beginning, as far back as we can go to the origin of New Testament Christology, we meet Jesus as person who

28. *Rediscovering the Teaching of Jesus*, p. 15. He expresses much the same opinion in *Jesus and the Language of the Kingdom* (Philadelphia: Fortress, 1976), pp. 1–12 (but cf. p. 12, n. 9).

29. *Christology in the Making: A New Testament Inquiry into the Origins of the Doctrine of the Incarnation* (Philadelphia: Westminster, 1980).

30. *Ibid.*, p. ix.

31. *Ibid.*, p. 248; compare pp. 249f. His italics.

makes categorical truth-claims through his speech and behavior that can only be called *personal* christological claims. Christology does not begin with abstract, apotheosized words, but with the person who speaks the words, accompanies them with appropriate action, and stands back of and indwells that linguistic activity with personal accreditation. Jesus already identifies the word of God with himself as he forgives sins and celebrates table-fellowship with sinners.

Origin of the Doctrine of Incarnation

Dunn's second statement requires careful examination. There seems to be a detectable development in the New Testament from Jesus' simple identification of God's word with his own person to the explicit doctrine of his preexistence — "Christ the incarnation of God's word uttered from the beginning of time in creative and redemptive power." Yet even here we must be careful not to draw hasty conclusions, for Jesus' implicit christological claims are also claims to divine equality that carry with them implicit claims to preexistence. The question I will address presently in this chapter is how conjunctive or disjunctive are *explicit* christological and preexistence claims with the impressive implicit claims of Jesus. Dunn asserts that "the identification of Christ with the word of God in a deliberately metaphysical way (John 1:14) must be regarded as marking a new stage in Christian thinking."[32]

Perhaps this is true in a specifically metaphysical way, but not in the voluntary sense in which Dunn has approached the subject of New Testament Christology. He seems to want to attribute to the fourth evangelist the sort of originative creativity for which there is abundant evidence in the language of Jesus himself. When one examines Dunn's brief treatment of the material about Jesus in the early section on "Jesus' Sense of Sonship,"[33] one finds him making the same category mistake as Perrin in assessing the material. He does allow that the historian can penetrate the self-consciousness (or self-understanding) of individuals and gain something of their feelings and consciousness through their language. In Jesus' case there are a few undeniable personal vignettes that express, in Bultmann's words, "the immediacy of eschatological consciousness,"[34] such as Matthew 11:5–6 ("the blind receive their sight and the lame walk, lepers are cleansed and the deaf hear,

---

32. *Ibid.*, p. 248.
33. *Ibid.*, pp. 22–33, 10 pages out of 268 pages of text.
34. *The History of the Synoptic Tradition*, p. 126.

and the dead are raised up, and the poor have good news preached to them. And blessed is he who takes no offense at me"; parallel, Luke 7:22–23); Matthew 13:16–17 ("But blessed are your eyes, for they see, and your ears, for they hear. Truly, I say to you, many prophets and righteous men longed to see what you see, and did not see it, and to hear what you hear and did not hear it"; parallel, Luke 10:23–24); Matthew 12:41–42 ("The men of Nineveh will arise at the judgment with this generation and condemn it; for they repented at the preaching of Jonah, and behold, something greater than Jonah is here. The queen of the South will arise at the judgment with this generation and condemn it; for she came from the ends of the earth to hear the wisdom of Solomon, and behold, something greater than Solomon is here"; parallel, Luke 11:31–32); Luke 12:54–56 ("He also said to the multitudes, 'When you see a cloud rising in the west, you say at once, 'A shower is coming'; and so it happens. And when you see the south wind blowing, you say, 'There will be a scorching heat'; and it happens. You hypocrites! You know how to interpret the appearance of earth and sky; but why do you not know how to interpret the present time?'").

To these few examples Dunn adds several other passages that embody a consciousness of eschatological power (Matt. 12:28; parallel, Luke 11:20), "But if it is by the Spirit [Luke: "finger"] of God that I cast out demons, then the kingdom of God has come upon you"; and a consciousness of authority ("Amen," "But I say . . ."). Dunn remarks that

> on the basis of these and other passages E. Käsemann comments: 'Jesus felt himself in a position to override, with an unparalleled and sovereign freedom, the words of Torah and the authority of Moses. . . . What is certain is that he regarded himself as being inspired. . . . It signifies an extreme and immediate assurance of knowing and proclaiming the will of God . . . he must have regarded himself as the instrument of the living Spirit of God, which Judaism expected to be the gift of the End' ("The Problem of the Historical Jesus," *Essays on New Testament Themes*, pp. 40–2).[35]

Yet in light of this formidable evidence Dunn is unwilling to allow that Jesus thought of himself as more than a prophet—unique, yes, but not free of the old prophetic mold. Let his argument speak for itself.

35. *Christology in the Making*, p. 279, n. 91.

Following a brief résumé of Matthew 12:28 (parallel, Luke 11:20); Isaiah 61:1-2; Luke 6:20-21 (parallel, Matthew 5:3-6); Matthew 11:4-5 (parallel, Luke 7:22); Mark 6:4 (compare Luke 13:33); Matthew 10:40 (parallel, Luke 10:16); Matthew 15:24, he writes,

> These passages have still more to tell us, for according to the same evidence it was not simply as a prophet that Jesus saw himself. Rather the clear implication is that he saw his role as unique: his was the role of eschatological prophet (Isa. 61:1), of the coming one, the anointed one of prophetic hope (Matt. 11:3-6//Luke 7:20-3); only through his Spirit-empowered ministry was the eschatological rule of God realized (Matt. 12:28//Luke 11:20; 'something greater than Jonah' — Matt. 12:41//Luke 11:32). *Yet nevertheless his concept of ministry, and so far as we can tell of his understanding of himself, did not break clear of prophetic language.* . . .[36]

The phenomenologist will immediately notice that Dunn is hedging on the data. He does not want to allow the evidence to take him where it is naturally leading. Of what biblical prophet can it be said that he uses the personal pronoun *I* with such authority, claims that he is the anointed one (Messiah) who fulfills prophetic hope, who sees the end times in terms of himself? Of course Jesus' explication of his activity employs the language of the prophets to evidence that he is fulfilling prophecy. But it is incorrect to say that Jesus' concept of himself "did not break clear of prophetic language," for Dunn cites evidence in the first two-thirds of the preceding passage that indicates Jesus did precisely that. Dunn's attempt to play down the astounding christological claims of Jesus as little more than "inspiration and empowering" of the Spirit[37] bypasses Jesus' personal intention to claim divine prerogatives as his own. There is an intimate association of Father (*Abba*) and Spirit in his eschatological activity, and this association is (to Jewish eyes) on the outlandish level of parity, not of mere prophetic subordination. Dunn comes close to the real significance of the phenomena, then backs away from their christological implications because he has already entered the hermeneutical circle farther down the line with his assumption of an evolutionary Christology created by the early church. By his own admission, on the first page of the preface (as I have noted), he is not concerned to make the quest of Jesus' own self-understanding a central

36. *Ibid.*, p. 137. My italics.
37. *Ibid.*, pp. 138ff.

endeavor; but if he is really interested to inquire into the origin of the doctrine of the incarnation, it is crucial that he start correctly with a thorough investigation of Jesus' own claims. Dunn's reiterated assumption is that the evangelists view Jesus as primarily "a prophet like Moses . . . , a man inspired by the Spirit."[38] Yet he has to qualify this oversimplified theme repeatedly: "Of course for the Evangelists Jesus was never just another prophet (cf. Matt. 12:41 par.; 13:16f. par.; Luke 16:16 par.); much more was he Messiah, the anointed of the Lord, the one who fulfilled the role of the Servant of Yahweh, the uniquely commissioned agent of God's purpose at the end of the age (see again Mark 8:28f.; Matt. 12:18; Luke 4:18)."[39]

How then can Dunn fall back to his notion of Jesus as "a prophet like Moses," as his very next sentence attests? "But this was a role which nevertheless they were able and content to describe in prophetic terms."[40] But that is just the point at issue. The verses that Dunn himself quotes are empirical evidence that Jesus and the evangelists were not content to describe him solely in prophetic terms. Let us look at the texts again with a phenomenological openness to what Jesus is claiming about his self-understanding and mission.

> ". . . behold something greater than Jonah is here . . . behold, something greater than Solomon is here." [Matt. 12:41–42]

Jesus is claiming that in his ministry both the prophetic and wisdom genres of the Old Testament are superlatively superseded. This is not prophetic or wisdom language in the old sense, but something unique and unexpected.

> "Truly, I say to you, many prophets and righteous men longed to see what you see, and did not see it, and to hear what you hear, and did not hear it." [Matt. 13:17]

Jesus is not able or content to describe his ministry simply in prophetic terms in this passage.

> "The law and the prophets were until John; since then the good news of the kingdom of God is preached, and every one enters it violently." [Luke 16:16]

38. *Ibid.*, p. 140.
39. *Ibid.*
40. *Ibid.*

Here Jesus explicitly dissociates himself from any mere extention of Mosaic or prophetic functions. He fulfills them and supersedes them in a radical pattern unique to his person.

Accordingly I can only conclude that Dunn has already made up his mind to settle on an extreme critical hypothesis of a late evolutionary development of christological themes, and is required to compromise the data that come from Jesus himself. The synoptic evangelists are described as evolving near the end of the first century a higher Christology in which Jesus is "presented as looking forward to the time when he will be the inspirer rather than the inspired."[41] Not only is this tendentious and circular in terms of dating the Gospels, which may be much earlier than Dunn assumes,[42] but also it insists on portraying Jesus in the passive voice as one who is only the agent of the Spirit of God and the recipient of power and inspiration. I read the data differently — and I think correctly — that Jesus is the creative originator of his unique Christology, on a parity with *Abba* and *Pneuma*, and uses the personal pronoun *I* with divine, not Mosaic, authority. The cumulative · evidence of my study, and the few texts cited by Dunn, all point in that direction. Hence I disagree further with Dunn's interpretation of the fourth Gospel, which he views as a late document that "is moving beyond the more limiting confines of a prophet christology," though still using the prophetic mold: "From Jesus himself to the Fourth Evangelist at the end of the first century Jesus is understood as a prophet — more than a prophet to be sure, but so far as the relation between Jesus and the Spirit is concerned the category of prophet consistently provides the most suitable language and understanding — *Jesus of Nazareth a man inspired and enabled by the power of God* to fulfill his eschatological role."[43] Notice here the patronizing characterization of Jesus as a man who functions largely in the passive voice: he is primarily a passive agent, not the creative and outspoken person of the Gospels who fashions a unique Christology by claiming to inaugurate the reign of God, forgive sins, and gather outcasts around the messianic banquet table. No mere prophet would dare to claim this right or so shape his behavior to conform to his spoken claims. Does not Jesus dispense the

41. *Ibid.*, p. 141.
42. See John A. T. Robinson, *Redating the New Testament* (London: SCM Press, 1976), and *Can We Trust the New Testament?* (Grand Rapids: Eerdmans, 1977), especially chapter 4.
43. *Christology in the Making*, p. 141. His italics.

Spirit through his own activity, ministering on a parity with the Spirit
and as the Son of the Father from his baptism on (Luke 3:22)?

Jesus' Sense of Sonship

As regards Jesus' sense of sonship, Dunn allows that *"it was a characteristic of Jesus' approach to God in prayer that he addressed God
as 'abba' and that the earliest Christians retained an awareness of this
fact in their own use of 'abba'."*[44] Jesus' unique use of "abba" is secure,
since there are only three instances of the term in Semitic material.[45]
In short, Dunn continues, the evidence points consistently and clearly
to the conclusion that Jesus' regular use of "abba" in addressing God
distinguished Jesus in a significant degree from his contemporaries.[46]
His is an intimate sense of sonship (Mark 14:36); it is an authoritative
sonship, which assumes that his disciples' sonship is dependent on his
own (Luke 11:2; 22:29–30). It is also an eschatologically unique sonship that is the climax to God's purposes for Israel (Mark 12:2–6) and
that is bringing about a new covenant intimacy (cf. Mark 14:24 and
I Cor. 11:25 with Jer. 31:31–34; and Matt. 7:7–11 and Luke 11:2 with
Hos. 1:10–11).[47]

This much Dunn is ready to allow as evidence of Jesus' unique sonship. In view of all the other unquestionably authentic passages that I
have gathered as intimations of Jesus' self-understanding, one should
expect Dunn to concede that here is sufficient phenomenological data
to indicate an original and originative Christology on Jesus' part that
implies preexistence through his awareness of being the divine Son of
God. But Dunn shies away at this crucial point and warns of dogmatic
theology outrunning exegesis. I would reply that dogmatic considerations might indeed be set aside at this point and a simple phenomenology of persons brought to bear on the data by asking, "In view of
all we know about Jesus' extraordinary claims, would it be coherent for
anyone other than a person who felt himself equal to God to assume
such divine prerogatives? And if he is aware of being equal to God, is

44. *Ibid.*, p. 26. His italics.
45. *Ibid.*, p. 280, n. 97, where P. M. Casey is cited as noting only bTaan. 23b, Targ.
Ps. 89:27, and Targ. Mal. 2:10, in "The Development of New Testament Christology,"
Aufstieg und Niedergang der römischen Welt, ed. Hildegard Temporini (Berlin and
New York: W. de Gruyter, 1972).
46. *Christology in the Making*, p. 27.
47. *Ibid.*, p. 28.

he aware also of his preexistence?" Surely that is the direction in which the criterion of coherence would lead us.

Dunn and other radical critics play a curious language-game in coming up to the data, then retreating. Jesus claims to be more than a prophet, they say, but he is really only a prophet; he is unique, but he is not really at all that unique. Because of their unwillingness to concede the full force of the core of authentic sayings arrived at by the criterion of dissimilarity, and because of their unwillingness to allow the criterion of coherence to come fully into play, extreme critics like Dunn do not really know their own mind. Dunn demands that in order for scholarly criticism to validate Jesus as the originator of New Testament Christology, Jesus must have been conscious of his sonship as "protologically unique" ("begotten before all ages"). But this must be done by means of a criticism in which all explicit claims to such protological sonship are rejected as creations of the early church. The argument is circular and not very scientific. A genuinely scientific phenomenology accords the core data their full meaning, namely, that Jesus must have thought of himself in virtually divine patterns to have spoken and acted as he did. Working then from this base I would ask why explicit christological texts are not coherent with that pattern.

Dunn cites three synoptic passages that suggest bolder claims to sonship—Mark 12:6; 13:32; and Matthew 11:27 (parallel, Luke 10:22). The first, however, he dismisses because "the distinction between 'servant' and (beloved) son' in Mark 12:2–6 provides no sure foundation since the contrast can be fully explained as part of the dramatic climax of the parable."[48] But is this good exegesis in light of the larger sense unit of Jesus' self-understanding, which I have already established? Of course the term *son* fits naturally within the dramatic parabolic framework,[49] but would we not expect that to be the case, considering Jesus' self-understanding; and would it not also be coherent, in view of that self-understanding, for Jesus to refer to himself on a deeper christological level as "beloved son"? I am arguing that in view of the core data the exegetical emphasis should now shift from suspicion to confidence that Jesus would utter more explicit claims about his person.

Regarding the other two sayings, Dunn again betrays his inclination toward the "when in doubt, discard" hermeneutic when he says "it is

48. *Ibid.*

49. See I. H. Marshall, *The Origins of New Testament Christology*, Issues in Contemporary Theology series (Downers Grove, IL: Inter-Varsity, 1976), pp. 115f.

precisely in Jesus' reference to himself as 'the Son' that most scholars detect evidence of earliest Christians adding to or shaping an original saying of less christological weight."[50] But surely that is circular, for explicit christological utterances need to be compared with the genre of Jesus' implicit christological sayings, and when they are, they cohere. That makes an especially strong case, since I have already demonstrated the absence of data for the notion that early Christians placed new sayings on the lips of Jesus. It is scientifically unsound to rely upon that hypothesis any longer. There is, accordingly, no basis for dismissing Jesus' use of "Son" in Mark 13:32 (especially as it occurs in a context where Jesus recognizes the incarnational limitations of his eschatological knowledge), or in Matthew 11:27 — "All things have been delivered to me by my Father; and no one knows the Son except the Father, and no one knows the Father except the Son and any one to whom the Son chooses to reveal him." This utterance is perfectly coherent with the implicit core sayings. One should note, however, Dunn's equivocation regarding the saying, how sadly deficient is his sense of biblical historiography, and his need of a valid phenomenology of persons. Of Matthew 11:27 he writes,

> We may well have a saying which confirms our earlier conclusion — that Jesus' sense of sonship was one of intimacy in the councils of God and of eschatological significance, unique in the degree and finality of the revelation and authority accorded to him (as compared with prophetic consciousness — Amos 3:2); but more than that we cannot say with any confidence. . . . Schweitzer's claim that Matt. 11:27 'may be spoken from the consciousness of pre-existence' is never more than a possibility, neither finally excluded nor positively indicated by careful exegesis. This is the frustrating character of our evidence. Just when our questioning reaches the 'crunch' issue (Was Jesus conscious of being the divine Son of God?) we find that it is unable to give a clear historical answer.[51]

Now that is a most revealing admission, and says more about where Dunn is hermeneutically than it says about the text. It is symptomatic of what is phenomenologically unsound about such extreme criticism in New Testament circles. If Dunn is convinced by the data, which he accepts as authentic, that Jesus' sense of sonship is "unique in the

50. *Christology in the Making*, p. 28.
51. *Ibid.*, p. 29.

degree and finality of the revelation and authority accorded to him (as compared with prophetic consciousness)," what is holding him back? What possible reason could there be for not going on and allowing Jesus to make explicit christological statements about himself that are fully in accord with his implicit christological intimations as person? I detect nothing but a long-standing prejudice in critical circles — now seen to be empirically without supportive data — that the church has created all explicit christological sayings and assigned them to the mouth of Jesus.

Surely if Jesus can be described as conscious of a unique and final revelation, and of an authority that is more than prophetic consciousness, and if he forgives sinners and welcomes them into eschatological fellowship, he must be seen as one who could have a sense of filial preexistence in his parity with the Father and the Spirit. Certainly the criterion of coherence would lead one to that conclusion, and Dunn himself admits the possibility. Why then does he reject that possibility as a reality and close off his discussion of the synoptic Gospels with a question mark? But he does not really close off the discussion with a question mark, for it is clear all through his analysis that he has an agenda, and that agenda is to advance the hypothesis that the early church evolved a high Christology, because Jesus, though more than a prophet, was really not more than a prophet.

Accordingly, we should not take too seriously Dunn's intimidating warning that if we had any intention of using the "I am" sayings of the Johannine Jesus (e.g., "Before Abraham was, I am," 8:58), *"it would be verging on the irresponsible to use the Johannine testimony on Jesus' divine sonship in our attempt to uncover the self-consciousness of Jesus himself."*[52] The pattern of the fourth Gospel is radically different from the Synoptics' picture, he avers, and cannot be used as historically reliable:

No one can dispute the vast differences between the discourse style in the Fourth Gospel and Jesus' teaching recorded in the Synoptics. The point is that the style is *so consistent* in John (whether in Galilee or Judea, to crowd or individual, to peasants or Pharisee, to disciples or hostile 'Jews') and *so consistently different* from the Synoptics that it can hardly be other than a Johannine literary product, developing and shaping the tradition according to a pattern largely imposed on it. The

52. *Ibid.*, p. 31. His italics.

best explanation still remains that the Johannine discourses are medi-
tations or sermons on individual sayings or episodes from Jesus' life,
but elaborated in the language and theology of subsequent Christian
reflection.[53]

That of course is a common attitude toward the fourth Gospel in
radical redactional circles, but we ought not allow Dunn's rather final
way of putting the matter to intimidate us into dismissing the Gospel
as a source of data for Jesus' self-understanding. Dunn makes much of
the difference between the Synoptics and John, but the phenomenologist
will be impressed by the multiple aspection that is evidenced among
the synoptic Gospels themselves, which are as varied and yet as unified
in their perspectives of Jesus' ministry as is the fourth Gospel compared
with the Synoptics as a whole. The clue to these variations on a common theme lies in a simple phenomenology of persons. No person is
exhausted by a single portrait of his many-faceted self. The beauty of
the four Gospels is their complementary aspection, each portraying an
aspect of the richly variegated person and ministry of Jesus.

Accordingly it is tendentious to play up the "consistently different"
theme in order to impugn the fourth Gospel as a historical source of
data for Jesus' self-understanding. Given his prior commitment to an
evolutionary motif, it is in Dunn's methodological self-interest to dismiss the witness of the fourth evangelist concerning Jesus' claims to a
high Christology. Otherwise his thesis fails and the book would have
to be completely rewritten. Let us ask then whether the Johannine
Christology is consistently different from that of the Synoptics. The use
of the first-person personal pronoun by Jesus is one primary datum in
all four Gospels that points to a high Christology in Jesus' consciousness of his messianic role. In the Synoptics his use of $eg\bar{o}$ and the
formulas "I say to you" ($eg\bar{o}\ leg\bar{o}\ hymin$) and "truly, I say to you" ($am\bar{e}n$,
$leg\bar{o}\ hymin$) carries such enormous authority that even on the level of
the implicit core sayings in which the use of the personal pronoun I
appears either explicitly or as part of the main verb, Jesus is seen to
claim divine powers. It would be irresponsible, therefore, not to ask
whether Jesus' use of the authoritative personal pronoun I in the Synoptics is consistent with the Johannine Jesus' use of the self-designating
pronoun, and vice versa. And when we compare the two by the criterion

53. *Ibid.*, p. 30. See also his *Unity and Diversity in the New Testament: An Inquiry
into the Character of Earliest Christianity* (London: SCM Press, 1977), pp. 75f.

of coherence on a purely phenomenological level, free of dogmatic considerations, we find it perfectly consistent that a person who makes
outrageous claims about himself implicitly also makes outrageous claims
about himself explicitly. Assuming as he does the very voice, authority,
and activity of God in the Synoptics, it is consistent when Jesus in the
Johannine account claims self-conscious preexistent divinity and a
Christology of conscious preexistent sonship. It is not patently clear on
any empirical level that the Johannine Christology has to be late and
highly developed, as Dunn insists.[54] If one has done his homework on
the synoptic data (as I have tried to do, and as Dunn has elected not
to do in any detail or with an unprejudiced methodology), the fourth
Gospel will be seen to be consistent with the Synoptics christologically,
and different only in the sense of dimensional aspection, as the evangelist wishes to highlight certain aspects of Jesus' many-sided ministry
which complement the synoptic account.

Moreover, it is essential to Dunn's evolutionary model that the fourth
Gospel be as late as possible, preferably near the end of the first century
in order to give sufficient time for a high Christology to evolve. It was

> John's inspired genius that he hazarded so much and yet pulled it off
> so successfully — shaping Christian thought about God and Christ for
> all time . . . : John is wrestling with the problem of how to think of God
> and how to think of Christ in relation to God in the light of the clari-
> fication of the nature and character of God which the Christ-event
> afforded.[55]

Now there is theological obfuscation at its best, or worst! It means that
John or his tradition has created all the "I" sayings and other explicit
Christology in the fourth Gospel. And I am saying that Jesus in the
fourth Gospel is not inconsistent with Jesus in the synoptic Gospels, if
we have done our homework with an adequate phenomenology of persons. Dunn's hypothesis requires time for evolution of ideas in the early
church. Suppose, however, that the fourth Gospel is actually earlier, as
it may well be if my line of argument is correct. Dating is a language-
game we play in a circular pattern — if we think the theology of a Gospel
or Epistle is late, we date the document late. But if the Christology of
John is not incoherent with the Christology of the Synoptics and both

54. *Christology in the Making*, pp. 31f.
55. *Ibid.*, pp. 264f.

are traceable to Jesus himself, then the fourth Gospel may have been written much earlier than Dunn believes. We ought to examine seriously the whole question of dating, which is radically reconsidered by John A. T. Robinson in *Redating the New Testament* and summarized in *Can We Trust the New Testament?*[56] Robinson's principal observation is that it is simplistic to set up the old dichotomy between John and the Synoptics, for all four are both historical and theological in nature and should be seen as closer together than has hitherto been the case in critical circles. John's doctrine and language do not need to be dated later than that of Colossians and Hebrews, which also speak of the preexistence of the cosmic Christ and which should be dated before the fall of Jerusalem in A.D. 70, since they make no mention of that cataclysmic event. Certainly in the case of Hebrews and John the destruction of the temple would have occasioned considerable comment had they been written after the event (cf. also John 5:2, where the sheep pool of Bethzatha is still in use, to be obliterated in the destruction of the city; and sacrifices are still offered in the temple, according to Hebrews, cf. 9:25). A very possible date for the fourth Gospel might be shortly after A.D. 65 in view of these points and the Gospel's thoroughly evangelistic and Palestinian setting. Hence, a good argument can be made that "this Gospel tradition was coming to fruition simultaneously with the others. . . ."[57]

The point is that Dunn cannot simply assume the end of the first century as an assured date for John in order to give adequate time for the evolution of its high Christology. In fact a high Christology is found throughout the Synoptics and is traceable, I am convinced, to Jesus himself. While Robinson himself may balk at ascribing to Jesus John 6:56–58 ("He who eats my flesh and drinks my blood has eternal life," v. 54) and 8:58 ("Before Abraham was, I am") because "no sane person" goes around saying such things, he is certainly correct about the "madness" theme: "Judge the Jesus of this Gospel purely at the level of psychological analysis, and you will probably conclude, with the Jews, that he is a megalomaniac."[58] Precisely. But I have argued the same for the Synoptics. Attending to the language and behavior of Jesus in the synoptic Gospels initially leads one to assume that he *is* a megaloma-

56. In the latter, see chapter 4, "The Generation Gap," pp. 62–79; and chapter 5, "John's Picture of Jesus," pp. 80–94.
57. *Can We Trust the New Testament?*, p. 88.
58. *Ibid.*, p. 91.

niac and that he is mad, because he is claiming a divine status. I say "initially" because a deeper phenomenology which is accessible only to faith discloses the truth of Jesus' claims, and this removes him from the suspicion of madness and megalomania and allows him to be seen for what he is claiming to be — correlative with God. And this parity necessarily entails both an implicit and an explicit claim to preexistence. The latter is coherent with the former, and the former is inherent in the verbal and behavioral claims in the core data.

The conclusion that can be drawn from our examination of Jesus' behavior, whether on this side or the other side of faith, is that he possessed an astounding opinion of his authority, in light of which both implicit and explicit intimations of his divinity and preexistence as Son of God are entirely appropriate and consistent. Accordingly I reject as altogether too skeptical Dunn's interpretation of an all-too-narrow sampling of the data when he concludes,

> ... if we are to submit our speculations to the text and build our theology only with the bricks provided by careful exegesis we cannot say with any confidence that Jesus knew himself to be divine, the preexistent Son of God.[59]

And yet note Dunn's equivocation, for as soon as he says that he seems to realize how dangerous it would be if all subsequent Christology were cut off from Jesus as he actually was. So he allows this confession, which, if followed through by an adequate analysis of Jesus as person, should bring him close to the conclusions I am espousing. Observe what he is willing to concede from the evidence:

> Nevertheless the christology of a sonship distinctive in its sense of intimacy and unique in its consciousness of eschatological significance and of the dependency of others on it, that can only be called *a high christology* — higher certainly than a christology of a righteous man or a charismatic exorcist, higher perhaps even than of a Davidic Messiah — though, if so, how much higher we cannot say.[60]

Now if Jesus' sense of sonship was *distinctive* in intimacy, if he was *unique* in his eschatological consciousness — so much so that he felt

59. *Christology in the Making*, p. 32. His italics. See also R. E. Brown, "How Much Did Jesus Know?", *CBQ* 29 (1967): 337f.

60. *Christology in the Making*, pp. 32f. His italics.

others to be dependent on it — then Dunn is absolutely correct in calling
that a *high* Christology. Obviously Jesus was more than a righteous
man or a charismatic exorcist; the evidence is clear about that. Why
then should one be in doubt whether Jesus saw himself as more than
a Davidic Messiah? Dunn should continue with a penetrating analysis
of what it would mean for Jesus to evince a distinctive sense of sonship
with the Father. It could mean only one thing, for many righteous people
have an intimate sense of sonship with God that is not ontologically
distinctive. The word *distinctive* is apposite because on examination of
Jesus' claims of correlativity with the Father and Spirit in the Synoptics
and the fourth Gospel, his self-understanding can only be interpreted
as a sense of distinctive *ontological* relationship. On the most skeptical
level of analysis, his language must be said at least to intimate this
consciousness. But if the language reveals this implicitly, then there is
no coherent reason to deny him the right to intimate his unity with God
explicitly. Thus for him to say, "You have heard that it was said, but
I say unto you" (*egō legō hymin*) is tantamount to assuming the privileged position of the divine personal pronoun *I* in Exodus 3:14 ("I AM
WHO I AM," *'ehyeh 'ašer 'ehyeh*), and is christologically and ontologically
no different from the explicit use of the personal pronoun *I* in the fourth
Gospel: "Truly, truly, I say to you, before Abraham was, I am" (*Amēn
amēn legō hymin, prin Abraam genesthai egō eimi*, 8:58). We note that
in the Johannine account "they took up stones to throw at him" (v. 59) —
they knew what he meant and read his claims, if not his deeper character, correctly. Nor is there anything unexpected or incoherent about
Jesus' other "I" claims in the fourth Gospel, in view of his "I" claims in
the Synoptics: for example, "I am the bread of life" (*egō eimi ho artos
tēs zōēs*, 6:35, 48); "I am the light of the world" (*egō eimi to phōs tou
kosmou*, 8:12; 9:5); "I am the door" (*egō eimi hē thura*, 10:7–9); "I am
the good shepherd" (*egō eimi ho poimēn ho kalos*, 10:11, 14); "I am
the way, and the truth, and the life" (*egō eimi hē hodos, kai hē alētheia
kai hē zōē*, 14:6); "I am the true vine" (*egō eimi hē ampelos hē alēthinē*,
15:1). A thoroughgoing analysis and comparison of Jesus' use of the
personal pronoun *I* in the Synoptics and the fourth Gospel (which lies
beyond my present scope) intensifies the identity of Jesus in the four
Gospels as one who now speaks guardedly, now more openly, and
always "in parables" (*en parabolais*, Mark 4:11), and "in figures" (*en
paroimiais*, John 16:25), but always plainly enough that one wants
either to stone him or to adore him — because one reads his fantastic
claims of parity with God as either blasphemous or true.

To sum up, Dunn's recent attempt to write a "state of the art" Christology must be deemed a failure because, like radical criticism in general, it enters the hermeneutical circle too late — in the twentieth century, as a matter of fact, with its predisposition to evolutionary models rather than an openness to the phenomena themselves. It is curious to observe how contradictory radical critics always seem to react when they come up against the facts of Jesus as person. The evidence, arrived at by the most skeptical critical methods, is absolutely convincing and compels the critic to concede the most remarkable facts about Jesus. He is described as radical, unique, distinctive — and yet when it comes to understanding what a person must be like who speaks and acts in such a radical, unique, and distinctive manner, negative criticism retreats and obscures the phenomena with a thousand qualifications. The twofold reason for this ought to be obvious by now. First, radical criticism confuses the freedom of the evangelists to paraphrase and adapt their material with the free creation of new material. There is hard data for paraphrastic redaction; there is not hard data for creative redaction *de novo*. This is the first error, and it requires considerable sensitivity on the part of New Testament scholars to achieve a sympathetic openness to the gospel data and to analyze properly both paraphrastic variety and unity in the Gospels. This is the proper function of redaction interpretation as I see it, and the techniques have already been articulated by the prescient New Testament scholar Ned B. Stonehouse[61] who, long before the days of Willi Marxsen and radical redactionist extremism, appreciated the multiple aspection of the evangelists and their fidelity to the personal intention of Jesus.

The Failure of Radical Criticism

A good deal of work remains to be done by New Testament scholars sensitive to a phenomenology of persons as they seek to describe Jesus' christological self-understanding and self-disclosure, and the parameters of the evangelists' complementary perspectives of that disclosure. But the hard data about Jesus must always be the basis for analyzing the theological adaptations of the evangelists. The most irreducible, undeniable facts which radical criticism is willing to ascribe to Jesus' own lips are still so unquestionably unique that even the most extreme

61. See *The Witness of Matthew and Mark to Christ* (Philadelphia: Presbyterian Guardian, 1944), and *The Witness of Luke to Christ* (Grand Rapids: Eerdmans, 1951).

critic cannot deny an implied Christology in the words of Jesus. My task has been to allow the force of this fact to fill my critical sails and drive us on to the point where we realize that Jesus' tacit claims to represent God are as good as his explicit claims, and that there is no way, really, to distinguish the two when once the first is conceded. It is not enough to apotheosize Jesus' *word* and *wisdom*, as Dunn inclines to do,[62] but to ask the question, "What sort of person was Jesus, what must he have thought of himself, to have spoken and acted on a parity with God?" If Jesus had such a tremendous effect on his followers as incarnate wisdom that Dunn can say, "God's love and power had been experienced in fullest measure in, through and as this man Jesus; . . . Christ had been experienced as God's self-expression, the Christ-event as the effective, recreative power of God,"[63] then this is equivalent to saying that Jesus is behaving as God incarnate, that the love and power of God, indeed God himself, is experienced in fullest measure not only in and through but also as Jesus. The hard data justify this conclusion. If Jesus is consciously acting *as* God, there is no coherent reason for denying him consciousness of his preexistence. Language to this effect, along with other explicit christological utterances that fall from his lips, are appropriate expressions of his self-understanding and cannot be facilely assigned to later stages of an evolving tradition. They are entirely coherent with the self-understanding of the "core" Jesus.

Hence Dunn's insistence that *"the pre-existence element in the Johannine Son of Man sayings is a distinctively Johannine redaction or development of the Christian Son of Man tradition"*[64] is, phenomenologically speaking, unwarranted and tendentious. Observe the uncertainty and vacillation in his summary description of Jesus' self-understanding in the following passage near the end of the book.[65] "What do we find?" he asks. (I have arranged the quotations in strophes for comparison.)

a We find one who was conscious of being God's son, a sense of intimate sonship, an implication that Jesus believed or experienced his sonship to be distinctive or unique;

62. *Christology in the Making*, p. 262.
63. *Ibid.*
64. *Ibid.*, p. 90. His italics. Interestingly, Dunn argues that even Paul did not teach the preexistence of Christ; see pp. 44, 119, 127, 143–149, 176–196, 211.
65. *Ibid.*, pp. 253f. His italics.

b   but the evidence did not allow us to penetrate further or to be more explicit.

a¹   We find one who may well have understood the vision of Dan. 7 to be a description or indication of his own role, as one who represented God's people at the climax of the present age, as the one who would be vindicated beyond his anticipated suffering and death and play the decisive role in the final judgment. We find one who claimed to be inspired by the Spirit of God, to be a prophet in the tradition of the prophets, but more than that, to be the eschatological prophet, the one anointed by God to announce and enact the good news of God's final rule and intervention. We find one who may well have claimed to speak as the final envoy of Wisdom, with an immediacy of revelatory authority that transcended anything that had gone before.

b¹   But there is no indication that Jesus thought or spoke of himself as having pre-existed with God prior to his birth or appearance on earth. Such self-assertions appear only in the latest form of the canonical Gospel tradition and presuppose substantial developments in christological thinking which cannot be traced back to Jesus himself.

a²   It may of course be the case that Jesus *was* more, much more than he himself explicitly claimed to be.

b²   But from the beginning Christianity's claims regarding Jesus have always been about the whole Christ-event, particularly his death and resurrection, and never simply his life as though that had an independent value distinct from his passion and exaltation. Consequently Christianity's claims regarding Jesus have never depended solely on Jesus' own testimony regarding himself, let alone on its accessibility or otherwise.

a³   On the other hand, a complete discontinuity between Jesus' own self-assertions and the subsequent claims made about him would constitute a fatal flaw at the foundation of the whole superstructure of subsequent christology, not least the doctrine of the incarnation. It is of crucial importance therefore for Christianity that a sense of climactic finality, of immediacy of divine authority, of unique intimacy in his relationship with God can be detected in the earliest and probably authentic stratum of the Gospel tradition.

b³   *We cannot claim that Jesus believed himself to be the incarnate Son of God;*

a⁴   *but we can claim that the teaching to that effect as it came to expression in the later first-century thought was, in the light of the whole Christ-event, an appropriate reflection on and elaboration of Jesus' own sense of sonship and eschatological mission.*

This oscillating uncertainty as to what Dunn believes can and cannot be said about Jesus is distressing when viewed in antithetic strophes (following his own order), but what is most striking is Dunn's failure to recognize that if so much can be said with confidence about Jesus' self-concept — that he was distinctive, unique, decisive, final, authoritatively transcendent, and probably much more — then his argument that Jesus could not have uttered explicit christological and preexistence claims is seriously weakened. Phenomenologically it is altogether coherent for Jesus to do so. It is not coherent to insist that the early church must have created these claims and placed them on Jesus' lips, unless it can be proved that the explicit claims are fundamentally incompatible with the authentic implicit claims. Dunn even tries to justify the assumed elaborations of the church on the ground that they are *appropriate* reflections and elaborations, tacitly admitting the essential coherence of the two. Thus the fatal critical question must be asked: By what scientific criterion does the radical redactionist know for certain that Jesus could not have uttered explicit christological and preexistence claims, when these are entirely appropriate to and coherent with implicit claims that are accepted as authentic? What sort of concept of persons is the radical school working with?

As I have insisted all along, a phenomenologist who is truly open to the data and aware that a person's intentionality is to be observed in his speech and behavior will not be surprised that Jesus would make extraordinary explicit claims about himself. One should not balk at this point, for there is no substantive difference between a person's implicit and explicit language, since both originate from the same self-concept. What is truly surprising (and nearly everyone concedes that fact in view of the data) is that Jesus' *implicit* claims are so outrageous. Once that fact registers, gospel criticism can no longer be carried out as a neat science that separates authentic sayings of Jesus from inauthentic church-created sayings, or traces radically disparate evolutionary theological tendencies in the Gospels. What *can* be profitably pursued by the gospel interpreter is a descriptive analysis of the polyphonic portraits of Jesus by the four evangelists, both in their unity of theme and in their complementary variations on that fundamental theme, as they explore the rich phenomena that comprise the person and creative orchestration of Jesus.

My second point is that related to this failure of radical criticism to be faithful to the wider implications of the phenomena surrounding

Jesus as person is a second failure of nerve. The inability to handle the logically odd phenomena of the supranormal in the New Testament is typical of post-Enlightenment historicism. Radically historicist criticism cannot allow the peculiar phenomenon of Jesus to be simply who he is and the evangelists to be who they are, but must superimpose upon the data an alien disbelief in the supernatural character of Jesus' claims and of the evangelists' witness. The underlying reason for the odd critical behavior of Bultmann, Käsemann, Perrin, Dunn, and others in the extreme redactional school is a curious attachment to naturalism, which is a method of interpreting supposedly supernatural phenomena wholly in terms of natural causation. This has been noted by Morton Smith, Walter Wink, and Peter Stuhlmacher,[66] among others. It finds a clear programmatic expression in Ernst Troeltsch's essay "Über historische und dogmatische Methode in der Theologie."[67] For Troeltsch, history is the unfolding of the divine Reason and contains everything within its network of natural and evolutionary causation. Accordingly, nothing truly unique can occur but is to be explained solely by analogy to other natural events. Since this is the underlying presupposition of the more radical wing of historical criticism, the open-minded phenomenologist can see immediately that a whole realm of religious phenomena is immediately excluded from the purview of any critical observer committed to the doctrine. Hence, just as one knows how Dunn is going to use the critical method in *Christology in the Making*, when on page 1 he decides prejudicially that he will not make an investigation of Jesus' own self-understanding a central endeavor in his search for the origins of the doctrine of the incarnation, so in an even more outspoken fashion Bultmann squeezes his phenomenological horizon narrowly within the limits of naturalism:

66. See Morton Smith, "Historical Method in the Study of Religion," in *On Method in the History of Religions*, ed. James S. Helfer, p. 12, quoted in Walter Wink, *The Bible in Human Transformation: Toward a New Paradigm for Biblical Study* (Philadelphia: Fortress, 1973), pp. 37ff.; Peter Stuhlmacher, *Historical Criticism and Theological Interpretation of Scripture*, trans. Roy A. Harrisville (Philadelphia: Fortress, 1977), for example, pp. 74–76. For a helpful review of recent German literature on the debate, see John Piper, "Historical Criticism in the Dock: Recent Developments in Germany," *JETS* 23 (1980): 325–334.

67. Written in 1898, it has recently been reprinted in *Theologie als Wissenschaft*, ed. Gerhard Sauter (Munich: C. Kaiser, 1978), pp. 105–127.

> The historical method includes the presupposition that history is a unity
> in the sense of a closed continuum of . . . cause and effect [and] cannot
> be rent by the interference of supernatural powers.[68]

With that sort of narrowness guiding the pattern of the critic's mind,
we can see exactly what will happen when he comes up against the
authentic core of Jesus' implicit christological claims — he will acknowledge their authoritative character and uniqueness, but then he will back
away and qualify the phenomena, for there is no way that he can allow
them their full supernatural impact. Precisely at this point we can see
why radical historicist criticism fails to allow all the data to appear as
they are. It is not that we should abandon the critical method, with its
valuable tools for text criticism, literary criticism, redactional analysis,
and the like, but that the phenomenological base must be broadened
and radical prejudices against the phenomena, as they appear on their
own terms, bracketed.

It is a salutary sign that Stuhlmacher is making a similar critique in
Germany. Although he is trying to occupy middle ground in the debate
and is less than clear in his view of Scripture, he is nevertheless on the
right track when he calls for the interpreter to stand sympathetically
within a text and say yes to it rather than no, to be humble and open
rather than superior, insolent, and closed.[69]

This is the phenomenological hermeneutic I have been employing in
this study. I am convinced that it is more vigorously scientific and truer
to the Gospels as phenomena than is a radical redactionalism that
superimposes modern and alien language-games on the text. In part 2
of this study I will address creative approaches to the Gospels, which
will afford as broad a horizon as possible to their phenomena from the
inside out. As I near the conclusion of part 1, I wish to continue the
analysis of the explicit christological sayings of Jesus from the outside
in, and test their coherence with the core implicit sayings.

---

68. "Is Exegesis Without Presuppositions Possible?" in *Existence and Faith* (New
York: Meridian Books, 1960), pp. 291–292.

69. *Historical Criticism*, p. 84; *Vom Verstehen des Neuen Testaments* (Göttingen:
Vandenhoeck & Ruprecht, 1979), pp. 199–220. Stuhlmacher acknowledges his in-
debtedness to Hans-Georg Gadamer's "Hermeneutic of Agreement" *(Einverständnis)*
in the epilogue to the third and fourth editions of *Truth and Method*; and to Adolf
Schlatter's principle of perception, or looking and seeing *(Prinzip des Vernehmens).*

5

Jesus, the Original Source of High Christology in the Gospels
Toward a Deep Phenomenology

In his balanced study on *The Origins of New Testament Christology*, I. H. Marshall demonstrates the logic of moving from the implicit to the explicit christological utterances of Jesus. Rebutting Ernst Käsemann's inadequate concept of persons and his equally inadequate exegesis of Jesus' self-understanding (to which I have had occasion to refer before),[1] Marshall observes,

> The indirect approach to Christology demonstrates that Jesus spoke and acted as Messiah. The presence or absence of Messianic titles cannot alter this proof. Jesus could well have considered himself to be the Messiah, and yet not have used the title publicly. If so, the presence or absence of the title is irrelevant if other considerations show that he did think of himself as the Messiah.

To which Marshall adds, "Then it becomes wildly improbable that the fact did not come to expression in some way in his teaching—if not to the public at large, at least to his closest followers." Accordingly,

> we have reached the conclusion that indirect Christology makes the existence of a direct Christology in the teaching of Jesus highly probable. The Messianic titles which appear in the Gospels need to be reassessed in the light of the fact that Jesus did know himself to be the Messiah. We can, therefore, . . . allow for the possibility that the origins of the church's Christology lie in the use of Jesus' own Christology.[2]

1. "The Problem of the Historical Jesus," in *Essays on New Testament Themes*, trans. W. J. Montague, Studies in Biblical Theology, no. 41 (London: SCM Press, 1964), pp. 43f. See my comments, pp. 37–38.

2. *The Origins of New Testament Christology*, Issues in Contemporary Theology series (Downers Grove, IL: Inter-Varsity, 1976), pp. 55–57. See also C. F. D. Moule, *The Origin of New Testament Christology* (London: Cambridge University Press, 1978), pp. 1–46, especially pp. 34f.

That is directly on target, though I would prefer to say that it is altogether logical to assume that Jesus speaks explicitly of his messiahship, not only because for him to do so is coherent with his implicit Christology, but also because the evangelists represent him as making such explicit statements and because there is no convincing evidence that they are in the habit of creating these on their own (I refer to David Hill's argument against the creativity of Christian prophets). The implication of this line of reasoning is that the criterion of dissimilarity, having served by providing authentic sayings that are unquestionably if implicitly christological, now begs for its own dismantling. We can now see that what was originally designed by radical criticism to assign all explicit high Christology to the faith of the early church self-destructs — not only its historicist hermeneutic but, as is the case with certain critics like Rudolf Bultmann and Käsemann, a curious neo-Gnostic application of the Reformation doctrine of *sola fidei* by which the Gospels are stripped of all christological security that might qualify as good works. Bultmann explains this curious hermeneutic:

> Demythologizing is in fact a parallel task to the formulation of Paul and Martin Luther in their doctrine of justification by faith alone without works of law. More exactly, demythologization is the radical use of the doctrine of justification by faith in the area of knowing and thinking. Like the doctrine of justification, demythologization destroys every demand for security. There is no difference between security on the basis of good works and security which rests on objectifying knowledge. The one who believes in God must know that he stands as it were in a vacuum.[3]

Both these prejudicial presuppositions are discredited when rigorously applied to the gospel material, for the critics who use them must finally come up against the hard evidence, which even they have to admit is unique, extraordinary, radical, and at least implicitly christological. Ironically, the beauty of the criterion of dissimilarity is its ruthless deployment in the service of radical criticism, its provision of the firmest evidence for Jesus' implicit christological self-understanding, and its final plea for self-destruction as a criterion. Having done its work, it begs to be dismantled because the Jesus it has discovered is now seen (in light of a rigorous phenomenology of persons) to be co-

---

3. Quoted in Peter Stuhlmacher, *Vom Verstehen des Neuen Testaments* (Göttingen: Vandenhoeck & Ruprecht, 1979), p. 181, and in John Piper, "Historical Criticism in the Dock: Recent Developments in Germany," *JETS* 23 (1980): 326.

herent in his own uniquely creative way with both Old Testament messianic motifs and the high Christology of the Gospels. Since that is the case, there is no reason to continue to bracket either the Old Testament background of Jesus' ministry or the explicit christological utterances that are assigned to him. The criterion itself now needs to be bracketed, since it is clear that its intent and formulation have arisen in the first instance from alien dogmatic considerations, though it may inadvertently serve a temporary useful purpose. Its further use, however, would impair a genuinely open and scientific analysis of the data. After it has done its work it no longer serves the expanding horizons of the descriptive method and should be replaced by the criterion of coherence.

Consideration of Problematic Sayings

The criterion of coherence is extremely useful to the interpreter as he now examines the discarded sayings of Jesus, this time with an eye sensitively focused on the analysis of persons as the proper methodology to discern what is appropriate for Jesus to say and do. This hermeneutic for continuing exegesis so completely turns the tables on radical criticism that now the burden of proof lies completely on the other side. No longer is the interpreter's exegesis guided by critical doubt ("when in doubt, discard") but by anticipation of behavior appropriate to what we already know about Jesus' extraordinary concept of himself. We must also bear in mind that in addition to the hard evidence for his spectacular claim to be acting with the authority of the divine personal pronoun *I*, there is hard evidence against the radical doctrine that the early church placed new sayings on the lips of the historical Jesus. Studying the question of Jesus' authentic language from these two complementary angles, we are compelled to proceed in our exegesis with a positive attitude ("authentic until proven spurious").

If the critic is loath to give up the criterion of dissimilarity at this point, I suggest that perhaps the criterion might be reformulated in light of its positive results in conjunction with a phenomenology of persons, namely, that whatever further activity attributed to Jesus could be proven generically dissimilar to his established form of life be bracketed as inauthentic. What would such inappropriate explicitly christological behavior be, in view of Jesus' established implicit christological behavior? I must admit that I fail to see anything that is attributed to Jesus in the Gospels, including the fourth Gospel, that can be demonstrably proven to be incoherent with what we already know about him through the application of the criterion of dissimilarity as first formulated. That, of course, undermines the radical use of redaction criticism, but we must be faithful to the established data if we are to be truly phenomenological and scientific. If the analysis of Jesus as person through the lens of the most pessimistic methodology still yields a portrait of one who makes astounding God-like claims for himself, and if there is no substantial evidence that the early church has created new sayings of Jesus and put them on his lips, then we must proceed with the assumption that the real source of high Christology in the Gospels is Jesus himself, and that the evangelists are reliable witnesses to that fact.

A few texts might be cited as problematic, such as Matthew 18:20; 28:18–20 and Luke 11:49–51; 21:20–24.[4] Matthew 28:18–20 is more detailed than Luke 24:48–49 and John 20:21, which are similar sayings, but there is no reason that it would be incoherent for Jesus to use a trinitarian formula explicitly when he has already employed it implicitly in Matthew 12:28 and in numerous instances where he claims a filial relationship with the Father and the presence of the Spirit in his ministry (so also John 14:15–26). Besides, if Jesus in his resurrected state is incapable of making an explicit trinitarian statement, where before he discloses an implicit trinitarian self-consciousness, that would be odd indeed. And if Jesus were to make an explicit reference to the Trinity, where but in his final hours with his disciples as risen Lord would he be likely to make it? Here is an instance where the risen Lord himself confers an explicit redaction of his earlier implicit trinitarian self-consciousness! At any rate, it is impossible to dismiss the saying as inauthentic by the criteria of dissimilarity or coherence, since the saying is entirely appropriate in view of his already established form of life and appears strange only to those who have not really appreciated his previous claims to parity with the Father and the Spirit.

As for Matthew 18:20 ("For where two or three are gathered in my name, there am I in the midst of them" [en mesō autōn]), this saying compares with Jesus' declaration in Luke 17:21, ". . . the kingdom of God is in the midst of you" (entos hymōn), where he is implicitly claiming himself to be the personified reign of God. Both texts are declarations of divine presence and are generically coherent in terms of Jesus' own person, though each audience is different. Matthew 18:20 may be

4. Cited by David Hill, *New Testament Prophecy* (Atlanta: John Knox, 1980), pp. 181f.

simply a prophetic present of what Jesus envisions will be the continued experience of his followers in the future (cf. the present-future context of vv. 15–20). In any event, is one forced by the genre of the saying to assign it to the early church? I think not.

Luke 11:49–51 could very well be Jesus' own *pesher* on Jeremiah 7:25–26 that he personifies the Wisdom of God (*hē sophia tou theou*) and as Wisdom weaves his own authoritative word with Jeremiah's against the present generation. Likewise Luke 21:20–24 is coherent with the prophetic office of Jesus who prophesies against the present generation and predicts the destruction of Jerusalem. Such predictive language is appropriate to Jesus' established self-understanding and could be assigned to the early church as "prophecy after the event" only if it could be shown to be incoherent with Jesus' form of life.

The enormous difficulty of attributing a dominical saying to the early church is underscored by my method of employing a phenomenology of persons to the data about Jesus. It might be possible to argue that I have overstated the case and am now overcompensating and challenging the critic to come forward with a single saying assigned to Jesus that could be proven to be unquestionably incoherent with his established self-concept. But the difficulty is also highlighted by Hill, who warns,

> To be open to the possibility of having an origin in inspired Christian prophetic speech in the name of the risen Lord a Jesus-saying must (i) fail to pass all the linguistic, environmental and other criteria for genuineness; (ii) be proved to be no part of the evangelist's editorial work; and then (iii) be shown to be consistent with what we know of the characteristics of Christian prophetic speech in the first century (which, unless we are too heavily dependent on Paul and Revelation, is not very much). In our opinion, not many sayings of Jesus in the Synoptics will pass these tests.[5]

After listing the handful of possible candidates I have considered, Hill concludes his study of the sayings of Jesus with this extremely important distinction and warning, which I have had occasion to quote before:

> ... there is no evidence that the liberty of adaptation — which, be it noted, is not the same as the creation of sayings *ex nihilo* — was taken casually. Even with regard to what we have just suggested . . . , we

5. *Ibid.*, p. 184.

must admit that we are dealing only with possibilities, not with certainties or assured results.[6]

The Evangelists' Paraphrastic Freedom

Assuming then that my phenomenological analysis of Jesus' sayings is valid, we must now address the fact that the evangelists arrange and paraphrase their data with considerable freedom. This is the area in which a redactional approach is helpful, as long as it is rigorously descriptive of the hard facts and does not bring inappropriate dogmatic assumptions to bear upon the data, as is the case with radical criticism where historicist presuppositions force the data into a ready-made mold. In separating the evangelists' paraphrastic adaptations of Jesus' authentic sayings and acts (for which there is hard data) from their assumed wholesale creation of sayings and events (for which there is not), I am arguing that redactional analysis must be limited to a phenomenological description of the paraphrastic data and the likely motifs that guide each of the evangelists to fashion the material as he does. Having established the factual and historical basis of the Gospels in Jesus' form of life, we may now turn our attention to the creative ways in which an evangelist experiences and reflects a particular aspect of that complex field of force. The evangelist is not its creator, for the original creator, speaker, and doer of the gospel story is Jesus himself; but as subcreator the evangelist reflects the original light of Jesus' field of force through the prism of his own self-understanding as well as that of his audience.

This is a limited use of redactional methodology but is truer to the actual phenomena than is the use commonly practiced by extreme critics. It opens up a different kind of language-game for the New Testament scholar in that it does not force positivistic and naturalistic prejudices upon the gospel data, but brackets these generically unsuitable prejudices and allows the phenomena to be exactly what they are.

6. *Ibid.*, p. 185. Hill cites with approval James D. Dunn's cautious article, "Prophetic 'I'-Sayings and the Jesus Tradition: The Importance of Testing Prophetic Utterances within Early Christianity," *NTS* 24 (1977–78): 175–198, in which Dunn argues that prophetic utterances in the early church would have been carefully tested in light of its kerygma. The only post-Easter utterances he is inclined to allow are Matthew 10:5; 11:28–30; 18:20; Luke 11:49–51, and possibly Luke 22:1a, b. One wonders what happened in Dunn's thinking between this conservative approach and the excessive evolutionary motif in *Christology in the Making*, which places the principal creation of high Christology in the hands of the early church.

If there is any value to the Husserlian phenomenology it lies precisely in this bracketing of prejudices and in an openness to the phenomena themselves.

It is at this juncture that we need to be especially clear-headed in order to understand where this phenomenological openness to the data is going to take us and what it demands of us as scholars and interpreters. Since there is no fact that is not already an interpreted fact, it is patently clear that the evangelists are writing their Gospels from the presupposition of Christian faith and do not share the "flat fact" approach of modern positivistic historiography. The latter has its own set of presuppositions and is flat because it rules out the transcendent and the supernatural and attempts to limit its investigation of history to the first and second dimensions, namely, to the empirical and the rational respectively, within a closed universe that is perceived in humanistic terms. A flat hermeneutic predetermines what the data will be allowed to say, and is the principal weakness of radical gospel criticism. The evangelists, on the other hand, assume a "round" hermeneutic, which moves freely within the third dimension of the supernatural and profoundly informs their understanding of empirical and rational phenomena. The third dimension of faith in the supernatural presence of God in Jesus Christ draws them, on their own tacit admission, into deep space and time where the sensory and the rational are themselves perceived with a new third-dimensional depth of field in stereoscopic fashion. Indeed, the "secrecy motif" in the Synoptics, which is generically akin to the "see, but do not perceive" motif of Isaiah 6:9–10, is precisely the inability of Jesus' unreceptive audience to see three-dimensionally; and the increasing clarification of Jesus' originative themes by the New Testament writers is due to their progressive experience of the depth of field that comes through faith within the third dimension.

Up until now my analysis of the gospel data has been, quite frankly, "flat." The use of Ludwig Wittgenstein and the school of person analysis, in conjunction with the radically skeptical criterion of dissimilarity, has produced remarkable results, but these results are still only flat perceptions without the full-bodied depth by which the evangelists perceive them, simply because they only "come up to" Jesus from the outside and confront his astounding claims. That is as far as a flat phenomenology "from the outside in" can take us. It says nothing about the truth of Jesus' claims and can make no judgments as to his madness or genuineness in making those claims. We need now to go further.

Having bracketed the prejudice of radical criticism against the quest

of Jesus as originative person, we now need to bracket whatever contemporary presuppositions would hinder us from entering sympathetically into the presuppositions of Jesus and the evangelists themselves.
In order to do this we will have to follow the deep phenomenology I
will describe hermeneutically in part 2, which will allow us to move
from the inside out. A true phenomenology of the Gospels is incomplete
until we can get at the data from the inside, as it were, in their richness
and depth of field. In order to do this we must sympathetically assume
the vision of Jesus and the horizon of the evangelists. We must, in other
words, become believing Christians, and by believing Christians I do
not mean those who subscribe to a modern theism that has denatured
the story to a liberal essence, or demythologized it to meet modern
existential criteria, or fused its horizon with ours. What I mean is that
the New Testament interpreter, if he is to avoid coming up wrong or
coming up short in terms of the New Testament data, must bracket all
alien prejudices and assume the evangelical presuppositions of the gospel writers, and thus enter into the originative mind of Jesus himself.
This is the ultimate phenomenology, for only in a fiduciary mode that
is at once empathetic and heuristic can the New Testament scholar
perceive the story with the mind of Christ and through the minds of
the evangelists.

When we enter the gospel data experientially as believers we begin
to appreciate that it would be a mistake for us to insist that the evangelists conform to our image of how we think they should present the
facts of Jesus. It would be a mistake for us not to allow them freedom
to write exactly as they do. Behind the adaptive language of the evangelists we discover the personal backing and signature of Jesus, as we
have seen. He generates a tradition such that his faithfulness to Old
Testament motifs and his creative originality engender an analogous
faithfulness and subcreativity on the part of the evangelists. The contemporary interpreter must not demand that the evangelists conform
to a style of reporting or historical writing that is not indigenous to
their own intention as authoritative interpreters of Jesus. They assume
a Spirit-given depth of vision in exegeting the meaning of Jesus' words
and works, a vision that the contemporary interpreter must seek to
enter into and to share from the evangelists' own Christian perspective.

Perhaps we can combine the two polarities that perplex the modern
historian—the desire to describe the facts as they really are or were,
and the realization that no fact is without interpretation. The two coalesce when the New Testament exegete enters empathetically into the

faith of the evangelists and is enabled to appreciate Jesus' complex form of life from the complementary perspectives of the evangelists themselves. One of E. Harris Harbison's illustrations addresses the issue. As a Christian historian he tried to combine objectivity with Christian commitment in his own area of Reformation studies and saw no contradiction between being a Christian believer and a professional historian. Harbison tells the story:

> A theologian who had written an eloquent history of the Reformation is said to have met the historian Ranke in Berlin and embraced him effusively as one would a confrere. "Ah please," said the father of scientific history, drawing himself away, "there is a great difference between us: you are first of all a Christian, and I am first of all a historian."

To which Harbison replies, suppose Leopold von Ranke (in a previous incarnation) experiences the rebuff in reverse as he enthusiastically embraces a great medieval saint, for example, Bernard, who draws himself away with the words, "Between us there is a great gulf fixed: you are first of all a historian, and I am first of all a Christian."[7]

Though one would not need to agree with everything Harbison says in his longer essay, he is right, I believe, in holding to the view that scientific objectivity and Christian faith are compatible. He is also correct when he criticizes modern historians for undue skepticism and cynicism as they interpret their textual material, a skepticism and dubiety we have observed among extreme New Testament critics. The Christian historian, Harbison writes, "will not bleach the moral color out of history by steeping it in corrosive skepticism. . . . He will know that to see any meaning at all in history is an act of faith, not a result of studying documents."[8] Accordingly, one may be "first of all a Christian *and* a historian."[9]

That is it exactly. The most scientific approach to Jesus is simply to describe the phenomena as they appear in the Gospels, from the inside out. I have already observed the phenomenon of Jesus as person with rigorous openness to his claims about himself, and now I am suggesting

7. "The Marks of a Christian Historian," in *God, History, and Historians: An Anthology of Modern Views of History*, ed. C. T. McIntire (New York: Oxford University Press, 1977), pp. 331–332. The first half of the anecdote was used by Lord Acton to support the doctrine of purely objective and scientific historiography.

8. *Ibid.*, p. 354.

9. *Ibid.*, p. 355.

that the only truly scientific way to describe the phenomena of the evangelists as interpreters of Jesus is to share their faith, observing how in complementary fashion they actually describe the phenomenon of Jesus. When we do this we discover that they also are both historians and believers who realize that every fact must be an interpreted fact whose meaning is vouched for by a responsible interpreter. Facts are not independent units that have isolable status apart from persons who invest them with significance. The evangelists implicitly attest their belief that Jesus has invested the primary facts of his person and ministry with significant meaning, that the Father and the Spirit have powerfully ratified that investiture of meaning by their presence in his words and works, and that they as evangelists are faithfully refracting the meaning of Jesus from many angles of perspective.

Accordingly, as a historian and a believer each evangelist is given the insight to focus his lens from one particular angle upon the three-dimensional and polymetric phenomenon of Jesus. He perceives the person of Jesus from a unique perspective that is complementary to the other evangelists' perspectives, yet allows him to see Jesus' utterances and acts in various sequences and combinations, and to present these to his readers in essential or paraphrastic form. It is the angle of perception that distinguishes the uniqueness of each evangelist, and the factuality of Jesus as person that accounts for the fundamental unity of the four portraits. We can illustrate the simplistic view of Ranke, who wanted only the facts without interpretation, as one-dimensional or at best two-dimensional. As long as one has this model in mind it is understandable that he will ask for literal uniformity in reporting words and events. See Figures 1 and 2. But when one views a phenomenon such as the person and ministry of Jesus in its polydimensional richness, there are going to be complementary aspections emanating from the phenomenon, and complementary perspectives on the part of the evangelist-observers, as shown in Figure 3.

We can expect a basic uniformity of description with this three-dimensional model, but it also guarantees considerable differences in

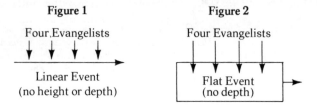

Figure 1

Four Evangelists

Linear Event
(no height or depth)

Figure 2

Four Evangelists

Flat Event
(no depth)

Figure 3

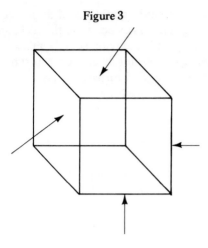

perspective. This is what we find when we examine the four Gospels. My analysis has led us to a substantial accreditation of the words spoken by Jesus. Because of the angle of each evangelist's perspective, which is gauged by his personal manner of perceiving from that particular angle, as well as his intention to represent that perception to the perceived needs of his readers, his portrait of Jesus may include a paraphrase or adaption of the essential meaning of what Jesus said, leaving in this detail, excluding another, or reordering a sequence of events in order to bring out its underlying theological significance. And this is exactly what we observe. On the very first page of the first Gospel we find Matthew adapting a factual genealogical list of Jesus' forebears in three groups of fourteen in order to sound the theme of his Davidic ancestry ($d = 4$, $w = 6$; $dwd = 4 + 6 + 4 = 14$). A one-dimensional genealogical chart with no names missing would satisfy a court of records but convey no particular meaning. The significance Matthew attaches to his abbreviated table conveys a profound theological truth about Jesus which is essentially true to the historical data.[10] This happens again and again in the Gospels, and the sensitive exegete begins to appreciate that the evangelists are doing this intentionally. Their interests are three-dimensional; through the person and ministry

10. See William Henry Green, "Primeval Chronology," BS 47 (1890): 285–303; reprinted in Classical Evangelical Essays in Old Testament Interpretation, ed. Walter C. Kaiser, Jr. (Grand Rapids: Baker, 1972) for a similar interpretation of the early genealogical tables in Genesis.

of Jesus they see the profound significance of deep time and deep space. A deep phenomenology affords us access to the real and ultimate meaning of the fact of Jesus, which may be entirely missed or misconstrued by the historian who focuses entirely on redactional differences in order or content in the narrative, and misses the point as to why the evangelists present the data in that way.[11]

The Interpreter's Approach

The New Testament interpreter must use the utmost discretion not to impose himself on the evangelist's historiographical style, but to understand his position theologically and to appreciate his conviction that this Gospel discloses an inner depth of meaning in the fact of Jesus. One finds this deep phenomenological approach employed by Ned B. Stonehouse in his two pioneer studies.[12] By a judicious blend of scholarship and empathy with the Christian faith of the evangelists, Stonehouse was able to hold a high view of the inspiration and authority of Scripture with a phenomenologist's ability to let the evangelists themselves determine the scope and meaning of their trustworthy witness to Jesus. He realized that only this methodology has exegetical fidelity, and that in fact the Gospels are seen to be far richer when, alongside their fundamental unity, we recognize their complementary diversity. Mark writes not only as a chronicler or biographer but also as a believer who is publishing the glad tidings of Jesus Christ:

> In Mark's thought the truth of his history is bound up with the truth of his presuppositions as a believer; likewise, these presuppositions are judged to have found their demonstration in his witness to the historical life of Jesus Christ. Hence, his record cannot be shown to be unhistorical merely by pointing to his presuppositions of faith; fact and meaning, the divine meaning and the divine action in deed and word, cannot be isolated with a view to separate evaluation.[13]

11. See Moises Silva, "Ned B. Stonehouse and Redaction Criticism, Part Two: The Historicity of the Synoptic Tradition," *WTJ* 40 (1978): 290, for a sample list of interesting variations in the synoptic accounts.

12. *The Witness of Matthew and Mark to Christ* (Philadelphia: Presbyterian Guardian, 1944); *The Witness of Luke to Christ* (London: Tyndale Press, 1951). See also his *Origins of the Synoptic Gospels* (Grand Rapids: Eerdmans, 1963).

13. *The Witness of Matthew and Mark to Christ*, p. 83.

Comparing Matthew with Mark, Stonehouse practices the rule of harmonizing where it is natural to do so, but astutely observes that on the basis of the data it would be false to the aim of the evangelists to judge them by hermeneutical criteria alien to their intention:

> The defender of the truth and authority of the gospels does not face the necessity of fitting all the details of the records into a continuous framework. The evangelists do not provide sufficient data for such an effort, and did not intend to do so. Consequently, it is not scientific to shout "discrepancy" whenever it appears that details are not presented in the same order in various records, or it develops that one evangelist disregards the precise framework which another delineates in connection with the narration of a particular phase of the ministry of Christ.[14]

Stonehouse carries the same brief for Luke, wisely recognizing the "various historical factors" which "must have included special aptitudes and qualifications as a writer, his opportunities for securing information, and his estimate of the needs of those for whom the finished work was intended."[15] Luke's witness to Christ is therefore "a superb work of devotion and adoration," but it is impossible to set it sharply against Matthew and Mark, for there is among them all a fundamental unity and testimony to the lordship of Jesus, his atoning death, and the coming of the kingdom of God.[16] The inspiration and authority of the Gospels are affirmed in view of their own testimony to themselves and in terms of what they actually are. This is the only sure ground for holding to a high view of Scripture.

It is worth noting that sixty years before Stonehouse's first study and one hundred years before our present situation, the great New Testament scholar and theologian, Benjamin Breckinridge Warfield, appreciated the same point regarding the aim of the evangelists as crucial to a scholarly defense of the plenary inspiration and authority of the Gospels, as of all canonical Scripture. Warfield held that Scripture is the Word of God in the phrases and idioms of human beings. The recognition of this fact is enormous:

> This at once sets aside as irrelevant a large number of the objections usually brought from the phenomena of the New Testament against its

14. *Ibid.*, pp. 163f.
15. *Ibid.*, p. 176.
16. *Ibid.*, p. 177.

verbal inspiration. No finding or traces of human influence in the style, wording or forms of statement or argumentation touches the question. . . . The current sense of a phrase is alone to be considered; and if men so spoke and were understood correctly in so speaking, the Holy Ghost, speaking their speech would also so speak. No objection then is in point which turns on a pressure of language. Inspiration is a means to an end and not an end in itself; if the truth is conveyed accurately to the ear that hears it, its full end is obtained.[17]

Warfield continues with this capital insight, which is astute, faithful to the facts, and is the working hermeneutic of those of us who aspire to do careful, scientific exegesis of Scripture:

And we must remember again that no objection is valid which is gained by overlooking the prime question of the intentions and professions of the writer. Inspiration, securing absolute truth, secures that the writer shall do what he professes to do; not what he does not profess. If the author does not profess to be quoting the Old Testament *verbatim*, — unless it can be proved that he professes to give the *ipsissima verba*, — then no objection arises against his verbal inspiration from the fact that he does not give the exact words. If an author does not profess to report the exact words of a discourse or a document — if he professes to give, or it is enough for his purposes to give, an abstract or general account of the sense of the wording, as the case may be, — then it is not opposed to his claim to inspiration that he does not give the exact words. This remark sets aside a vast number of objections brought against verbal inspiration by men who seem to fancy that the doctrine supposes men to be false instead of true to their professed or implied intention. It sets aside, for instance, all objection against the verbal inspiration of the Gospels, drawn from the diversity of their accounts of words spoken by Christ or others, written over the cross, etc. It sets aside also all objection raised from the freedom with which the Old Testament is quoted, so long as it cannot be proved that the New Testament writers quote the Old Testament in a different sense from that in which it was written, in cases where the use of the quotation turns on this change of sense. This cannot be proved in a single case.[18]

17. B. B. Warfield, *The Inspiration and Authority of Scripture*, ed. Samuel Craig (Philadelphia: Presbyterian and Reformed, 1948), pp. 437f.

18. *Ibid.*, p. 438. This statement is part of a longer inaugural address about "Inspiration and Criticism" given by Warfield upon the occasion of his induction into the Chair of New Testament Literature and Exegesis in the Western Theological Seminary, Pittsburgh, April 25, 1880. It is one of the finest statements on inspiration I have read.

Appreciation of Perspective

Every good exegete will recognize the importance of appreciating the perspective from which the evangelist is writing and will attempt to understand his intention for presenting the material as he does. But a warning must be sounded at this point because it is altogether too easy in the climate of present-day research about the Gospels and Christology to assume that it was the intention of the evangelists to create sayings and stories about Jesus freely in order to make theological points. Once one begins playing the language-game of intentionality without checkpoints or guidelines, there is no end to what can be ascribed to the imagination of the evangelists. That is why I have given considerable space to establish the evangelists' foremost criterion, namely, Jesus' own remarkable vision of his person and ministry and the genre of his claims. On the basis of this criterion I am convinced that none of the sayings attributed to him in the Gospels are inappropriate to his established self-concept, including explicit statements about his correlativity with God and his consciousness of preexistence. Redaction methodology is useful in describing the distinctive perspectives of the four Gospels, but the scholar may easily fall into the temptation of thinking that whatever does not fit into his preconceived picture of Jesus must be the creation of the evangelists. There may be evidence of divine humor here in regard to the nature of the critical method, for we sometimes fail to recognize limits and assume that a methodology can do more than it is capable of doing.

Of course I am wise enough, I hope, to realize that it is theoretically possible that a number of sayings of Jesus could have been inspired by the risen Christ and placed on the lips of the historical Jesus by the evangelists. Many evangelical New Testament scholars subscribe to this as true to some degree or other. So would I if the evidence convinced me that that was really the case. But the data seem to indicate otherwise. There is no compelling evidence that the evangelists have created or received from the risen Christ *de novo* sayings and placed them on Jesus' lips. What they often do, as we see when we compare the phenomena of the four Gospels, is to adapt an original saying or act of Jesus in order to bring out its intended meaning on a deep level, so that their readers and hearers may be effectively confronted by the person of Jesus and his redemptive work. Different evangelists and audiences provide complementary lines of access to the complex richness of Jesus' self-disclosure. Hence we expect to find and do find a providential

freedom on the part of the gospel writers to modify, adapt, or paraphrase the original saying or event as they feel led to do so. The value
of a controlled redactionism (controlled by the limits Jesus himself tacitly imposes in his language-game and form of life) is that it allows us
to see what Matthew, Mark, Luke, and John are doing, and what are
their complementary angles of vision of Jesus as person.

Beyond that we cannot go with any confidence, for to do so is to
make oneself vulnerable to the charge that personal preference is controlling the data, and the data would say otherwise. The scholar cannot
say on the basis of the phenomenological data that Jesus' implicit claim
about himself requires the exclusion of any explicit claim attributed to
him in the four Gospels. Exegetical evidence that the evangelists intended to write semihistorically must be extraordinarily persuasive to
explain the absence of external support for the view. Accordingly, if I
read in print or hear in lecture a critic's opinion that, for example,
John 8:58 ("Truly, truly I say to you, before Abraham was, I am") cannot possibly have been spoken by Jesus, or that it is probable that he
never spoke it, my response is, "Have you done your homework on
Jesus' use of the personal pronoun *I* in the synoptic Gospels and his
extraordinary enunciation of correlativity with the Father and the Spirit
in his speech and behavior? What concept of persons are you working
with that has led you to that opinion? Let us review the evidence
phenomenologically."

Limits of the Redactional Method

In this connection I am glad to see that a New Testament scholar of
the younger generation, Moises Silva, has expressed a sensitivity to the
limits of the redactional method. In discussing Stonehouse's interpretation of Matthew and the modern tendency among evangelical scholars
to accept the semihistorical, Silva writes,

> *A semi-historical interpretation of Matthew's Gospel does not in prin-
> ciple appear to be incompatible with verbal inspiration, nor would the
> presence of some unhistorical material in one gospel by itself cast doubts
> on the historicity of Jesus' life and work. Nevertheless, the available
> evidence suggests that we need not interpret the gospel material in a
> substantially freer manner than Stonehouse did.* [19]

19. "Redaction Criticism," p. 298. His italics. But compare the extreme redactionalism in Robert H. Gundry, *Matthew: A Commentary on His Literary and Theological
Art* (Grand Rapids: Eerdmans, 1982), for example, pp. 5–10, 19–26, 122, 235,
275–280, 623–640. See also the appendix for an extended critique.

Silva acknowledges that Stonehouse has not said the last word on gospel research but argues, I think correctly, that we need to build on his judicious sense of scholarship and faithfulness to the intent of Scripture, submitting ourselves to its authority in order to be responsible exegetes who are responsive to the divine counsel. This kind of exegesis I find to be most worthy of the word *fidelity* because such exegesis works from the inside out with a truly deep phenomenological method that affirms the presuppositions of the evangelists and their conviction that what they are writing corresponds to true historical events under the guidance of divine providence.

The first sentence in the quotation from Silva describes the posture of many evangelical New Testament scholars who accept a more or less radical reading of the Gospels as semihistorical, on the assumption that Bultmannian exegesis has proven the presence of nonhistorical sayings in the gospel records. This does not trouble them, however, since their belief in verbal inspiration guarantees the truth of a saying; if Jesus did not actually say it, the risen Christ did, and it doesn't make any difference. Ralph P. Martin, as I have indicated, takes this approach when he says,

> A larger issue looms in the question whether the Gospel writers even felt free to read back from the post-resurrection ministry of the Lord and the experience of the congregations any sayings of Jesus that we now find embedded in the context of the earthly ministry. A case in point is Matthew 18:15–20, which clearly has a later church situation in view. Is Jesus giving instruction in advance, or does this entire passage reflect the mind of the Lord communicated to the congregation through the prophets of the New Testament Church in a way similar to the *verba Christi* recorded in Revelation 2–3? The former alternative, though possible, seems strange, for why should Jesus give a promise (Matt. 18:20) that can only be understood in the light of the later Christian experience of public assembly? So the question is left wide open. If we knew more about the authority of early Christian prophets (cf. the *Didache*), we would be better able to answer it. Perhaps, however, it is more academic than vital, since the words of Jesus are now embedded in canonical Scripture, and for that reason gain their authority *regardless of their origin*, just as we read Revelation 3:20 as a true word of Christ today.[20]

20. *New Testament Foundations: A Guide for Christian Students*, vol. 1, *The Four Gospels* (Grand Rapids: Eerdmans, 1975), p. 159. My italics. Compare p. 158.

There is no question about Professor Martin's posture as an evangelical scholar, but several serious difficulties attend the position he has taken. First, it is not really a matter that is "more academic than vital." The practical effect of a hermeneutic that blurs the distinction between the historical sayings of Jesus and the utterances of the risen Christ leads him virtually to contract the person of Jesus out of his book. He has in effect abandoned any serious attempt to confront the historical Jesus; the study is wholly kerygmatic and redactional. Except for its evangelical spirit (its major redeeming characteristic) the book could, redactionally speaking, have been written by a Bultmannian — except that even Norman Perrin devotes far more space in his studies to the question of Jesus' authentic claims. The evangelical critic is found to be in the embarrassing position of showing less interest in the person of Jesus, and of being more neo-Gnostic, than the Bultmannian critics!

Of course, *if* it were probable that New Testament prophets were inspired to utter new sayings of the risen Christ and to assign them freely to Jesus of Nazareth, then we could afford to play that language-game and take refuge in the final canonical result of the process, although that would give us a house with second and third stories and no ground level to support them. But perhaps we could settle for a Gnostic house if the facts compelled us to do so. What happens, however, when the scientific evidence from two directions lays the theory of creative New Testament prophets to rest? While there is a good deal in Martin's study that is valuable — historical background, helpful redactional insights regarding the evangelists' perspectives — the study is not on the whole phenomenologically accurate. Like Dunn's *Christology in the Making*, it begins too far down the line, focusing almost exclusively on creative responses to Jesus by the evangelists rather than on the author of the tradition, Jesus himself. Phenomenologically speaking, it is Jesus who is the archetype, the original, and the evangelists who are ectypal and derivative, not the other way around.

If I were to diagram the situation in gospel research as I perceive it at the present, a possible model would resemble Figure 4.

Reading the chart from left to right, we observe that radical critics generally proceed from nonsupernaturalist assumptions and are inclined to explain away explicit christological sayings attributed to Jesus as creations of the redacting evangelists. Scholar A (Perrin, let us say) goes about as far in this direction as is possible without doing total violence to the data. There are, of course, variations regarding the degree to which the radical scholar views the redactional activity of the

Figure 4

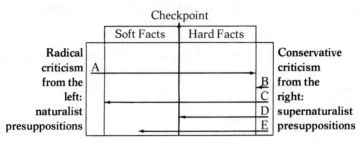

evangelists, but the differences are relatively minor and academic once the phenomena of the Gospels are forced into a nonsupernaturalistic mold. The results of such research are quite predictable. Scholar B, approaching the data with supernaturalist assumptions but skeptical of redactional methods, tends to downplay the multiple aspection of the Gospels and tries to harmonize them into one composite picture. This would be typical of very conservative exegesis. I am in favor of harmonizing as long as one honors the distinctive perspectives of each evangelist (but I object as strongly to the opposite extreme, represented by Werner H. Kelber, who so overplays the diversity among the Gospels that he sees little possibility of any harmonization at all).[21] Scholar C, also a supernaturalist, goes to the other extreme and (like Martin) seems willing to overlap the redactional system to the full extent if necessary, convinced that all Scripture is canonical because inspired by the Holy Spirit; therefore the question is academic. This is also typical of contemporary Roman Catholic exegesis. Bruce Vawter, for example, subscribes to the inspiration of Scripture but interprets the intention of the evangelists in such a way as to allow them freely to create stories about Jesus as parables of his significance for faith:

> When all the probabilities are weighed, and without any at all of the primitive rationalistic prejudice against the possibility of the miraculous, it can easily appear that passages like Mk 6.47–52 (parallels in Mt 14.23b–33, Jn 6.17b–21) or Mk 11.12–14 (parallel in Mt 21.18–19) may be parables that do indeed have something truthful to tell about the person of Jesus and His impact on the first Christian consciousness but that offer no factual details about His life. The results of form and

21. See "Redaction Criticism: On the Nature and Exposition of the Gospels," *Perspectives on Religious Studies* 6 (1979): 4–16, especially pp. 14f.

redactional criticism have had much to contribute in making such conclusions possible, the more it has been recognized how much subject
to such influences the inspired writers were.[22]

Scholar D (my own position) appreciates the valuable insights of a
judicious redactionist like Stonehouse who is sensitive to the multiple
aspection of the evangelists, yet is also convinced by the phenomena
that since Jesus implicitly claimed correlativity with God, he also made
explicit christological statements about himself, as the evangelists attest. Redaction is thus limited to what I call the "hard facts," namely,
the recognizable nuances of perspective and intention of the four evangelists. The checkpoint is at the line where one is tempted to move from
hard facts (what actually is the case) to soft facts (what is not necessarily the case). Hence it is not necessarily the case (indeed, from my
point of view is very likely not the case) that the evangelists have created
explicit christological sayings and placed them on Jesus' lips. The latter
is an unfounded assumption on the part of radical criticism and reflects
an external hermeneutic that is prejudicial to the intrinsic supernatural
genre of the Gospels. Accordingly, I would appeal to my evangelical
colleagues not to buy too heavily into a methodology that is presup-
positionally alien to the phenomena of the Gospels and seriously inadequate in regard to interpreting the central christological claims of
Jesus. Redaction analysis is valuable up to a point, but beyond that
point it is enervated by its biases. I realize that evangelical New Testament scholars, while generally conservative in their use of redaction
criticism, are nonetheless arrayed across a wide spectrum represented
by the three points of left, right, and center on my chart (Scholar E
would be typical). I understand the reasons for their respective positions but hope that the evidence adduced in this study will press them,

---

22. *Biblical Inspiration*, Theological Resources series (Philadelphia: Westminster,
1971), p. 143. Edward Schillebeeckx, while allowing that the Gospels show a loyalty
to the historical Jesus of Nazareth, is deeply committed to the creative redactional
activity of the early church and hence is skeptical of the authenticity of many of the
sayings attributed to Jesus. See *Jesus: An Experiment in Christology*, trans. Hubert
Hosleins (New York: Seabury, 1979), pp. 85–100. Although he holds correctly that a
person is finally to be understood by his actions (p. 258), he does not really know what
to do with the idea, and cannot go very far with it in any case because of his redactional
assumptions (cf. pp. 79; 200–213). See also his *Christ, the Experience of Jesus As
Lord*, trans. John Bowden (New York: Seabury, 1980), pp. 19–25, where he disavows
the possibility of getting back to a direct experience of Jesus apart from the horizon of
modern constructs — the process is dialectical (pp. 31–36; 62–64; 78–79).

along with critics on the radical left, to reconsider the assumptions and applications of redaction criticism, principally in regard to the explicit christological sayings of Jesus in the four Gospels. The burden of proof against the authenticity of these sayings shifts to the shoulders of those who would question them, in light of Jesus' implicit christological claims and the absence of support for the hypothesis about Christian prophets. The grounds for assigning an explicit christological saying to the early church rather than to Jesus must be evidentially solid to be convincing.

A Hermeneutic from Within

I have spoken often of the biased assumptions of radical criticism. It is now time to confront these presuppositions hermeneutically in part 2 of this study, where I will offer what I think are challenging approaches to the Gospels through a hermeneutic from within. Until we are able to carry on our exegesis from within the presuppositions of the Gospels (from the inside out), we will never really grasp the meaning of that pivotal figure who *is* the story, Jesus himself. Exegesis from the outside in invariably misses the point if its underlying philosophy of history is inimical to the supernatural third dimension which provides depth for the natural and the rational.

In concluding part 1, which has focused on exegetical applications of a phenomenology of persons, and in making the transition to part 2, I could not sum up my own sentiments better than to refer to Stonehouse's concluding words in his last book. I quote him at length:

> . . . it should not be overlooked that *Jesus himself in the fullness of his self-disclosure, in the precise way in which he employs various titles as self-designations and describes the various activities of his ministry, provides the final and complete portrayal of what it meant to be the Messiah.* . . .
>
> As we reflect upon the disclosure of Jesus concerning his person and messiahship we observe that a distinctive view of history — and especially of the gospel history — confronts us. And this view of history is in irreconcilable conflict with others which have dominated the thinking of modern students of the Gospels. Historicism is clearly found wanting. For it lays violent hands upon the witness of the Gospels. In the name of criticism and exegesis, it modernizes that witness, first, as it relativizes the absolute and unique in the person of Jesus Christ and, subsequently, in the interest of abiding religious value, seeks, after a fashion, to absolutize the so-called historical Jesus. And the virtual repudiation of the significance of history for Christian faith, whether

inspired by Hegel or Heidegger, as it has come to expression in Strauss, Schweitzer and Bultmann, is thoroughly at variance with the once-for-all place assigned to the history of Jesus in the gospel as both Jesus and the apostles proclaimed it. . . .

Only if the witness of the Gospels to Jesus and that of Jesus' self-revelation are taken at face value, therefore, will one be able to establish genuine continuity between Jesus and the Gospel tradition. And once it is acknowledged that the divine Messiah alone can explain the origin of that tradition will one be in a position to discern how, as a part of a single historical movement, the Gospels not only as matchless historical documents but as integral parts of Holy Scripture came into being. Only if he was the divine Messiah, can we understand the history in which those who from the beginning were eyewitnesses and ministers of the Word, acting with his authority, delivered over to the Church a knowledge of the Gospel tradition. And this history is intelligible also only as we grasp the fact that the divine Messiah, who was endowed with the Spirit of God in a unique fashion, himself qualified his spokesmen and representatives with an enduement of the Spirit from on high that they might bear faithful witness to him.[23]

It is the distinct advantage of evangelical exegetes that we interpret the Gospels from within the story as believers and as disciples. While Wittgenstein was not writing expressly from a Christian point of view, his phenomenology of persons has afforded us a useful secular model in assessing the self-understanding of Jesus from the outside in. But the analysis could take us only so far. We need to move from surface grammar to depth grammar, such as a believer has when he or she enters the story by believing it, or more accurately, by believing in the One who is the story. I do not vouch for everything the six hermeneuts in part 2 ever wrote; Gabriel Marcel tends to be antipropositional, which is typical of existentialists; Michael Polanyi is not theologically orthodox enough for my tastes; J. R. R. Tolkien tends to come at everything obliquely; C. S. Lewis I find most compatible with my Christian perspectives, though his views on the inspiration of Scripture are less satisfactory. I. T. Ramsey and Cornelius Van Til will not meet everyone's tests either. But what they all share in common is a marvelous sense of belief and wonderment as the means of really understanding on a deep level. I consider them deep Christian phenomenologists and have freely drawn on their profound images and insights to interpret

23. *Origins of the Synoptic Gospels: Some Basic Questions* (Grand Rapids: Baker, 1979), pp. 184, 190–191, 192. His italics.

the Gospels and to allow the Christ of the Gospels to encounter us personally as interpreters of the Word which he embodies. I hope that the reader will find as much help in these writers as I have for the continuing task of appropriating and interpreting the good news of Jesus the Messiah to a generation as needy of his supernatural grace as the first.

Part Two

A Phenomenology
from the Inside Out

6

On Transposition and Attentiveness
C. S. Lewis's Approach to Jesus and the Gospels

In his presidential address before the Society of Biblical Literature in November 1973, Norman Perrin threw out a significant challenge for future New Testament studies. In his paper on "Eschatology and Hermeneutics: Reflections on Method in the Interpretation of the New Testament,"[1] he remarked that

> one of the tasks to which I believe we have to commit ourselves as biblical scholars is the investigation of the function or evocative power of biblical symbols. This will, of course, take us into the field of psychology and the psychological process of human understanding, but then one of the characteristics of the contemporary situation in biblical scholarship is that it challenges us to do things we have not done before. Our situation as biblical scholars is, quite simply, that our traditional understanding of the nature of our task is no longer adequate to its fulfillment. We are all of us trained in historical criticism, but if we are to achieve our goal as hermeneuts there is the whole field of human understanding for us to explore.

Coming from a New Testament critic who had become increasingly skeptical in his interpretation of the synoptic Gospels in midcareer, that is quite an admission, and perhaps signals a major modification of the hermeneutical rationalism and naturalism that have tended to dominate biblical criticism to the present day. I am not exactly certain what Perrin had in mind when he spoke of "psychological process" and "the whole field of human understanding," though his later New Testament studies shed some small light on the matter. But I concur that a willingness to investigate this large area ". . . opens up a third dimension of our hermeneutical task . . . ," to quote his concluding words.[2] Perrin appeared to be searching for a method of interpretation that would be more truly

1. *JBL* 93 (1974): 13f.
2. *Ibid.*, p. 14.

descriptive of early Christianity as we find it expressed in the writings of the New Testament and as we experience it in the present. His query seems to echo the complaint of many people in recent times that the methodology of historical biblical criticism is seriously deficient and requires considerable rethinking. Walter Wink offers a more trenchant appeal in his study, *The Bible in Human Transformation: Toward a New Paradigm for Biblical Study*,[3] where he makes a case for nothing less than communal exegesis on the part of teacher and students.

The Hermeneutic of Transposition

All of this brings us to C. S. Lewis. Though he was not a New Testament scholar by profession, he was nonetheless a first-class linguist and literary critic who knew his New Testament well, understood the strengths and foibles of the critical method, and got hold of the "third dimension" in a rather remarkable way. In his penetrating address on "Transposition," which I shall use as a model piece in this first section, Lewis argues that our emotional life is richer, more varied, and therefore "higher" than the life of our sensations.[4] The transposition of the richer spiritual and emotional realm into the poorer realm of sensations and syllables takes place when elements in the poorer system carry more than one meaning: the transposition is algebraical, not arithmetical. It is like transposing a full orchestral score into a piece for piano, where a single limited instrument must make do for the sonority of the flutes, the subtlety of the strings, the reedy nuances of the oboe, and the cutting timbre of a trumpet; or, as in the art of drawing a three-dimensional world on a flat sheet of paper, where it is necessary to scribe the appearance of depth and space by using lines and curves in multiple ways that give the illusion of the real world, such as drawing a straight road receding from the spectator in a shape similar to a dunce's cap. Shading too must serve many purposes to achieve the desired effect of snow, flesh, or a lake in evening light.[5]

Now the point of this, says Lewis, is that it illustrates how the poorer realm of sensations (the first dimension) is given higher significance by means of symbols which are in a very real sense sacramental (the third

3. (Philadelphia: Fortress, 1973).
4. C. S. Lewis, "Transposition," in *The Weight of Glory* (Grand Rapids: Eerdmans, 1965), pp. 20f.
5. *Ibid.*, pp. 21f.

dimension). Lewis is not speaking merely of signs that signify something conventional, such as the relation between speech and writing.
He is rather describing the relationship of a picture to the visible world:

> Pictures are part of the visible world themselves and represent it only
> by being part of it. . . . The suns and lamps in pictures seem to shine
> only because real suns or lamps shine on them: that is, they seem to
> shine a great deal because they really shine a little in reflecting their
> archetypes. The sunlight in a picture is therefore not related to real
> sunlight simply as written words are to spoken. It is a sign, but also
> something more than a sign: and only a sign because it is also more
> than a sign, because in it the thing signified is really in a certain mode
> present.[6]

Although he is only on the fringe of the third dimension, Perrin suggests
something similar as a working model for future New Testament study.
Following Paul Ricoeur and Philip Wheelwright, he distinguishes between sign and symbol, or between steno-symbol and tensive symbol.
In *The Symbolism of Evil*, Ricoeur defines a sign as that which is
usually transparent and exhausted by its "first or literal intentionality,"
while a symbol is opaque and leads one to a second intentionality, and
by analogy to even deeper meanings.[7] Similarly Wheelwright distinguishes steno-symbols from tensive symbols. Steno-symbols are one-to-
one relationships with what they represent — signs, in Lewis's and Ricoeur's terminology — while tensive symbols have a set of meanings that
cannot be exhausted by one referent; they are true symbols in the sense
in which Lewis and Ricoeur describe them.[8]

Now it is interesting to note that more than forty years ago C. S.
Lewis was already thinking in these terms and had worked out the
implications in theology and imaginative Christian fantasy writing. He
employed a word that does more than distinguish between sign and
symbol or steno and tensive symbols, a term that illustrates his point
of the lower being taken into the higher by means of transposition:

6. *Ibid.*, pp. 23f.
7. Trans. Emerson Buchanan (1967; reprint ed., Boston: Beacon Press, 1969),
p. 15. See Perrin, "Eschatology and Hermeneutics," pp. 11f. For a critique of Ricoeur,
see my remarks, p. 146.
8. Philip Wheelwright, *Metaphor and Reality* (Bloomington: Indiana University
Press, 1962), p. 62. See Perrin, "Eschatology and Hermeneutics," pp. 10–13, and *Jesus
and the Language of the Kingdom: Symbol and Metaphor in New Testament Interpretation* (Philadelphia: Fortress, 1976), pp. 29–31, 84–85.

If I had to name the relation I should call it not symbolic but *sacra-mental.* . . . The emotion descends bodily, as it were, into the sensation and digests, transforms, transubstantiates it. . . .[9]

This description of the nature of being and the nature of knowing has a crucial bearing upon all of Lewis's thought and carries profound implications for questions of ontology, epistemology, and soteriology, and especially for biblical studies. What is the nature of reality, how do we come to know what it is, and how do we become redemptively related to it? These are the most fundamental questions of human existence, and Lewis addresses each of them with directness and imagination. His most significant contribution is, perhaps, in the field of epistemology, for he is constantly addressing the question, "How do we know?" Ontological and soteriological matters must at last come down to the level of consciousness and empirical experience where persons begin their quest.

Lewis makes imaginative use of sensory experience with a profusion of illustrations drawn from the empirical world. This empirical realm of immediate sensory experience may be regarded as the first dimension. But Lewis does not limit himself to the empirical; he is not a thoroughgoing naturalist. His apologetic writings and religious fantasies are always cogently reasoned and systematically consistent with each other, and evince the fact that he employs the second dimension of reason and rational argument to a rather remarkable degree. Yet while he is a rationalist, he does not end his epistemological quest with the canons of rationalism.

That brings us back to what I think is Lewis's principal contribution to theology and biblical interpretation, namely, his deep appreciation of the third dimension, the realm of the Spirit and the spiritual, where the higher transposes itself sacramentally into the lower. If one approaches the higher from the lower medium only, one may see the facts and miss the meaning; indeed, by missing the meaning one will not see the facts at all. It is like trying to direct a dog's attention to a dish of food on the floor by pointing one's finger. But the dog doesn't understand pointing; instead of looking at the floor, he sniffs at the pointing hand. Lewis draws this conclusion:

A finger is a finger to him, and that is all. His world is all fact and no meaning. And in a period when factual realism is dominant we shall

9. Lewis, "Transposition," in *The Weight of Glory*, pp. 23f.

find people deliberately inducing upon themselves this doglike mind. A man who has experienced love from within will deliberately go about to inspect it analytically from outside and regard the results of this analysis as truer than his experience. The extreme limit of this self-binding is seen in those who, like the rest of us, have consciousness, yet go about to study the human organism as if they did not know it was conscious.[10]

Lewis considered that the canons of critical analysis in many dominant academic schools disallow serious consideration of the third dimension and follow a naturalistic reductionism, which emphasizes the empirical first dimension, or a rationalistic reduction, which stresses the second dimension of reason. He never felt that the first and second dimensions should be sacrificed to the third dimension, but he was insistent that the third dimension of the Spirit and the spiritual be allowed to function along with the other two and properly inform them. Indeed, the first and second dimensions are understood only in light of the third.

Through the hermeneutic of transposition, which is so apparent in his theological studies and in the imaginative retelling of the original Christian story (his *Space Trilogy* and *The Chronicles of Narnia*), Lewis allows one a new appreciation of the power and the importance of story and of the third dimension. But there is need to practice something akin to Edmund Husserl's *epoché* or bracketing of presuppositions when we read the New Testament story, though in a much broader sense than Husserl entertained. The student as well as the teacher should accordingly permit the story to speak to him before he addresses it with questions of doubt and criticism. Analysis then follows as a secondary interest, but rather chastened and disciplined because it has first listened within the realm of the third dimension to what the story has to say. Otherwise, Lewis avers, critics resemble the skeptical dwarfs in *The Last Battle*, the concluding eschatological book of the Narnia chronicles, who find themselves at last in the presence of the divine Aslan who has come to release them from the dark little stable in which they seem to be trapped; but they are so afraid of being taken in, they cannot be taken out; they see only what they choose to see.

Of this refusal to see the higher in the lower Lewis remarks,

As long as this deliberate refusal to understand things from above, even where such understanding is possible, continues, it is idle to talk of

10. *Ibid.*, p. 28.

any final victory over materialism. The critique of every experience from below, the voluntary ignoring of meaning and concentration on fact, will always have the same plausibility. There will always be evidence, and every month fresh evidence, to show that religion is only psychological, justice only self-protection, politics only economics, love only lust, and thought itself only biochemistry.[11]

Transposition, Lewis argues, confronts such simplistic reductionism head-on. He then counterbalances his criticism of lower-level reduction with a positive affirmation of transposition:

I said before that in your drawing you had only plain white paper for sun and cloud, snow, water, and human flesh. In one sense, how miserably inadequate! Yet in another, how perfect. If the shadows are properly done that patch of white paper will, in some curious way, be very like blazing sunshine: we shall almost feel cold while we look at the paper snow and almost warm our hands at the paper fire. May we not, by a reasonable analogy, suppose likewise that there is no experience of the spirit so transparent and supernatural, no vision of Deity Himself so close and so far beyond all images and emotions, that to it also there cannot be an appropriate correspondence on the sensory level? Not by a new sense but by the incredible flooding of those very sensations we now have with a meaning, a transvaluation, of which we have here no faintest guess?[12]

I began with Perrin's plea that New Testament scholars should henceforth explore tensive biblical symbols in some third dimension of human understanding. This dimly promising groping for a new method of interpretation beyond the limitations of naturalism and rationalism could be considerably aided if it were to give Lewis's hermeneutic of transposition careful attention. Nor is Lewis alone in offering such advice to the modern intellectual. Michael Polanyi has made a penetrating critique of modern skepticism and a strong case for third-dimensional commitment in his study on epistemology.[13] And Morton Kelsey has recently reviewed the weaknesses of modern critical thought

11. *Ibid.*, pp. 28f.
12. *Ibid.*, p. 29.
13. *Personal Knowledge: Towards a Post-Critical Philosophy* (New York: Harper & Row, 1964). See especially chapters 8, "The Logic of Affirmation"; 9, "The Critique of Doubt"; and 10, "Commitment." See my remarks, pp. 168–189.

and argued persuasively for a new appreciation of the third dimension of the Spirit and the spiritual.[14]

Lewis appears to have been one of those gifted forerunners who see things clearly and well in advance of their contemporaries. Beyond his apologetic interests as a Christian scholar, he had a phenomenological interest in letting things be themselves in all their multidimensional richness. According to Lewis's hermeneutical view, the Bible must also be allowed to be itself, to function within the spiritual as well in the empirical and intellectual domains. Anything less, he felt, amounts to a serious misrepresentation of the meaning and intention of the story. One hopes that is what a growing number of New Testament hermeneuts and exegetes will begin to appreciate as they prepare to move beyond the limitations of traditional criticism to an approach that is more appreciative of the spiritual dimension of the biblical narrative.[15]

The Approach to Criticism

One of Lewis's original contributions to literary criticism is his compelling study, *An Experiment in Criticism*.[16] Where traditional criticism judges books first and taste among readers second, Lewis reverses the order and judges readers and types of reading first, and books as a corollary. The desired end is to define a good book as one that is read in a certain way (and bad books as those read in another).[17]

14. *Encounter with God: A Theology of Christian Experience* (Minneapolis: Bethany Fellowship, 1972). See especially chapter 5, "Opening the Door to Spirit – a Counter Revolution."

15. I had hoped that Perrin's later studies would subject Enlightenment presuppositions to the same critical scrutiny that he applied to the New Testament. His publication, *The New Testament, An Introduction: Proclamation and Parenesis, Myth and History* (New York: Harcourt Brace Jovanovich, 1974), unfortunately does not seem to challenge the negative presuppositions of the modern period sufficiently; nor does his use of the hermeneutic of myth, as entirely separate from the radical skepticism of the historical-critical method, seem to hold much promise. See his discussion, "The New Testament as Myth," *ibid.*, pp. 21–37. His later published works, while coming on a bit, still do not make a satisfactory transition to the third dimension of the supernatural. See *Jesus and the Language of the Kingdom*, in which he seems to avoid the possibility that Jesus might be the King of the Kingdom, and thus does not allow Jesus' language to say anything directly about himself and his intentionality. He also is deeply influenced by the opaque symbolism or Mircea Eliade and Ricoeur at this stage of his pilgrimage.

16. (Cambridge: Cambridge University Press, 1966).

17. *Ibid.*, p. 1.

This approach has significant implications for the New Testament scholar who is, after all, only one among many readers of the Scriptures, and not necessarily the one who understands or appreciates their central themes best. We scholars tend to be drawn to the Gospels not as stories to be listened to but as texts to do something with, such as analytical sleuthing regarding origins and editing, as though the reader of a story were more interested in psychologizing the author's reasons for redacting his experiences and materials and anticipating his audience than in reading the story on its own merit.

The first mark of a good reader, says Lewis, is that he will read great works again and again. Most people read a book only once and then discard it like a burned-out match. "Those who read great works, on the other hand, will read the same work ten, twenty or thirty times during the course of their life."[18] Second, the majority read only when they have to, while the person who loves to read seeks every occasion to find undisturbed quiet where he may devote himself to his book; else he feels impoverished. Third, the reading of a great literary work is so moving for the person who loves to read that his whole consciousness is changed, as in experiences of love, religion, or bereavement. Fourth, what is read is continually in his mind and conversation; his thoughts are permeated by scenes and characters from the great works he has read.[19]

Ways of Reading

The principal question has to do with different ways of reading. What is surprising, Lewis observes, is that those who might be expected to have a deep and continuing appreciation for literature because they earn their living at it are often mere professionals who feel they are under pressure to say something new about the literary work in question and get it into print as soon as possible, or status seekers in circles of literary conversation where to be in latest fashion is of first importance. The true reader and genuine devotee of real works of art, on the other hand, seeks modestly to improve himself by staying close by the established great works rather than following the current vogue. But more importantly,

> the true reader reads every work seriously in the sense that he reads it whole-heartedly, makes himself as receptive as he can. But for that very

18. *Ibid.*, p. 2.
19. *Ibid.*, p. 3.

reason he cannot read every work solemnly or gravely. For he will read "in the same Spirit that the author writ."[20]

Otherwise the solemn readers read on with Puritan conscience without the saving grace of Puritan theology, too solemn to be seriously receptive:

> Solemn men, but not serious readers; they have not fairly and squarely laid their minds open, without preconception, to the works they read.[21]

It is important, says Lewis, to appreciate what the work of art is, not what it is "of," otherwise it will soon die once it has been used and its work is done. With considerable irony he addresses the utilitarian reader who merely uses the text:

> In other words, you "do things with it". You don't lay yourself open to what it, by being in its totality precisely the thing it is, can do to you.[22]

Doing things with a text is like treating it as an icon or a toy which evokes in its user, whether worshiper or child, imaginary pictures of something else. Real appreciation of a work of art, however, is quite the opposite:

> We must not let loose our own subjectivity upon the pictures and make them its vehicles. We must begin by laying aside as completely as we can all our own preconceptions, interests, and associations.[23]

Then comes the positive effort, after the negative:

> We must use our eyes. We must look, and go on looking till we have certainly seen exactly what is there. We sit down before the picture in order to have something done to us, not that we may do things with it. The first demand any work of any art makes upon us is surrender. Look. Listen. Receive. Get yourself out of the way. (There is no good asking first whether the work before you deserves such a surrender, for until you have surrendered you cannot possibly find out.)[24]

20. *Ibid.*, p. 11.
21. *Ibid.*, p. 12.
22. *Ibid.*, pp. 16–17.
23. *Ibid.*, p. 18.
24. *Ibid.*, p. 19.

Simply put, Lewis's hermeneutic of art observes that where the many *use* an artistic work, the few *receive* it, and art must be received if it is really to be understood. The implications for a New Testament hermeneutic are enormous, and may account for the fact that there is such a disparity between biblical scholars and lay Christians, not so much on content of technical knowledge, which goes without saying, but on the level of attitude and receptivity to the gospel itself. Speaking from personal experience, a danger greater than lay naïveté is scholarly utilitarianism, where tools of trade are applied to the Gospels as "useful for" illustrating this development or that tendency. But a receptive posture of surrender before the work of art, in this case the gospel, is requisite, says Lewis, to understanding what it *is*. In his own way Husserl was after much the same thing by bracketing presuppositions that distort the essential object; and following Husserl, E. D. Hirsch, Jr., has argued for the priority of the original author's meaning in understanding a text properly.[25]

Obedience to the Text

Lewis forewarns that surrender does not mean simply being passive or lacking in imaginative activity, but rather that the right reader is obedient to the work of art, is making sure of his orders. If the orders are bad he turns away; if they are good he becomes more obedient to the work and crosses the frontier into a new region where he begins to grasp the structure of the whole work with intelligence and emotion. The principal attitude for understanding deeply is to look, listen, wait, attend. Jesus bids the disciples of John, who ask whether he is the one who was to come or whether they should look for another, to "go and tell John what you hear and see . . ." (Matt. 11:2–5). One must not be critical of the lens by only looking *at* it; one must look *through* it. It is not simply the event that must be sought in a story (in John's case the event of the promised Messiah as John understood him) but the way in which the present messianic story is being unfolded by its author, Jesus: "Look and see." Strict attention and obedience to his words and acts are important if one is to divine their meaning. It is the demand for realism of content on John's part, and coincidentally on the part of the religious establishment, that throws them off in their frustration with Jesus' style and shape in his ministry, which does not conform to the

---

25. *Validity in Interpretation* (New Haven: Yale University Press, 1967), and *The Aims of Interpretation* (Chicago: University of Chicago Press, Phoenix Books, 1978).

Old Testament patterns of messianic prophecy as they interpreted them. They cannot assimilate the novel and peculiar way — it seems out of character and deeply disappointing to John and blasphemous to the scribal scholars — in which Jesus carries out his ironic ministry.

Hence much literary and gospel criticism today cannot brook the fantastic and logically odd. Jesus' activity must conform to "scientific" canons of repeatability and radical realism; otherwise he is questioned, dismissed, or demythologized. Lewis observes that until the nineteenth century nearly all stories were about the remarkable, not the perfectly ordinary,[26] and that it is important to reinstate the fantastic and ironic element in story once again, for without it the reader can be deceived by what passes as "real fact," and is not. Likewise John and the Pharisees, though on different levels, had lost the Old Testament sense of God as "round" and logically odd in his dealings with Israel. Theirs is sober-faced realism that lacks a sense of imagination for the novel and misses the meaning of the central person of the gospel stories, with his recondite, elusive, and ironic announcement that in himself, in this poor Galilean carpenter, the kingdom of God is being inaugurated, the wedding feast of heaven and earth has begun, and forgiveness of sins is available to sinners and outcasts. Logically odd language indeed!

Of the child, for all its fickle weaknesses, yet of whom Jesus made a splendid example of faith (Matt. 18:2–4), Lewis remarks,

> But who in his sense would not keep, if he could, that tireless curiosity, that intensity of imagination, that facility of suspending disbelief, that unspoiled appetite, that readiness to wonder, to pity, and to admire? The process of growing up is to be valued for what we gain, not for what we lose. Not to acquire a taste for the realistic is childish in the bad sense; to have lost the taste for marvels and adventures is no more a matter for congratulation than losing our teeth, our hair, our palate, and finally our hopes. Why do we hear so much about the defects of immaturity and so little about those of senility?[27]

The grown-up characteristic of "chronological snobbery"[28] is most to be avoided; and when we have done with it, "what then would become of the criticism which attaches so much importance to being adult and instills a fear and shame of any enjoyment we can share with

---

26. *An Experiment in Criticism*, pp. 62–63.
27. *Ibid.*, p. 72.
28. *Ibid.*, p. 73.

the very young?"[29] Lewis's criticism of criticism is roundly biblical, is indeed in keeping with Jesus' criticism of scribal criticism which had lost the true and childlike sense of wonder at the odd and round grace of God, a wonder known by the pious children of Israel in earlier days and now again being felt by seeking sinners in Jesus's day. A primary hermeneutic for gospel interpretation comes out of this plaintive call "to become a child again," to rediscover an original naïveté beyond the second naïveté of Ricoeur (which refuses to relinquish the right of the critic to stand over the text with authority), and to recapture the posture of belief through the logically odd, the marvelous and fantastic, and the awesomely wonderful in the words and works of Jesus.

Attentiveness to the Text

Attention to what the creator, artist, or author is doing — what Jesus the primary "author" of the gospel story is saying (Logos) and making (Poiema) — is the first step in "receiving" rather than "using."[30] We must allow ourselves to be open to "the complex and carefully made objects" of his creation:

> Our feelings and imaginations must be led through "taste after taste, upheld with kindliest change." Contrasts (but also premonitions and echoes) between the darker and the lighter, the swifter and the slower, the simpler and the more sophisticated, must have something like balance, but never a too perfect symmetry, so that the shape of the whole work will be felt as inevitable and satisfying.[31]

Lewis goes even further — and here the gospel critic will be stretched to the utmost not to "use" the text to try to prove this evolutionary trajectory or that, but simply to let it be what it is in itself, as it is:

> As little as possible must exist solely for the sake of other things. Every episode, explanation, description, dialogue — ideally every sentence — must be pleasureable and interesting for its own sake.[32]

The critic will be self-deceived, Lewis warns, to ignore a statue's shape in view of the sculptor's view of life, since the sculptor's view of life is

29. *Ibid.*
30. *Ibid.*, pp. 82–83.
31. *Ibid.*, p. 83.
32. *Ibid.*, pp. 83–84.

known through the shape he gives to the statue.[33] Applying this observation to Jesus' creative use of spoken and acted language, we come to know him and his intention in no other way than through the shape of what he says and does, so that attention to the details of his dialogue discloses his intentional "I" — an important insight that Ludwig Wittgenstein employs in his phenomenology of persons and that I have discussed in chapter 1.

Accordingly, a fresh immersion in what a Gospel *is* as we approach it in the spirit of true receptivity takes precedence over a mere desire to *use* the text to find what we want:

> The supreme objection to this is that which lies against the popular use of all the arts. We are so busy doing things with the work that we give it too little chance to work on us. Thus increasingly we meet only ourselves.[34]

To receive is to enter fully into the opinions, the attitudes, the feelings, the total experience of Jesus as he speaks and acts and takes us along roads we have never yet explored.[35] The content of Jesus' self-disclosure is not to be used by the "user" as a pastime for solving puzzles or games (which is downward), but received by the recipient as a place to rest in, as religious contemplation (upward), as "exquisitely detailed compulsions on a mind willing and able to be so compelled."[36] It is the willing and receiving mind that comes openly to the gospel and experiences the deep "magic" of heaven, the evocation of "color," "flavor," "texture," "smell," or "race of words."

Lewis now lets loose his disdain for criticism that uses rather than receives the text: "That is why the inevitable abstraction of content and words seems to do such violence to great literature."[37] Critical reading has its place, of course; but only after the good reader has first received a work does he have anything to evaluate. The ideal of first receiving, then evaluating is, says Lewis with a trenchant critical eye, realized less and less the longer we move in professional circles, as we "fail of that inner silence, that emptying out of ourselves, by which we ought to make room for the total reception of the work."[38]

33. *Ibid.*, p. 84.
34. *Ibid.*, p. 85.
35. *Ibid.*, pp. 85, 88.
36. *Ibid.*, p. 89.
37. *Ibid.*, pp. 89–90.
38. *Ibid.*, pp. 92–93.

For this reason, Lewis writes, it is a mistake to force the young constantly to express opinions when they are reading great works, for that aggravates the natural disposition to use a work as we professionals do when we are under pressure to review a book or send a manuscript to the publisher. An attitude of doubt is cultivated in the young reader who is always encouraged to look at every work with suspicion. To be able to discern propaganda and muddled thinking is meritorious, but to become impervious to the good is meretricious.[39] The Gospels will not give up their secrets about Jesus to the reader who approaches them with the suspicion that sayings attributed to Jesus are really creations of the early church, unless proven otherwise. "When in doubt, discard," says Perrin, for "the burden of proof always lies on the claim to authenticity."[40] Compare that with Lewis's challenge of such arrogance:

> No poem will give up its secret to a reader who enters it regarding the poet as a potential deceiver, and determined not to be taken in. We must risk being taken in, if we are to get anything.[41]

It is on grounds of imported assumptions and not of the work itself that much literary and gospel criticism of the last hundred years has been undertaken. Critics "get the right answer, not because their method leads to it, but because they knew it beforehand. Sometimes, when they don't, a revealing answer may give the teacher cold doubts about the method itself."[42]

The next gust of fashion may blow a critic's conclusions away. Indeed, in criticism, "dethronements and restorations are almost monthly events."[43] None of them can be trusted to be permanent. But what does not change is the distinction between the attentive and inattentive, the obedient and willful ways of reading; and this distinction always works in the open. The standard by which one properly judges readers and

39. *Ibid.*, p. 93.

40. *Rediscovering the Teaching of Jesus* (London: SCM Press; New York: Harper & Row, 1967), pp. 11–12. One cannot help comparing the overconfident claim of Perrin in the midsixties with the careful work of David Hill which demolishes the argument. See *New Testament Prophecy* (Atlanta: John Knox, 1980), especially chapter 7, "Christian Prophets and the Sayings of Jesus."

41. *An Experiment in Criticism*, p. 94.

42. *Ibid.*

43. *Ibid.*, p. 105.

books is this: what those who read deeply judge to be good is probably good, and this would include the Gospels read by ardent believers, regardless of their level of formal education or critical acumen. Though they may make mistakes on this particular exegesis or that (and all do, including the scholars), their attentiveness and obedience to the text guarantee that they will hear the story and be confronted by the Jesus who announces the arrival of salvation and the commencement of the messianic wedding feast. But "all probability is against those who attack."[44]

The Art of Interpretation

What then defines good professional criticism? Lewis finds in Matthew Arnold a helpful mentor who stays clear of evaluation and aims to see the work in itself as it really is, getting himself out of the way and letting humanity decide.[45] Evaluative criticism is least helpful; Lewis admits that he owes far more to editors, textual critics, commentators, and lexicographers, who stand at the top of his list:

> Find out what the author actually wrote and what the hard words meant and what the allusions were to, and you have done far more for me than a hundred new interpretations or assessments could ever do.[46]

Second come good literary historians who help to put the works in their proper settings. But it is only in knowing the work itself that one can appreciate the nuances of insight that the commentators and historians bring to the text. Attentiveness and obedience to the text come first.[47] Best of all is "an independent rereading in a happy hour."[48] But there is an unhappy tendency in modern schooling to encourage students to see books wholly through other books, and thus they are "drenched, dizzied, and bedevilled by criticism to a point at which primary literary experience is no longer possible."[49]

This, I fear, is the state of many of our seminarians and pastors who no longer are capable of a primary experience of the texts of the Gospels because critical theories (many of them long since revised or discarded)

44. *Ibid.*, p. 112.
45. *Ibid.*, pp. 119–120.
46. *Ibid.*, p. 121.
47. *Ibid.*, p. 123.
48. *Ibid.*, p. 124.
49. *Ibid.*, p. 129.

have short-circuited them with doubt and waning confidence in the story; or worse, have engineered an arrogance toward the text that makes attentiveness and obedience to the words extremely difficult, if not impossible. Meanwhile the unhappy parishioner, chafing in the pew, prays that what he or she sees in the text will be confirmed by the trained expert behind the pulpit; or perhaps, which is worse, is simply encouraged to become as diffident and as inattentive to the gospel as the cleric himself. Accordingly, Lewis calls for a fast from criticism (with tongue in cheek of course; the image is hyperbolic for effect.) But imagine what would happen in New Testament studies if the plan were even partially put into practice:

> I suggest that a ten or twenty years' abstinence both from the reading and from the writing of evaluative criticism might do us all a great deal of good.[50]

Summing up his case, Lewis concludes that when we read the Gospels (I have all along been transposing his literary agenda to our special New Testament concerns) we must treat the reception of the Gospel we are reading as an end in itself, not as a means to uncovering, by some theory or other, ostensive "facts" that lie hidden behind the words and are supposed to explain the narrative in purely naturalistic terms; or as a repository of morals to be distilled by a theory of essences. Listening and attending to the words of the text allow the Spirit to speak to the reader through the living Word, as the Word appears both as Logos (something said) and as Poiema (something made). It both *means* and *is*. Lewis summarizes nicely these two functions of the living text as the believer and the New Testament scholar (one would hope he is also a believer) are confronted by its claims:

> As Logos it tells a story, or expresses an emotion, or exhorts or pleads or describes or rebukes or excites laughter. As Poiema, by its aural beauties and also by the balance and contrast and the unified multiplicity of its successive parts, it is an *objet d'art*, a thing shaped so as to give great satisfaction.[51]

The implications for gospel interpretation are large. The interpreter first listens attentively to the story, responds obediently to its pleading,

50. *Ibid.*
51. *Ibid.*, p. 132.

and only then proceeds to analyze and appreciate its esthetic unity in multiplicity and diversity in unity. The movement of deep interpretation is from the higher to the lower, from the inside out; from "attending to" the Story-Logos, to "attending from" the Story-Logos, to Poiema. When we "attend to" and "attend from" the shape of a Gospel we are interpreting in the presence of its archetypal author, Jesus, and under the ectypal spell of the writer who has shaped his Gospel under inspiration. As we read, immersed, "we entertain various imaginations, imagined feelings, and thoughts in an order, and at a tempo, prescribed by the poet."[52]

True obedience to the gospel text thus becomes a pleasure here and now; as the fashioner of the story, like a master of the dance, takes us through our paces,

> the rests and movements, the quickenings and slowings, the easier and more arduous passages will come exactly as we need them; we shall be deliciously surprised by the satisfaction of wants we were not aware of till they were satisfied. We shall end up just tired enough and not too tired, and "on the right note". It would have been unbearable if it had ended a moment sooner — or later — or in any different way. Looking back on the whole performance we shall feel that we have been led through a pattern or arrangement of activities which our nature cried out for.[53]

Accordingly, Lewis would say, the primary art of gospel interpretation is not to analyze the gospel to pieces, assigning this pericope to the creation of the church community and that to Jesus, this to one supposed level of development and that to another, as though what we were after were some ostensive "real facts" beyond the artistry of the text, arranged in the "real" evolutionary order of their happening. That would be just the opposite of what Lewis is saying and what (I believe correctly) his comments on criticism ought to say to us who do professional biblical criticism, and to the laity. The gospel is to be entered into on its own account, for it is in the inspired shape of Logos-Poiema that God addresses us with his grace and challenge. Of course in the case of the Gospels we intend them to be true, because in obedience to

52. *Ibid.*, p. 133.
53. *Ibid.*, p. 134.

their claim to be factually true they are different from other great literary works, which make no such claim.[54]

The Gospels thus interpreted are not windowless monads in the Leibnizian sense, but windows and doors through which one can say, "I have got out," or "I have got in."[55] What matters is the power through which we are permitted to relive the Gospel of the inspired evangelist, and are admitted (if we are attentive and obedient) to experience other than ourselves, to be drawn into an "enormous extension of our being," to be confronted by Jesus, the expression of God, and his saving work:

> Here, as in worship, in love, in moral action, and in knowing, I transcend myself; and am never more myself than when I do.[56]

---

54. So Lewis's note that "the mark of strictly literary reading, as opposed to scientific or otherwise informative reading, is that we need not believe or approve the Logos" (ibid., p. 136) does not hold in the case of the Gospels, which go beyond purely imaginary literary creation in their claim of actual happening, and are in that sense sui generis and all the more demanding of the reader's attentiveness and obedience.

55. Ibid., p. 138.

56. Ibid., p. 141.

7

Jesus and the "Logically Odd"
I. T. Ramsey's Logical Empirical Approach to Jesus and the Gospels

One of the more fascinating approaches to the Jesus of the Gospels is I. T. Ramsey's study of those experiences in life that require discernment and commitment and lead to a disclosure situation that is "more than" one would expect to find on the surface. The language of such situations is "logically odd" but wholly appropriate. In the following pages it will be my purpose to explore Ramsey's empirical description of persons in religious disclosure situations and make generous use of his notion of the "logically odd" in interpreting Jesus' language in the Gospels.[1]

Ramsey's goal as a Christian philosopher and apologist is to use rather than to disdain the insights of contemporary logical empiricism and so provide a novel inroad into the problems of theology.[2] His discerning understanding of contemporary interest in language provides valuable clues to a new method of approaching Jesus in the Gospels. The method is to elucidate the logic of theological assertions. Ramsey asks what kind of situations religious language appeals to and what sort of empirical anchorage theological words have.[3]

Ramsey begins to answer these questions by affirming, as Ludwig Wittgenstein did before him, that living agents have a self-awareness that is not exhausted by reference to simple scientific verification. In the religious situation there is something *more than* just the spatio-temporal; there is a depth that leads one to discernment, then to a total commitment appropriate to a "question of great consequence," like a man who can hardly swim jumping into a river to rescue a drowning child. Such discernment and total commitment go beyond mere logical

---

1. I. T. Ramsey, *Religious Language: An Empirical Placing of Theological Phrases* (New York: Macmillan, 1963).
2. *Ibid.*, p. 11.
3. *Ibid.*, p. 15.

considerations which are matters of speculation only.[4] Both discernment and commitment are necessary, since commitment without discernment is bigotry and idolatry, while discernment without commitment
is the vice of religious insincerity and hypocrisy.[5] Jesus speaks profoundly of both discernment and commitment, for instance in Mark
8:27 where his question of discernment, "Who do men say that I am?",
is coupled with a demand for total commitment: "For whoever would
save his life will lose it; and whoever loses his life for my sake and the
gospel's will save it" (v. 35).

One notices such discernment-commitment utterances are logically
odd, since their meaning cannot be discerned through ordinary logical
and empirical testing, but only in the moment of discernment-commitment when they "come alive," the "light dawns," and the "penny drops."[6]
We can see this to be the case in Jesus' parables and his proclamation
of the arrival of the kingdom of God, and in his own person. It is only
when Jesus' claims are met "eye to eye" that his words and acts "come
alive" and the disclosure situation takes on depth and a certain spatio-
temporal elusiveness, simply because it is a *characteristically personal*
situation where the situation is more than "what's seen" and has the
character of "vision."[7] The entire Gospel of Mark has this elusive characteristic of personal disclosure by Jesus in language that only the discerning and committed can understand in depth. Then and only then
does the penny drop. But the other Gospels, including John, are also
characteristically personal and require discernment-commitment before
the enigmatic Jesus reaches to the roots of one's understanding.

This is to say that religious language is not a mere set of labels for
hard, objective facts, though facts are included in the disclosure situation. Rather, the deep meaning of Jesus' disclosure is penetrated when
one attentively hears him speak one's name, and when in turn one
speaks the name of Jesus in expectant faith, like the speaking of names
between the risen Jesus and Mary in the garden (John 20:16). We can
know all kinds of things about another person through knowledge by
external description, but only when he offers his hand and his name
does the ice break and the penny drop. Even inanimate things like hills
and buildings and ships take on a personality when we name them,

4. *Ibid.*, pp. 17–19.
5. *Ibid.*, p. 19.
6. *Ibid.*, p. 20.
7. *Ibid.*, pp. 21–22.

because they are drawn into a characteristically personal disclosure situation and become familiar friends.[8]

In matters of free will and decision making, especially where Jesus lays upon his hearers the challenge to discern his person and mission and to make a decision to follow him, we have a situation that is "not exhausted by any tale, however comprehensive, of bodily behaviour; not exhausted by the scientific language of determinism, be this ever so complex — involving biochemistry, physiology, psychology, economics and the rest."[9] These are wise words for gospel criticism, which can exhaust the historical, psychological, economic, and sociological settings of the Gospels, yet miss the point. The claims of Jesus "will not be exhaustively unpacked in scientific language, however far those languages go."[10]

Discernment and Commitment

Ramsey makes an important point when he distinguishes the commitment one has in doing mathematics (which is always a loose or partial commitment, since it depends on what language-game or geometry one is working with), and personal commitment, which is a localized loyalty. The first is broad and universal, the second deep and local. Religious commitment — the kind Jesus personally evinces and requires of his followers — is best described by the word *agapē* and combines one's localized total commitment to a pastime or a person with the universal breadth of mathematical commitment. It is a commitment that is deep *and* universal. It is a commitment to something "from outside us," like Jesus' claim in John 15:16: "You did not choose me, but I chose you." Religious commitment in the gospel sense is total commitment to the whole universe, or more accurately, to the Lord of the whole universe.[11] Such discernment and commitment are characteristic of Jesus' spoken and acted language.

But surely this is all very odd language, for the purpose of the Gospels is "to tell such a tale as evokes the 'insight,' the 'discernment' from which commitment follows as a response." The Gospels employ key expressions whose logic has to do with personal loyalty, "final" endpoints of explanation, "specially resistant posits" and "apex" words:

8. *Ibid.*, p. 29.
9. *Ibid.*, p. 31.
10. *Ibid.*, pp. 31–33.
11. *Ibid.*, pp. 39–41.

In particular the Christian religion focuses such a cosmic commitment on Christ — on Christ as Jesus of Nazareth, born, dead and buried, but also on the risen and ascended Christ, the cosmic Christ of Ephesians and Colossians, the Christ who is organic to the old Israel and to the new Israel of his Church and through them to the whole of history.[12]

The use of ordinary empirical situations to illustrate the depth of disclosure in the religious setting suggests that religious language, and so the language of the Gospels, is logically odd in several ways. First, the use of the personal pronoun *I* and the logic of nicknames or surrogates for "I" will give us some insight into the grammatical proper names used in the Gospels, and of the logical priority of "I" as Jesus uses it. Pressing the question as to *why* Jesus speaks and acts as he does, we find we cannot assign his behavior to forces working beyond him over which he has no control and which compel him to do what he does. We can only assign his behavior in the end to who he is — like the man who is asked why he has done such and such and who finally replies, after a series of questions in infinite regress, "Because I'm I." That is where the logic finally ends, with a logically odd tautology, the assertion of the logical priority of the responsible, choosing, willing "I." "I" is the final form.[13]

Jesus' observers ask of him, "Why do you say what you say and do what you do?" To which his reply in effect is, "Because *I am I* and *I choose* to do what I do: that is the person I am." As Ramsey says, "In the case of a 'free' response we reach a position in the question-answer game beyond which no more is possible along the same lines. There has been declared for that particular question-answer game, a 'final option.' "[14] Here, in Jesus' free decision to be this sort of person, doing and saying these kinds of things, he is exerting an authoritative claim to be the "I" he is, with his logically peculiar discernment, obligation, and focus of loyalty: "I am I." It is the irreducible tautology. Jesus, of course, claims to be sent from the Father and to be doing his will, especially, ironically, in the fourth Gospel, where explicit Christology and the use of "I" are strongest; but the unity of will between Father, Son, and Spirit in all four Gospels is so evident that Jesus, in using "I," appears to be claiming the divine tautology as authoritatively as Yahweh's "I AM WHO I AM" in Exodus 3:14. The personal pronoun *I* is

12. *Ibid.*, p. 41.
13. *Ibid.*, p. 46.
14. *Ibid.*

the "irreducible posit" of divine authority beyond which in the most ultimate sense it is impossible to go, and Jesus claims it.

"Why," Jesus is asked, "do you and your disciples do this?" And Jesus replies, "Look and see what my discernment and commitment specify. I am *showing* you by my words and acts." Whether it is table-fellowship, feasting rather than fasting, healing the sick, forgiving sins, proclaiming the kingdom's arrival, or making logically odd claims for himself, Jesus' language consists of final tautologies which sponsor key words and declare a divine commitment.[15] The questioner either sees it or he does not, depending on his own discernment-commitment. The Pharisaic and scribal questioners ask for convincing empirical signs as proof of Jesus' claims, but what they do not understand is that unless they are willing to come to the point where doubt and hostility give way to personal trust, the ice will never break, the light will not dawn, the penny will not drop. No number of spatio-temporal "signs," even in infinite regress, will exhaust what Jesus is claiming. But for the discerning and committed, his words of forgiveness, healings, and miracles are sufficient to disclose his authoritative "I."[16]

Accordingly, in the Gospels, Jesus claims to be the "Irreducible Posit"[17] of the new age of salvation which is breaking in precisely in terms of his "I." His name *Jesus*, his personal pronoun *I*, together with the other surrogate titles, such as "Son of man," are the irreducible posits, like the axioms of mathematics, which bespeak the particular yet universal redemptive system he is introducing. These personal names and surrogates are tautologies on the order of "I am who I say I am," and convey irreducibly the necessary proposition of the particular convention he is positing. In positing his authoritative claim "I am I," Jesus makes the tautology significant by telling and enacting "stories" until a characteristic discernment is evoked and is followed by the commitment of the believer. Hence his ordinary object-language is qualified by the logically odd shape he gives to it as he evokes the odd kind of situation.

The good exegete and hermeneut will train himself to discern Jesus' odd language and the logical improprieties in the Gospels that qualify ordinary models of experience. One may sensitize himself to the logically odd by becoming aware of odd logical behavior in other areas of

15. *Ibid*., p. 47.
16. *Ibid*., p. 48.
17. *Ibid*., p. 50.

human discourse, such as in poetry and in science. They may not all have logical behavior that could be called religious, Ramsey allows,

> but I am saying that a useful antidote to the craze for straightforward language might be found in suitable doses of poetry or greater familiarity with the curiously odd words thrown up in scientific theories. Such doses would at any rate begin to suggest to us that there is an important place for odd language; that odd language may well have a distinctive significance, and we might even conclude in the end that the odder the language the more it matters to us.[18]

Now a fascinating aspect of Jesus' claim of authority in forgiving sins, which is a prerogative of God alone, or in controlling nature by stilling storms, multiplying food, healing the sick, and raising the dead (all prerogatives of God) is that he is speaking and acting with an odd kind of language designed to evoke in the attentive and obedient a situation of discernment. This discernment moves one along a logical route until he sees, at the end of the series, that Jesus "completes" and "presides over" the rest of human language, which is a tremendous implication. Jesus, speaking with the authoritative "I am I" of God himself, "may be pictured as the centre of a maze — the spot where we finally arrive if we walk long enough and make the correct logical moves."[19]

Hence Jesus' own logically odd Christology is constructed out of ordinary language with ordinary models drawn from human experience, but is qualified with attributes of deity. For example, "you have heard that it was said" is an instantly recognizable model with qualifier words that invoke a divine authority far above the authority of Moses: "But *I* say to you . . ." (Matt. 5:21–48). The personal pronoun *I* is a recognizable empirical model of everyday discourse which Jesus qualifies with claims to divine authority and which is designed, in its logically odd way, to evoke a situation of discernment-commitment. It is in terms of "this *and more*" that Jesus' claim leads one on to "something 'mysterious' which eludes the grasp of causal language," and "satisfies" the attentive hearer.[20]

18. *Ibid.*, p. 54.
19. *Ibid.*, p. 68.
20. *Ibid.*, p. 70. The whole of chapter 2, "Some Traditional Characterizations of God: Models and Qualifiers," contains excellent materials for understanding how Jesus models and qualifies traditional language to make his claim of divine authority.

In each of the antitheses of the Sermon on the Mount, as in all his words spoken, stories told, and acts performed, Jesus' "I" completes the causal sequence and is at the same time logically prior. An attentive analysis of even the most cautious core of "authentic" sayings arrived at by the most radical criticism evidences, as we have seen, a logical status of authority in Jesus' use of "I." "I am I" is emphatic and final, a logical stop-card. Now that we have traced the causal series of words and acts back to Jesus, "a different logical move can be made, and it is when this kind of move is made that we talk of the causal story 'being completed.' "[21] Jesus' authoritative use of "I" has the same status as the "I am I" of God himself — he is claiming, as it were, to be the "First Cause," and the word is final. No wonder the guardians of traditional Mosaic authority were offended by what appeared to them to be the highest blasphemy. They read his language properly as far as straightforward logic would take them; the logically odd they could not understand or accept. But for the attentive it was the proclamation of good news, a disclosure-commitment situation in which the light dawned, the ice broke, the penny dropped. Jesus' name is accordingly given a certain logical placing of priority in the Gospels, as is the name *God*, where it is placed first at the head of all the stories, presiding over and uniting all causal explanations: "Jesus" = "I AM WHO I AM" = "divine authority."

The Pharisees and scribes were not willing to accept the odd logical priority of Jesus' "I" but wanted the causal regression continued to the "real" cause of his behavior: "It is only by Beelzebub, the prince of demons, that this fellow drives out demons" (Matt. 12:24, NIV). Jesus' reply identifies his activity with the Spirit of God: "But if I drive out demons by the Spirit [Luke: "finger"] of God, then the kingdom of God has come upon you" (Matt. 12:28; parallel, Luke 11:20, NIV). The recognizable models of Jewish theology are all qualified by his use of the authoritative "I" in terms of which a new salvation grammar is being introduced. In the prototrinitarian claims of Jesus there is a virtual sharing of divine authority and power with the Father and the Spirit. Beyond the divine "I am I" one cannot go, any more than on the ordinary level of human discourse one cannot go beyond the "I" in the reply, "I did it because I chose to do it."

The claim of Jesus in the use of "I say unto you" and "I am" gives

21. *Ibid.*, p. 72.

him "a distinctive placing, a presidential position over the whole language route."[22] His "I" fills the attentive believer with wonder, awe,
and astonishment; the situation takes on depth and disclosure. But only
for those who pursue, not with a doubting mind, but with an acquisitive
mind that is hungry for answers, do the intricate, purposive, and fascinating connections unfold with the self-disclosure of Jesus. He develops "purposive stories" which point to himself as the embodied purpose-
story of salvation, and which he prosecutes in the direction of belief
until wonder is evoked.[23]

Jesus' language is odd but suitable currency, empirically based on
Jesus' personal activity and qualified with divine qualifiers so that it
becomes logically appropriate language for the situation of revelation
and redemption, which in turn culminates in wonder, awe, and worship.
But we must not imagine that the breaking in of the light is wholly in
our hands, as though the listener and beholder of Jesus' words and acts
will automatically be drawn into a discernment-commitment response.
Perhaps this is the meaning of the "hard" saying about the parables in
Mark 4:11: "The secret of the kingdom of God has been given to you.
But to those on the outside everything is said in parables" (NIV). Re-
marking on the fact that it is not given everyone to see the ice break
and the penny drop, Ramsey remarks,

> Need this trouble us? Is not this only what has been meant by religious
> people when they have claimed that the "initiative" in any "disclosure"
> of "revelation" must come from God?[24]

We must never assume, then, that we have a privileged access to God's
private life, to his what, when, and where, other than what he has been
pleased to reveal to his people in Jesus and through the evangelists and
the inspired apostles who interpret him on even odder levels of theological reflection.[25] That question notwithstanding, Jesus is the one who
in the Gospels plots and maps the theological phrases of salvation; he
is the empirical anchorage of belief par excellence. Of the latter, Ramsey
says,

22. *Ibid.*, p. 74.
23. *Ibid.*, pp. 87–88.
24. *Ibid.*, p. 90.
25. *Ibid.*, pp. 104–105.

Without such an empirical anchorage all our theological thinking is in vain, and where there is controversy and argument we are to look for their resolution where they are fulfilled: in worship.[26]

Limitations of Scientific Historical Criticism

In an excellent section on "The Language of the Bible," Ramsey reiterates a major point that the inspiration of Scripture lends it a logically odd flavor, or better, a logical structure of its own, which cannot be fitted precisely into the logically simplistic and straightforward jacket of "scientific historical criticism" by those who think that "history is science, neither more nor less," and that "odd" and repetitive passages in the Gospels are of no value.[27] Ramsey does not mean to ridicule the "scientific" approach to the Scriptures, for it has value in a limited sense as long as those limitations are respected. But its main weakness is that from a Christian standpoint it can allow nothing distinctive and "odd" about the Bible.[28]

This is certainly correct (as far as "science" has up to now been understood), and is the point Ben F. Meyer makes so well in his study, *The Aims of Jesus*, where he follows Bernard Lonergan's open empirical approach to the Gospels (very similar to Ramsey's) and calls into question two main prejudices of post-Enlightenment biblical criticism: that the universe is a closed system (e.g., D. F. Strauss and Rudolf Bultmann), and that the only way to judge the past is by the present (e.g., Martin Kähler and Ernst Troeltsch).[29] And just as Meyer, following Lonergan, condemns these doctrines because they rest on underlying epistemological assessments that are defective ("an old mistake" dating from the seventeenth century), and calls for a new assessment of the nature of empirical science, Ramsey observes that "there is no single homogeneous scientific language; we are at the present moment very puzzled as to what science is about."[30] Moreover, "we have now come to see, by the development of biblical criticism itself, that the empirical anchorage of the Christian faith is not the kind of situation with which *any* scientific language, as such, could adequately deal."[31]

26. *Ibid.*, p. 102.
27. *Ibid.*, pp. 108–109.
28. *Ibid.*, p. 110.
29. (London: SCM Press, 1979), pp. 16–17.
30. *Religious Language*, p. 111.
31. *Ibid.*, p. 112.

Ramsey is aware, as increasingly all of us in New Testament studies are, that the "scientific" drive of earlier gospel criticism has now given way in many quarters to literary criticism, to form and redaction criticism and a fascination with the parables of Jesus. But the problem still remains: Where lies the distinctiveness of Christianity and the uniqueness of Jesus? In answering the question Ramsey breaks away altogether from the "facts" plus "meaning" school, which follows the old picture of isolated and objective "facts" that can be organized objectively by minds peering at them from a distance without any personal commitment. He agrees with those whose position is "based from the outset on a conviction that the situations to which the Christian appeals are nothing if not odd, that they are ontological peculiars. . . ."[32]

This means that the way to approach the Gospels is not via "brute historical facts" plus certain post-Easter "interpretations" that the evangelists give them (and that are believed to be easily separated from the "facts" by the knowledgeable scholar); rather, the "facts" are already complex and logically odd proclamations that are inseparably linked with the ontological affirmation that God's Word has become enfleshed in Jesus (so John 1:14). This is an impropriety to the natural mind, which wants only the controllable model of causally related · events within a closed universe. The Gospels witness a violent mixing of categories: observable, tangible *sarx* is mixed with *logos* beyond the perceptual world and linked by the verb *egeneto*. To understand the meaning of this odd language there must be evoked just the right disclosure-commitment situation,[33] which Jesus does with the appropriately odd (and to the "scientific" mind offensive and hence post-Easter) language of *egō eimi* in the fourth Gospel and *egō legō* in the Synoptics.

My point in reviewing this important material in Ramsey is to encourage the New Testament interpreter who wants to be truly phenomenological with respect to the Jesus of the Gospels not to be intimidated by the widespread tendency in gospel criticism to insist on construing Jesus in ordinary human terms without the divine qualifiers he claims for himself. The clear evidence, even with the minimal pillar sayings, is that his words and acts are quite extraordinary and odd. Any other conclusion leads to unsatisfactory results that do not faithfully reflect the empirical data as they are phenomenologically. As Ramsey remarks

32. *Ibid.*, p. 115. See the whole discussion, pp. 107–124, part 1, "Some General Reflections."

33. *Ibid.*, pp. 118–119.

in his summary, there has never succeeded any attempt to make the Bible conform to "scientific" currency, for the paradigm of the Gospels is in language that is appropriately "odd" as it announces the inbreaking of the supernatural: "The Word became flesh." Jesus and the Gospels have their own logical structure in telling of the "wonderful works of God." The Word of God evokes for the attentive and faithful listener a situation of discernment and commitment:

> To talk of the Bible as "the Word of God" or as "verbally inspired" is then to claim that if we take the words of the Bible and follow out the verbal pattern they form, the light will dawn, the ice will break, and so on. There will be once again a situation of "challenge" and "response" — the sort of situation which is called "holy."[34]

Sensitivity to the "Logically Odd"

In part 2, "Some Particular Examples" (pp. 124–174), Ramsey adduces considerable evidence to support his paradigm of the logically odd disclosure situation. Much of the material is relevant to my investigation of the phenomenon of Jesus' use of "I," especially the first section about "Naming God." To be told someone's name is an occasion for the ice to break, as in Exodus 3:14 and Jesus' naming himself in terms of "I say" and "I do" and "Son of man." This, as we have already seen,[35] is the logical point of the tautology, the claim that this is the end of the road, the farthest you can go, the final authority — "I AM WHO I AM." Only Jesus knows his own name and the meaning of his "I," only he knows the name of the Father who sends him and with whom he identifies his own name. And he vouchsafes only so much as he deems necessary for the discernment-commitment of his people, which leads to eternal life. There is an inevitable and systematic elusiveness about the divine names, of both Yahweh and Jesus, of the "I" of Exodus 3:14 and the "I" of Matthew 12:28, which are ultimately unpronounceable in their full meaning.[36] This would account for Jesus' hesitancy to vouchsafe the explicit meaning of his name in the Synoptics, and his avoidance of explicitly claiming kingship in the fourth Gospel (John 6:15).

34. *Ibid.*, p. 123.
35. See my comments, p. 39.
36. Ramsey, *Religious Language*, p. 129.

I think Ramsey is right when he says that the weaknesses of biblical criticism to the present time and its failure to perceive the inherent logical structure of the Gospels call for a new logical approach that will more fully appreciate the logically appropriate, if odd, language of Jesus and the Gospels.[37] But this will require that the New Testament hermeneut let the Gospels be what they are, with miracles and supernatural improprieties and all that is odd to the natural mind, and let Jesus' "I" be what it is, with its implicit and sometimes explicit claim to supernatural authority. Ramsey would call this approach not so much logical criticism as logical analysis, in the sense that it would describe phenomenologically the appropriate logical structures in the gospel narratives. For example, Jesus' reply to the woman at the well in Samaria, "I who speak to you am he" (*Egō eimi, ho lalōn soi . . .* , John 4:26), is a prophetic disclosure of his "odd" messianic self-understanding. Ramsey says of this passage:

> Here is not only the "I am" to which we have referred already; but here is "I" embracing the description "Messiah" *and more*; there is so much more in *this* challenge than every descriptive theology could cover. Here is a disclosure which has only been evoked when "thirsty Jew" becomes "strange water purveyor," becomes "prophet," becomes "Messiah," becomes "I . . . speaking to you." Only then does the light break, eyes are opened, and there is a *Christian* disclosure. Once again we see that a Gospel situation is one for whose expression language must be used with logical impropriety.[38]

Ramsey employs the word "impropriety" and elsewhere the word "odd" because Jesus' claim to messiahship is not an exact fit with current messianic expectations, not in the fourth Gospel or in the Synoptics. It does fit Old Testament paradigms when one looks closely enough and in light of the new disclosure that Jesus' "I" brings, but the logic of his declaration is *more than* what was expected in the Messiah — in fact, in view of his oddness, it is *logically* impossible for Jesus to be "the Messiah" on the grounds of contemporary Judaism.[39] He makes contact with Old Testament paradigms but fulfills them in unexpected and odd ways that are offensive to all but those for whom the penny

37. *Ibid.*, p. 141.
38. *Ibid.*, p. 145. His italics.
39. *Ibid.*

drops — usually those who are vulnerable in their sinful need and discern in Jesus' personal "I am I" the word of divine grace and forgiveness.

That is why such outlandish texts as those cited by Norman Perrin as authentic can pass the test of dissimilarity. They do not fulfill in a straightforward and logical way either the messianic picture of Judaism or the explicit Christology of the early church; there is a mysterious "more" to the sayings that goes beyond what an ordinary rabbi or prophet would have dared to say. In their own suitably odd fashion, the words and works of Jesus in both the Synoptics and John bespeak a "something more" that attests Jesus' intention to say in his own creative way that he is the Christ, the Messiah, who is ushering in the new age of forgiveness and salvation. This can be divined, not by a straightforward "scientific" analysis of the "facts," but only in the disclosure situation where the ice breaks, the light dawns, the penny drops.

When the interpreter approaches the Gospels with an appreciation of the subtle and suitably odd language of Jesus and sees the creatively appropriate logic of his christological claims, the hard and fast wall of "straightforward" criticism breaks down. It is no longer possible to separate so easily the "authentic" sayings of the historical Jesus from the post-Easter pronouncements of the early church. The criterion of dissimilarity, so useful in giving the critic a straightforward core of authentic and undisputed sayings, self-destructs as soon as one realizes that in all the authentic core passages Jesus is using a peculiar logic that is wholly appropriate for claiming indirectly (as he intends) that he *is* Messiah, *and more*. He is speaking as the "straightforward" Messiah of Judaism would never speak, namely, as God himself, in terms of the tautological, irreducible posit, "I AM WHO I AM," "I say to you," "I am he."

Such a fresh approach to the odd language of Jesus explains why his hearers were often offended: they missed the point; or, more accurately, they understood what he was saying and claiming about himself, but refused to enter into the oddity of it by faith. So great was their love of the familiar straightforward phrases of tradition that they preferred unbelief to Jesus' logical improprieties. This explains the puzzlement of Jesus' disciples even after Peter's incisive declaration (divinely disclosed, Jesus says, Matthew 16:17), who are enjoined not to tell anyone (odd), and are further instructed about something *more* and offensively odd, namely, that the enigmatic Son of man must suffer many things (Mark 8:30–31). Peter's earlier answer to Jesus' question concerning the meaning of his "I" is not the full story:[40] "When the light dawned and the penny dropped, 'Messiah' had to become 'crucified and risen Messiah' — a logical impropriety indeed. . . ."[41]

The same sort of sensitivity to the odd is required of the interpreter when he comes to the miracle episodes of the Gospels, each of which is a personal situation that requires *more than* scientific language. The miracle situation "neither denies nor asserts the applicability of the language of scientific law to the spatio-temporal features it contains, but it claims that such language never tells the full story."[42] In gospel research and interpretation, accordingly, the hermeneut would do well to heed Ramsey's warning not to try to force the special logic of Jesus and the evangelists into a language frame from which person words have been deleted. Scientific language has its own story to tell, but it is concerned only with straightforward causal relations for the most part. Each logical area therefore must be acknowledged as distinct,[43] and the logic of causal scientific analysis must not sit heavy upon the logically odd claims of Jesus. Indeed, as we shall see in our study of Michael Polanyi's hermeneutic,[44] science has its own peculiar personal component and a fair share of appropriately odd logical beliefs.

In the remaining section of his study Ramsey demonstrates how patristic theology offers to make logical sense in terms of its own cultural setting of the "riotous mixture of phrases" that comes from Jesus and his apostolic interpreters as they map the "logical geography" of Jesus for the Jewish and Greek worlds.[45] But always, as Ramsey wisely reminds us, the words and works of Jesus (and the second and third orders of theological interpretation that follow him) do not exhaust the profound mystery and systematic elusiveness of his person. The odd logical qualifiers that modify the straightforward empirical anchorage of Jesus in ordinary situations always lead us on to the inexhaustible disclosure where we begin to understand only if we are in a posture of

40. *Ibid.*, p. 161.
41. *Ibid.*, p. 166.
42. *Ibid.*, p. 171.
43. *Ibid.*, p. 177.
44. See pp. 168–189.
45. See Ramsey, *Religious Language*, pp. 201, 215–216. For further explorations by Ramsey that are especially useful for the purpose of understanding gospel hermeneutics, see "Religion and Science: A Philosopher's Approach," *The Church Quarterly Review* (vol. 162, 1961), and "Paradox in Religion," *Proceedings of the Aristotelian Society* (supplementary vol. 33, 1959), both reprinted in *New Essays on Religious Language*, ed. Dallas High (New York: Oxford University Press, 1969).

discernment and commitment. What is important for the New Testament scholar is that he be sensitive to the oddities of Jesus' language, both verbal and acted, that he conscientiously describe that language *as it is* in a truly phenomenological fashion, and that he aid the scholarly enterprise by appropriate logical mapping of Jesus' use of the personal pronoun *I*. The pronoun *I*, as Ramsey says, is the best clue to all genuine mystery, all sublime paradox, and all revealing impropriety. It is logically explorable, but never logically exhaustible. So it is with the Jesus of the Gospels.

8

Jesus and the Tacit Dimension
Michael Polanyi's Postcritical Hermeneutic

Michael Polanyi has played a dominant role in my theological pilgrimage ever since I was introduced to his thought in the mid-sixties. His approach to knowledge rejects the ideal of impersonal scientific detachment (though he was himself a scientist) and follows an alternative ideal of knowledge based on action that is accomplished by skills of which we are only tacitly or subsidiarily aware and which are learned in trust. When we focus on doing something and attend to this project, we tacitly attend *from* clues and tools that are not observed but tacitly used. At every moment we are committed (whether we know it or not) to the paradox that "we can know more than we can tell and we can tell nothing without relying on our awareness of things we may not be able to tell."[1] Things we can tell we know by observation, and those we cannot tell we know by indwelling them with personal commitment in the fiduciary mode of belief and trust. The latter is fundamental to the first; hence tacit or subsidiary knowing is more basic than explicit or focal knowing and provides the heuristic basis for all new discovery.

Polanyi's approach and vocabulary may seem very different from those of Ludwig Wittgenstein, I. T. Ramsey, Gabriel Marcel, and especially C. S. Lewis and J. R. R. Tolkien, but these men are all saying much the same thing, each in his own way, namely, that "into every act of knowing there enters a passionate contribution of the person knowing what is being known, and that this coefficient is no mere imperfection but a vital component of his knowledge."[2] Polanyi, a neo-Augustinian-Platonist, contends that there is an objective truth and a

---

1. Michael Polanyi, *Personal Knowledge: Towards a Post-Critical Philosophy* (New York: Harper & Row, 1964), p. x. See also *The Tacit Dimension* (New York: Doubleday, 1966), pp. 3–25.
2. *Personal Knowledge*, p. xiv.

rationality to reality which is not only tacitly presupposed by the scientists, but which also (whether we recognize it or not) "trains" us to recognize its inner qualities. Scientific achievement, including the science of gospel interpretation, rests always upon an "intuition" of rationality in the object of research which precedes empirical verification. This corroborates the Augustinian principle of "faith seeking understanding" (*fides quaerens intellectum*). Scientific methodology is first subsidiarily fiduciary, then in the testing of a hypothesis focally fiduciary. The combination of the fiduciary and the intuitional overcomes the purely relativistic pragmatism of positivism, which Polanyi sees as the most serious threat to the stability of Western culture.

The Nature of Knowledge

Because of the fiduciary nature of all knowing, particularly in its tacit component, Polanyi cautions the reader that the purpose of his study "is to show that complete objectivity as usually attributed to the exact sciences is a delusion and is in fact a false ideal."[3] No theory can be relieved of the scientist's personal conforming judgment as long as that theory is held to be true. Acts of personal judgment form an essential part of science and of gospel criticism, as we have seen throughout this study. This is not to ascribe a purely subjective value to our research as scientist-scholars, since we assume the universal validity of our appraisals of reality and tacitly assume that we are making statements about probable events and not probable statements about events.[4] In other words, it is by my *personal* appraisal that *I believe* what a sentence says.[5]

In his analysis of acquiring skills the strength of Polanyi's epistemology comes to clearest expression. Applying his phenomenology of skills to gospel interpretation, we may come to appreciate in a new way that what Jesus is announcing cannot be learned merely in precept but only by example and imitation of that example through the practice of the art of discipleship. In the art and acts of Jesus and in his teaching of the skills of discipleship, Christian faith eventually flowers and bears fruit. Such art can be passed on only from master to apprentice or disciple, since there is no precise prescription for such unspecifiable

3. *Ibid.*, p. 18.
4. *Ibid.*, pp. 22–25.
5. *Ibid.*, p. 28.

art. What Polanyi has to say on the subject is very close to Lewis's insistence that attentiveness and obedience to a text are requisite to understanding it. Here a comparison could be made between the gospel and its interpreters and Jesus and his disciples, where Jesus is the master teacher and the interpreter the apprenticed disciple. "To learn by example is to submit to authority," says Polanyi.

> You follow your master because you trust his manner of doing things even when you cannot analyse and account in detail for its effectiveness. By watching the master and emulating his efforts in the presence of his example, the apprentice unconsciously picks up the rules of the art, including those which are not explicitly known to the master himself. These hidden rules can be assimilated only by a person who surrenders himself to that extent uncritically to the imitation of another. A society which wants to preserve a fund of personal knowledge must submit to tradition.[6]

That is an especially important passage for the gospel interpreter. Polanyi's hermeneutic requires an obedience to the text and an attentiveness to the art of Jesus the master teacher, whose skill consists of the unspecifiable art of servanthood on behalf of the sinner, the poor, the sick, the oppressed, the widow, and the orphan. A genuine understanding of the Jesus of the Gospels does not come from some supposedly objective and uncommitted position assumed apart from discipleship, but only from obedience to the master teacher who exercises skills of discipleship to a consummate degree. With practice these develop into master skills, or what Polanyi calls "connoisseurship": "Connoisseurship, like skill, can be communicated only by example, not by precept; . . . you must go through a long course of experience under the guidance of a master."[7]

In the practice of attentiveness and obedience an apprentice gradually develops two kinds of awareness, one a subsidiary or distal awareness, which transposes him from knowing what to knowing how (the tacit component of thought and action); and focal or proximal awareness, which is the application of the skill or connoisseurship to the practical need at hand. The good New Testament interpreter, like Lewis's good reader and Polanyi's good scientist or craftsman, increasingly speaks and acts with a genuine transparency to the gospel language of which he is tacitly aware in personal commitment. That is, he indwells

6. *Ibid.*, p. 53.
7. *Ibid.*, p. 54.

a certain set of presuppositions, just as he indwells his body;[8] his guiding principle in gospel interpretation becomes an openness and commitment to the One who confronts and invites the disciple to follow him. True knowledge of the Jesus of the Gospels comes only through commitment to him and by practicing his art. Apprenticeship and connoisseurship require an element of passivity and trust, of discovery and submission, of feeling one's way in humble obedience. One lives in it as in the garment of his own skin:

> The act of personal knowing can sustain these relations only because the acting person believes . . . that he has not *made them* but *discovered them*. The effort of knowing is thus guided by a sense of obligation towards the truth: by an effort to submit to reality.[9]

In describing the grammar of the tacit component, Polanyi illustrates how important a limited language is for finite human beings and its repeated usage and consistency. The first he calls the law of poverty, pointing out that from an alphabet of twenty-three letters we could conceivably construct 23^8, that is, about one hundred thousand million eight-letter code words. Each sentence could thus be replaced by a different word. But this would mean the destruction of language, although it would mean its millionfold enrichment, for no one could possibly remember all the code words. The relatively simple repetition of a few words and their associated actions makes language meaningful. It also makes the language of Jesus and the Gospels possible. From the law of poverty "it follows that a language must be poor enough to allow the same words to be used a sufficient number of times."[10] ". . . that though he was rich, yet for your sake he became poor, so that by his poverty you might become rich" (II Cor. 8:9) has implications that are far-reaching, not least of all regarding the poverty of expression by which Jesus communicates divine grace, and by poverty of action conveys redemptive servanthood. Complementing the laws of poverty and grammar are the laws of iteration and consistency, where the repeatability of speech with consistent action makes the language-game under-

8. *Ibid.*, p. 60. Compare this approach with that of Cornelius Van Til, who is also a presuppositionalist. See his introduction, pp. 3–68, especially p. 68, in B. B. Warfield, *The Inspiration and Authority of the Bible* (Philadelphia: Presbyterian and Reformed, 1948). See my comments, pp. 221–243.

9. Polanyi, *Personal Knowledge*, p. 63. His italics.

10. *Ibid.*, p. 78.

standable and manageable (hence the additional law of manageability).[11] All of Jesus' language in the Gospels, both spoken and acted, contains a tacit component of unspecifiability, which requires the obedient apprenticeship of the disciple if he is really to understand the Master and learn his art of servanthood.

Polanyi observes that in our use of ordinary scientific language, from the descriptive sciences to the exact sciences to the deductive sciences, there is a sequence of increasing formalization and symbolic manipulation and a decreasing contact with experience.[12] As I apply this to gospel criticism, I find that the more the gospel material is analyzed without a sympathetic personal commitment, the more abstract become the theories adduced to explain the redaction of the sayings and acts of Jesus, so that every step toward the behavioral ideal of causal reduction is achieved by a progressive sacrifice of content. This is exactly what has happened in radical criticism since the Enlightenment: the Jesus of the Gospels is interpreted according to a transitory cultural ideal and not according to the claims of the gospel texts, only to have the ideally constructed portrait of Jesus in one generation demolished by the criticism of the next generation of scholars; in fact I am intending in these chapters to encourage the day when gospel interpreters will relearn the basic art of discipleship and listen to the Gospels as they are before undertaking to reconstruct them in our own image. Increasingly lay Christians are rejecting radical approaches to the Gospels, and a growing number of New Testament scholars (among them neo-evangelicals like me, latterly converted from a liberal orientation) are coming to appreciate that redaction criticism can be used either positively or destructively, either from within the story or outside it, and that a fiduciary commitment or lack of commitment to the principal figure of the Gospels determines the outcome of one's research.

Objectivity As an Impossible Ideal

Polanyi's major theme is that we deceive ourselves when we think that we can achieve truth by approaching an object of study like the Gospels in a spirit of critical doubt and "scientific" objectivism. There is no such impersonal objectivity and precision to be found. Polanyi cites Kurt Gödel's important mathematical discovery of the early thir-

11. *Ibid.*, p. 81.
12. *Ibid.*, p. 86.

ties to illustrate that the scope of mathematics itself, the very basis of science, is indeterminate and cannot function without commitment to its ultimate validity. Every mathematical system assumes one's tacit trust in some higher metasystem. And so it is with gospel criticism. If it is skeptical of the truth-claims of the evangelists that Jesus actually said and did what is reported, it reveals not so much the truth about Jesus but the tacit commitments of the critic. The tacit beliefs of the more radical redactional critics can be seen to lie not with the commitments of Jesus and the evangelists but with modern assumptions as to what is possible in a closed universe where the supernatural and the logically odd are ruled out. (More profitable than extreme redactional studies of the Gospels might be an analysis of the intentions and assumptions that compel the radical redactionists to redact as radically as they do!)

There is an attitude of humility in Polanyi's epistemology when he acknowledges the risk and commitment that are tacitly required in every field of knowing. Fully understanding an object of study is an impossible ideal, for not only is such uncommitted objectivity impossible, but also — as Polanyi will later argue — the object discloses itself only to the attentive and obedient beholder who approaches it with heuristic expectation. Hence the unspecifiability of our knowing, which rests upon personal commitment to the validity of our quest:

> For just as, owing to the ultimately tacit character of all our knowledge, we remain ever unable to say all that we know, so also, in view of the tacit character of meaning, we can never quite know what is implied in what we say.[13]

When this hermeneutic is applied to the gospel material and focuses not on an assumed conspiracy of the evangelists to redact a nonsupernatural Jesus into a supernatural Messiah, but allows the Gospels to be what they are, then Jesus may make his claim upon us. In this heuristic approach to the Gospels, Polanyi's words take on special meaning:

> We have seen already that whenever we make (or believe we have made) contact with reality, we anticipate an indeterminate range of unexpected future confirmations of our knowledge derived from this contact.[14]

13. *Ibid.*, p. 95.
14. *Ibid.*, p. 124.

But in the case of Jesus, where we have incarnate "genius," the contact with reality is on an extraordinarily wide range. The following passage is helpful in describing what Jesus' self-disclosure brings to light:

> Moreover, by deploying such powers in an exceptional measure — far surpassing ours who are looking on — the work of a genius offers us a massive demonstration of a creativity which can neither be explained in other terms, nor taken unquestioningly for granted. By paying respect to another person's judgment as superior to our own, we emphatically acknowledge originality in the sense of a performance the procedure of which we cannot specify. Confrontation with genius thus forces us to acknowledge the originative power of life, which we may and commonly do neglect in its ubiquitous lesser manifestations.[15]

So it is with the self-disclosure of Jesus. Receiving a disclosure requires the interpreter to experience something like an "ecstatic vision." It is not enough simply to be guided by experience and to pass through experience. The disclosure needs to be experienced in itself; and since the self-disclosure is inseparable from Jesus' own person who stands back of it, it is Jesus who is experienced in terms of his very words and acts. The experience of Jesus as he is in the Gospels requires on the part of the interpreter an intellectual passion of "contemplation," which "dissolves the screen" of a manipulative conceptual framework,

> stops our movement through experience and pours us straight into experience; we cease to handle things and become immersed in them. Contemplation has no ulterior intention or ulterior meaning; in it we cease to deal with things and become absorbed in the inherent quality of our experience, for its own sake.[16]

Polanyi interprets this indwelling as something akin to Christian contemplation, like the communion of the Christian mystic and his experience of redemption. There is a joy, but a joy mixed with guilt and mounting tension in the ritual of worship, which moves from anguish to surrender to hope. The only valid access to the Jesus of the Gospels (following this train of thought), therefore, is through the initial bracketing of conceptual prejudices and the passive reception of the redeeming grace he offers:

15. *Ibid*.
16. *Ibid*., p. 197.

It is man's surrender to the love of God, in the hope of gaining His forgiveness, and admission to His presence. The radical anti-intellectualism of the *via negativa* expresses the effort to break out of our normal conceptual framework and "become like little children". It is akin to the reliance on the "foolishness of God", that short-cut to the understanding of Christianity, of which St. Augustine said enviously that it was free to the simple-minded but impassable to the learned.[17]

Jesus is therefore not authentically "observed" by the critic who makes a sustained effort of breaking out; rather he is met only by one who shows love and desire for the holy and divine by breaking in:

> Proximity to God is not an observation, for it overwhelms and pervades the worshipper. An observer must be relatively detached from that which he observes, and religious experience transforms the worshipper. It stands in this respect closer to sensual abandon than to exact observation.[18]

Strong advice for the scientific historian and critic! Yet it is a necessary antidote to the kind of gospel criticism that observes and handles and uses, but misses the point because it stands outside the story. Like Ramsey with his hermeneutic of the logically odd, Polanyi fearlessly assails the opaque dogmas and prejudices of the modern critical mind. The proper approach to knowledge is not even like the indwelling of a great theory, or immersion in a musical masterpiece, "but the heuristic upsurge which strives to break through the accepted frameworks of thought, guided by the intimations of discoveries still beyond our horizon. . . ." This is especially true of the Gospels: "Christianity sedulously fosters, and in a sense permanently satisfies, man's craving for mental dissatisfaction by offering him the comfort of a crucified God."[19] The modern alternative to the Christian model of contemplation focuses instead on an atomized and depersonalized universe where everything at last becomes absurd and hostile, fragmented, and full of despair.[20] The radical doubt of our age has carried over into New Testament studies, but only because of a faulty hermeneutic based on a mistaken notion of what the scientific enterprise really is.

17. *Ibid.*, p. 198.
18. *Ibid.*
19. *Ibid.*, p. 199.
20. *Ibid.*, p. 200.

Conviviality among Believers

A gospel hermeneutic that will bring the interpreter into a real meeting with Jesus will not come from individual efforts of the scholar, but only within the conviviality of the believing community where the mind and heart are apprenticed by master believers and interpreters. Such is the implication of Polanyi's next discourse on "Conviviality,"[21] and such is the opinion of a number of biblical scholars and theologians who are beginning to appreciate again the inseparability of biblical scholarship and the believing community.[22] The secular academic setting alone is not sufficient for the work of apprenticing valid interpreters of the Word, though it does provide the principal means of conviviality for many other disciplines. Since the reigning attitude in most quarters of learning today is secular and positivistic, and the fiduciary hermeneutic of Polanyi and others little appreciated, the milieu of conviviality afforded by the secular university is largely hostile to the peculiar and logically odd content of the Gospels. The biblical scholar takes many professional risks if he maintains the integrity of the Gospels in such a setting. The tacit assumptions of positivism intimidate all but the hardiest, and little creative conviviality is possible, though professional conviviality can be very enjoyable.

Accordingly, authentic gospel interpretation will be nurtured only in the believing community as it flows from adults to young people, and from believer to believer:

> This assimilation of great systems of articulate lore by novices of various grades is made possible only by a *previous act of affiliation*, by which the novice accepts apprenticeship to a community which cultivates this lore, appreciates its values and strives to act by its standards. This affiliation begins with the fact that a child submits to education within a community, and is confirmed throughout life to the extent to which the adult continues to place exceptional confidence in the intellectual leaders of the same community.[23]

In the final view, it is a cultural apprenticeship within the believing and worshiping community of Christians that is more important than the cultural apprenticeship in the secular critical community, for the

21. *Ibid.*, chapter 7, pp. 203–245.
22. See especially Paul Hanson, "The Responsibility of Biblical Theology to Communities of Faith," and David Steinmetz, "The Superiority of Pre-Critical Exegesis," in *ThT* 37 (1980).
23. Polanyi, *Personal Knowledge*, p. 207. His italics.

latter, if not vitally informed by the first, will simply shift its fiduciary allegiance to the canons of secular scientism. That is what has happened within the guild of gospel scholarship, wherever secular conviviality has become a substitute for the church. Hence my call for New Testament scholars to rediscover the "heuristic intimations" of the believing and worshiping Christian community and its colleges and theological seminaries, where apprenticeship with integrity goes on in obedience to the original call to discipleship. In so pleading, I follow Polanyi's dictum that one must continually endorse the existing consensus or dissent from it, and in so doing affirm his fiduciary commitment to what he thinks the true consensus ought to be.[24]

The "primitive sentiments of fellowship" previous to articulation are the basis of shared experience and of joint activities. The fellowship that underlies genuine gospel interpretation cannot be limited to the academic office, classroom, or professional society, but must include at center the worshiping body of believers who are faithful to the patterns of tradition. Hence my deeper satisfaction with the conviviality of the neoevangelical community, where apprenticeship in the classical tradition is carried on, than with my former liberal setting where deep commitment to the integrity of the Gospels was missing. Polanyi's observation I would apply directly to the need of New Testament scholars to be true believers within a believing community:

> By fully participating in a ritual, the members of a group affirm the community of their existence, and at the same time identify the life of their group with that of antecedent groups, from whom the ritual has descended to them.[25]

My call for the New Testament scholar to return to the Christian rituals of convivial celebration will perhaps incur the hostility of secular and individualist critics, but the losses inflicted on gospel criticism by the latter have been so great that the risk needs to be taken. Polanyi describes four coefficients of societal organization that are necessary to form a stable institution,[26] and each is directly applicable to the subject of conviviality. Affirmation and indwelling are articulated as, respectively, the *sharing of convictions*, and the *sharing of a fellowship*; to which is added a third coefficient of *cooperation*, and a fourth, the

24. *Ibid.*, p. 209.
25. *Ibid.*, p. 211.
26. *Ibid.*, p. 212.

exercise of authority or coercion. Of the modern institutions that embrace the four, universities and churches are the most prominent. My concern is that for the New Testament interpreter the university or college not become a substitute for the church from which the Gospels arose and in which they have been preserved and transmitted. The Christian scholar's allegiance is first to the believing community and then to the university; otherwise he will find that his allegiance in the end is only to the university with its secular norms of interpretation which preempt the fiduciary trust the church has traditionally placed in the Jesus of the Gospels.

The New Testament scholar needs to see that the secular university does not provide an objective perspective on the gospel facts as they really are. That has been the mistake of post-Enlightenment criticism, which has culminated in the present crisis in biblical studies. It is Polanyi's point that no opinions, no matter how scientific they are claimed to be, are outside a believing community, including those of the university. The major difference between the conviviality of the believing Christian community and the conviviality of the secular community is that the latter is functionally atheistic in its approach to the religiously odd. Walter Wink illustrates the dilemma of the New Testament scholar who assumes the tacit commitments of the secular university community. Quoting Morton Smith and his admission that such a biblical critic does not allow for uncontrollable divine interventions in history (thus excluding the supernatural from the historical method), Wink observes,

> Few practicing biblical scholars would take exception to this, even those who speak of God's acts in history, since these are generally viewed as mediated through the selfhood of human agents. So acclimated are we to this attitude of functional, methodological atheism that we may no longer be shocked by the vast gulf between this view and the Bible's, where God is depicted as directly intervening in nature and history at will! From the outset, therefore, the biblical scholar is committed to a secularist perspective. If he wishes to discover meaning in the texts at all, he has but three choices: he may attempt to interpret the text by a program of demythologization; he may opt for a practicing atheism, whereby references to God in the text are in every case reducible to another explanation; or he may delude himself into believing that there is no hermeneutical problem.[27]

27. *The Bible in Human Transformation: Toward a New Paradigm for Biblical Study* (Philadelphia: Fortress, 1973), pp. 38–39.

What about a fourth choice: Accepting what Christians have always believed (until very modern times) about the reality of God's supernatural interventions in history, and about the authoritative witness of the Scriptures to these workings of God on behalf of a fallen race? This is where we evangelicals, irenic though we are on a host of lesser issues, see the line drawn. Wink himself, though he correctly surmises that historical biblical criticism is bankrupt, is unwilling to return to the conviviality of historic Christianity, but reverts to the warmth of an older liberalism and a subjective psychologizing communal exegesis.

The evangelical community really affords the best milieu, I think, for arriving at the real Jesus of the Gospels, for while its quest for truth is described by certain tacit beliefs — such as the reality of God and his supernatural working in history and nature, the inspiration of Scripture, the deity of Christ, and his substitutionary atonement — these beliefs imply a deep respect for scriptural revelation and form the parameters within which the Gospels can once again say what they were intended to say by the believing evangelists and by Jesus the genesis of the enacted story. The evangelical shares the same supernatural faith of the evangelists and has confidence in their divinely appointed authority to report correctly who Jesus was, what he said and did, and what his significance is. Hence there is a free and open reformist dynamism within the framework of evangelical belief that is like the reformist dynamism of the sixteenth-century reformers, while it is the functionally atheistic critic who is not free to interpret Jesus and the Gospels correctly because he is locked into a closed and anthropocentric universe. Functionally atheistic criticism is methodologically incapable of being truly phenomenological; it cannot allow the phenomenon of Jesus and the phenomena of the Gospels to be what they are in themselves and were originally intended to be.

Ostensibly free, Polanyi notes, the conviviality of the secular community contains a "menacing contradiction," which some of us see in radical gospel criticism:

> The great movement for independent thought instilled in the modern mind a desperate refusal of all knowledge that is not absolutely impersonal, and this implied in its turn a mechanical conception of man which was bound to deny man's capacity for independent thought. . . . For when open profession of the great moral passions animating free society are discredited as specious or utopian, its dynamism will tend to be transformed into the hidden driving force of a political ma-

chine, which is then proclaimed as inherently right and granted absolute dominion over thought.[28]

Polanyi, whose personal experience spanned the European horrors of
Marxist and fascist totalitarianism, unmasks the false ideal of the critical mind in a telling description of how doctrines of behavioral causality have undercut the morality of the Christian tradition and have
ended in political and social bankruptcy. He underscores the fact that
there is always a core of personal authority, a conviviality of some sort
in every system of thought. But which shall it be: liberal or conservative? Speaking of the social malaise of our time, Polanyi asks,

> Can the beliefs of liberalism, no longer believed to be self-evident, be
> upheld henceforth in the form of an orthodoxy? Can we face the fact
> that, no matter how liberal a free society may be, it is also profoundly
> conservative?[29]

The political lessons of the twentieth century, with its totalitarian powers bent on radical reforms ostensibly in pursuit of justice and broth-
erhood, impressed Polanyi with the fact that the right of moral self-
determination and religious freedom can be preserved only within the
conviviality of the conservative free society. The truth is unpalatable to
our consciences, he writes, but there is no other way to preserve the
free society than to correct unjust privileges within by carefully graded
stages, realizing that our duty lies in the service of ideals that we cannot
possibly achieve.

This holds true, I argue, in the interpretation of Scripture, the authority of which must be held with conservative allegiance within the
confessing community. In gospel criticism radical attempts to reinterpret the evangelists' claims in terms of a hostile hermeneutic have consistently failed, and I can personally attest its failure in my own
theological pilgrimage. I have come to affirm once again my conservative theological heritage, which involves a commitment with other believers to Jesus as the dominical source of authority who generates a
faithful tradition.[30]

28. *Personal Knowledge*, p. 214.
29. *Ibid.*, p. 244.
30. Polanyi's remarks on the conservative component (*ibid.*, pp. 244–245) are
applicable to my renewed Christian orthodoxy.

Justifying Personal Knowledge

The conservative commitment to a creative tradition now brings Polanyi to a powerful articulation of his postcritical hermeneutic, the justification of personal knowledge in the logic of affirmation, a critique of doubt, and commitment. These chapters contain, in my estimation, some of the finest hermeneutical thought of modern times and encourage a fresh interpretation of Jesus and the Gospels. In chapter 8, "The Logic of Affirmation," Polanyi opens his exposition by reviewing succinctly his appraisal of the epistemological situation: we know much more than we can tell, but we know much less than we previously had thought we could know through the exercise of freedom. He is now intent to focus upon the narrow range of knowledge that forms the hard core of greatest certainty.[31] The formal point that is central to his hermeneutic, and to that of Wittgenstein and Ramsey, is that we can escape the problem of indefinite regress when we realize that only a speaker or listener can mean something by a word, and that a word in itself means nothing; that is, persons stand behind meaning with personal commitment. Therefore all knowledge is personal knowledge (hence the title of the book, *Personal Knowledge*).

Applied to Jesus' language, this means that the words he speaks mean nothing in themselves; it is only Jesus as "I am" and "I say to you" who means something *by them*. His words do not have an open texture in and of themselves but convey meaning only through *his* sense of fitness, and our confident responsiveness to his sense of fitness.[32] Precise positivistic rules for determining the "authentic" words of Jesus are bound to fail because Jesus personally asserts the factual truth of his statements with "heuristic or persuasive feeling," and understanding comes only from implicit belief in his authority to speak in this manner:

> Any attempt to eliminate this personal coefficient, by laying down precise rules for making or testing assertions of fact, is condemned to futility from the start. For we can derive rules of observation and verification only from examples of factual statements that we have accepted as true *before* we knew the rules; and *in the end* the application of our rules will necessarily fall back once more on factual observations,

31. *Ibid.*, p. 249.
32. *Ibid.*, pp. 252–253.

the acceptance of which is an act of personal judgment, unguided by any explicit rules.[33]

The history of gospel criticism has proven this to be true, as again and again the cultural presuppositions of a period predispose the critic to enter the hermeneutical circle at the point of his tacit critical commitments and according to what is in vogue at the time. Two personal presuppositions whose factual truths are beyond any possibility of testing but which have been assumed by every radical critical school are the dogmas of the closed universe and the autonomy of the critic to interpret the past in terms of the present. But when these Enlightenment presuppositions are exposed as personal judgments which have no factual basis other than personal preference, the way is then open to offer a hermeneutic more sympathetic to the gospel texts and the language of Jesus. As Polanyi has pointed out earlier, the situation is akin to Gödel's discovery that in mathematics axioms are never self-demonstrable but continually refer to some wider system which always remains richer and ultimately undemonstrable. On the horizon of every form of knowledge one moves toward discovery by shifting from intuition to computation, and from computation to intuition: "The act of assent proves once more to be logically akin to the act of discovery: they are both essentially unformalizable, intuitive mental decisions."[34]

Hence the criteria of radical gospel criticism — dissimilarity, coherence, multiple attestation — are in themselves insufficient to tell us anything we do not already know, depending on our intuitive presuppositions. If we come to the Gospels attentively and obediently, the principal force of Jesus' "I" will address us through the fiduciary mediation of the evangelists; if we disclaim Jesus' supernatural claims and those of the early church because of prior allegiance to the anti-supernatural bias of secular criticism, we will hear only as much as can comfortably fit into that hermeneutical circle. But the latter will lack phenomenological integrity because it is unwilling to bracket its epistemological prejudices against the Gospels as they are.

Polanyi attacks this prejudice of scientism as a commitment that is burned out. The incandescence of the past four or five centuries has combusted on the fuel of the Christian heritage and Greek rationalism. Now we need to go back to our sources:

33. *Ibid.*, p. 254. His italics.
34. *Ibid.*, p. 261.

Modern man is unprecedented; yet we must now go back to St. Augustine to restore the balance of our cognitive powers. In the fourth century A.D. St. Augustine brought the history of Greek philosophy to a close by inaugurating for the first time a post-critical philosophy. He taught that all knowledge was a gift of grace, for which we must strive under the guidance of antecedent belief: *nisi credideritis, non intelligitis*.[35]

With John Locke and his successors faith was separated from knowledge and the first and second dimensions of observation and reason become the sole determiners of factual truth. But now that empiricism and rationalism have not produced indubitable certitude or the promised utopia, Polanyi calls for a return to belief and the fiduciary mode which all along has been functioning surreptitiously in this age of unbelief:

We must now recognize belief once more as the source of all knowledge. Tacit assent and intellectual passions, the sharing of an idiom and of a cultural heritage, affiliation to a like-minded community: such are the impulses which shape our vision of the nature of things on which we rely for our mastery of things. No intelligence, however critical or original, can operate outside a fiduciary framework.[36]

Hence we must seek liberation from the enervating and bankrupt objectivisim of our day, voicing our ultimate convictions from within our convictions, realizing that these are logically prior to any particular assertion of "fact." All knowledge is at root *personal* knowledge, asserted by the "I" who intends the world in this way and who stands behind his words with the commitment of belief. We should freely confess these beliefs that are tacitly taken for granted, and accept personal responsibility for them. Knowledge begins not with doubt but with the precritical posture of belief.

This brings Polanyi to the central chapter in his hermeneutical triad, "The Critique of Doubt." The Cartesian mode has deeply influenced the modern age with its call to purge the mind through universal doubt, ridding it of all opinions held on trust. The methodology of doubt goes hand in hand with objectivism and elevates itself into a creed of scien-

---

35. *Ibid.*, p. 266. Augustine, *De libero arbitrio*, 1. 4: "The steps are laid down by the prophet who says, 'Unless ye believe, ye shall not understand.' "
36. *Personal Knowledge*, p. 266.

tism that is blind and deceptive and leads ultimately to nihilism. All the great discoveries, on the contrary, have been made by believing and intuiting minds in contact with a reality that discloses itself to the indwelling and obedient. So in coming to know the Jesus of the Gospels, the truth or authenticity of his language cannot be unlocked by objectivist doubt, which approaches it impersonally, but only by an attitude of worship and indwelling. Apprehending the sayings and works of Jesus at their deepest level comes only in serving him who speaks and performs them:

> This will lead us back to the conception of religious worship as a heuristic vision and align religion in turn with the great intellectual systems, such as mathematics, fiction and the fine arts, which are validated by becoming happy dwelling places of the human mind.[37]

Unpopular as it may be to the objectivist critic, there can be no success in focal analysis of the gospel texts until there is first a subsidiary awareness of trust in the mode of "I believe":

> Only a Christian who stands in the service of his faith can understand Christian theology and only he can enter into the religious meaning of the Bible.[38]

With that sentence Polanyi presents the case as clearly as it can be made. This approach to the Jesus of the Gospels is radical or "rooted" in an exactly opposite direction from the radicalism of objectivist criticism. It means that a genuine interpretation of Jesus can be found only from within one's personal commitment to Jesus' personal claims about himself. No profound truths about him can be discovered through the objectivist method of radical doubt.

While Polanyi betrays some of his own theological liberal and non-supernaturalist biases in the course of the discussion, and makes too much of the difference between theological statements and factual assertions,[39] he nonetheless is persuasive when he describes the circularity of a conceptual system and the way it reinforces itself in contact with fresh topics: it is a kind of "magical framework," like the "spell"

37. *Ibid.*, p. 280.
38. *Ibid.*, p. 281.
39. *Ibid.*, pp. 282–284. His acceptance of Paul Tillich's two domains is especially weak.

Tolkien describes, which provides a certain stability.[40] Hence it is inconceivable that any program of comprehensive doubt could succeed. But what makes the "when in doubt, discard" hermeneutic of radical gospel critics dangerous and deceptive is that the advocacy of rational doubt is simply the skeptics' way of advocating their own beliefs.

The Gospel Tradition's Stability and Coherence

Polanyi sums up the case for his fiduciary hermeneutic in an important chapter appropriately entitled "Commitment." The leading axiom of his thesis should not be missed:

> Any inquiry into our ultimate beliefs can be consistent only if it presupposes its own conclusions. It must be intentionally circular.[41]

The logic of any argument is but an elaboration of this circle, a systematic course in teaching oneself to hold one's own beliefs. If this sounds subjective it must be remembered that it is undertaken within a community where one is held to be personally responsible for his beliefs. That the basic axiom is true, Polanyi has no doubts. The personal participation of the knower in his knowledge is held within a flow of passion and intellectual beauty. Hence the personal conviction and flow of passion with which Jesus is portrayed in the Gospels, as he confidently intends what he says and does to be universally valid.

The dilemma of the radical objectivist critic is that he is "caught in an insoluble conflict between a demand for an impersonality which would discredit all commitment and an urge to make up his mind which drives him to recommit himself."[42] What the radical objectivist often does, if he is a New Testament critic and a Christian, is to play two language-games at once: one with the secular circle where the credo of conviviality is radical skepticism, and the other with a worshiping community where the credo of conviviality is religious belief. But how do the two worlds come together?

> The answer is this. The "actual facts" are accredited facts, as seen within the commitment situation, while subjective beliefs are the con-

40. *Ibid.*, pp. 289–290.
41. *Ibid.*, p. 299. Again note the similarity of this presuppositional approach to that of Van Til.
42. *Ibid.*, p. 304.

viction accrediting these facts as seen noncommittally by someone not sharing them.[43]

This is to say that the authenticity of the sayings of Jesus in the Gospels may be arrived at by a number of different routes, but that at base a skeptical objectivism that dismisses the supernatural will inevitably end up with a shorter list. In that case Jesus will not be allowed to make any explicit claims that he considers himself Messiah or God incarnate. As I have already argued, however, the objectivist approach is self-defeating because on its own grounds it must admit that the core sayings of Jesus bear witness to claims that are implicitly christological and messianic. Thus an open fiduciary approach to the Gospels (recognizing that they are truly representing the intention of Jesus) is more stable simply because it fulfills the requirements of the criterion of coherence. Since Jesus makes implicit messianic claims, it is in character for him to make explicit messianic claims as well. There is, accordingly, no impersonal objective criterion by which to distinguish the early church's Christology from the claims of Jesus himself. Jesus is the genesis of the tradition.

The phenomenological method I have been using affirms the stability and coherence of the gospel tradition because Jesus is seen to indwell its truth-claims that the new age of salvation has come, and that he is, in his own creative way, the Christ, the promised Messiah. This classically orthodox affirmation of the gospel's empirical truth-claims rests on the authority of Jesus' "I say," "I am," and "look and see." Of such empirical truth-claims Polanyi writes,

> An empirical statement is true to the extent to which it reveals an aspect of reality, a reality largely hidden to us, and *existing therefore independently of our knowing it*. . . . The enquiring scientist's intimations of a hidden reality are personal. They are his own beliefs, which— owing to his originality—as yet he alone holds. Yet they are not a subjective state of mind, but convictions held with universal intent, and heavy with arduous projects. . . . In a heuristic commitment, affirmation, surrender and legislation are fused into a single thought, bearing on a hidden reality.[44]

That describes my own project and commitment as I reaffirm the convictions of the historic Christian community in a contemporary evan-

43. *Ibid.*
44. *Ibid.*, p. 311. His italics.

gelical setting, finding there a "happy dwelling place" of the mind. There the hidden reality of God speaks with more stability and coherence through the empirical disclosure of the authoritative Jesus who generates an authentic tradition. This is my intellectual commitment for which I accept personal responsibility: *"This acceptance is the sense of my calling."*[45]

What then of the "hard" questions, the variations among the Gospels? My reply is that one must first look at the overall evidence and the larger picture of personal commitment, stability, and coherence before dealing with smaller difficulties inductively. This is, after all, the way all of us, including practicing scientists, function. One of the most widely held theories in secular Western culture is the evolution of the species, yet there are many inductive problems in the theory with which the believing scientist makes peace, simply because the theory offers an ordered picture, given his personal commitment to mechanism. Polanyi observes that "neo-Darwinism is firmly accredited and highly regarded by science, though there is little evidence for it, because it beautifully fits into a mechanistic system of the universe and bears on a subject — the origin of man — which is of the utmost intrinsic interest."[46] Now if the practicing scientist is dependent on personal commitments to theories that contain evidential problems, the practicing Christian cannot be faulted for making personal commitments to a view that he believes brings the greatest coherence and stability to human existence. The fiduciary commitments of competing systems must be addressed first: Is the interpreter open or closed to the logically odd world of the Gospels, does he claim autonomy over the gospel texts and the authoritative claims of Jesus; or is he willing to be attentive to what they say? The results of inductive analysis will be determined by one's answers to these two principal questions.

I am convinced that radical New Testament criticism is embarrassed by its meager results and its largely negative effect on the role of the Bible in the church because it sees only its own face reflected in the gospel texts. An obedient hearing of the Gospels, on the other hand, has historically brought about great results in the life of the Christian church and in its mission, as we are once again witnessing among those who have evangelical commitments. Once this postcritical hermeneutic is adopted, the major variations among the Gospels may be largely

45. *Ibid.*, p. 322. His italics.
46. *Ibid.*, p. 136.

resolved by the criteria of complementary aspection and paraphrastic freedom with which the evangelists present and adapt the words and works of Jesus. Redaction criticism has been much overused as an interpretive tool by those who, on their own fiduciary commitment to impersonal objectivism, have sought to prove the overwhelming creativity of the church in placing on Jesus' lips his claims to christological and divine authority. I have tried to show the illogic of such radical redaction in view of the phenomena of Jesus' implicit claims, and have argued for a greater appreciation of the logically odd in Jesus' use of language. We have seen how David Hill has recently re-examined the evidence for New Testament prophets who supposedly created new sayings of Jesus and placed them on his lips, and found no empirical data to support this widely held theory.[47] What smaller oddities in detail remain among the gospel accounts are insignificantly small in view of the larger picture. If one is committed to a high view of scriptural inspiration it is not amiss to claim that the Holy Spirit, like love itself, has its reasons, and that the evangelists know more than they can tell.

Accordingly, if problems remain in the neoevangelical hermeneutic I have proposed, it would not be surprising in light of Polanyi's view of personal knowledge, for we all know more than we can tell, and can tell less than once we thought we could in scientific terms. A truly postcritical hermeneutic is not concerned primarily with the minutiae of analytical questions, though these are a secondary focus of interest, but with the larger issue of how the interpreter reads the gospel texts — whether in doubt as a disbeliever who undertakes to uncover a conspiracy of sorts, or in commitment as a believer to the ability of the evangelists to convey authentically the person and mission of Jesus. Once that initial posture is decided on (and both are fiduciary), the analytical details of the texts can be addressed. There may be unresolvable problems facing the interpreter at points, but as Polanyi says,

> A fiduciary philosophy does not eliminate doubt, but (like Christianity) says that we should hold on to what we truly believe . . . , trusting the unfathomable intimations that call upon us to do so.[48]

The acceptance of the truth-claims of Jesus in the Gospels as self-conscious and self-acclaimed Messiah arises from my sense of calling

47. *New Testament Prophecy* (Atlanta: John Know, 1980). See my comments, pp. 87–108.
48. *Personal Knowledge*, p. 318.

and response to the criteria of stability and coherence in Christian scholarship within the church. This study reflects my own pilgrimage and affirmation of personal convictions with universal intent. In the performance of this obligation I openly commit myself to belief in the integrity of the evangelists who, I believe, have authentically presented Jesus as the genesis of the story that continues to cast its logically odd and powerful spell of grace over all of us who are willing to be so enchanted.

9

Jesus As Incarnate "Thou"

Gabriel Marcel's Analysis of Incarnate Being and Creative Fidelity

Yet another contemporary voice may be applied to the debate on the meaning of Jesus, again in an oblique but challenging and imaginative way, and in general agreement with the approaches we have already considered. Gabriel Marcel is concerned to describe the phenomenon of the existing, thinking, and choosing self in relation to other selves, and in so doing discovers that region where the personal "I" stands in creative fidelity to other persons.

A number of fresh ways of looking at Jesus emerge from such a study and dissipate the staleness of ordinary analysis of the gospel texts. A fundamental phenomenon of human existence is the inescapability of incarnate being, not only for my personal experience where I and my body are inseparable, but also for my relationship with others and they with me in copresence. Indeed, for Marcel *esse est co-esse*, "to be is to be together," incarnate and proximate to each other, revealing to and being revealed to. Personal existence is charged with significance because of self-revelation to others: when I assert that I exist I mean to imply more than that I am only for myself, but that I am manifesting myself to others. The prefix *ex* in the word *exist* conveys a centrifugal movement toward the external world:

> I exist: that means I have something by which I can be known or identified . . . : "There is my body."[1]

If we think of Jesus in this sense, the Marcellian themes of centrifugal revelation clarify Jesus' self-disclosure and incarnate hospitality by which he invites us to participate in a certain plenitude. Incarnate being, hospitality, receptivity all describe the phenomenon who is Jesus.

1. *Creative Fidelity*, ed. and trans. Robert Rosthal (New York: Noonday Press, 1964), p. 17.

Thus the ambiguous term "receptivity" has a wide range of meaning extending from suffering or undergoing to the gift of self; for hospitality is a gift of one's own, i.e. of oneself.[2]

As incarnate "I" Jesus "takes upon himself" and "opens himself to" participation through the language of good faith as opposed to bad faith, in terms of "I," "thou," and "we." As incarnate, Jesus is present to the interpreter as "thou" and addresses him in the second person. Marcel is concerned to reinstate the priority of the first-and second-person personal pronouns against the distant third-person personal pronouns *him*, *her*, or *it*. This hermeneutic helps us to see how Jesus evinces his presence by giving priority to the personal pronoun *I* and to the pronouns *thou*, *you*, and *we* in his address. Gospel interpretation should focus on the presence-language of Jesus and not on an analysis of absence-language, which happens when interpretation makes him the object of distant critical analysis and does not permit him to address the critic on the personal level of "I am" and "do thou likewise."

Interpretation Begins with Openness to Jesus

The key to interpreting Jesus (as the evangelists themselves interpret him) begins with an appreciation of ordinary address and response. Marcel writes,

> . . . I address the second person when what I address can respond in some way — and that response cannot be translated into words. The purest form of invocation — prayer — embodied imperfectly in the uttered word, is a certain kind of inner transfiguration, a mysterious influx, and ineffable peace.[3]

But the distant analysis of another can destroy the uniqueness of "I," "thou," and the unity of "we":

> When I consider another individual as *him*, I treat him as essentially absent; it is his absence which allows me to objectify him, to reason about him as though he were a nature or given essence.[4]

2. *Ibid.*, p. 28.
3. *Ibid.*, p. 32.
4. *Ibid.*

However, there is also a presence that is really an absence, that is, when we act toward somebody who is present as though he were absent. For instance, if I merely talk about the weather with someone or gather biographical bits of information from him as though he were filling out a questionnaire, I treat him as essentially absent. Or if someone asks me similar questions as an external questioner, I too become a third person and am no longer "I" or "thou," but only a pen that traces words on paper. The real meaning of persons comes when there is a bond of feeling between the "I" and the "thou," when "a unity is established in which the other person and myself become *we*, and this means that he ceases to be *him* and becomes *thou*. . . ."[5] When the other person ceases to be a mere object of conversation and to intervene between me and myself, we then coalesce and fuse into a living unity of mutual openness: "The path leading from dialectic to love has now been opened."[6]

An open and authentic interpretation of the Gospels, following Marcel's phenomenological model, will first set out to describe Jesus' "I" and his address of "thou" and "you," and the response of "we" among those with whom he shares the joy of the new age that is breaking in. Those who hear and see him but keep him in the distant third person treat him as though he were filling out a questionnaire and were essentially absent. Accordingly, an authentic interpretation of the Gospels requires that the interpreter be open to the presence of Jesus in terms of his first-person personal pronoun *I*, and who addresses the interpreter as personal "thou." This is perhaps the hardest demand of a healthy hermeneutic, but it is the only way of getting around the falsification that comes from objectifying Jesus as a mere "him" to be analyzed from outside without personal confrontation. There is no neutral ground. Marcel's hermeneutic of persons-in-relation requires that the gospel interpreter be open to the presence of Jesus as he appears incarnate in his works and acts. When one allows himself to be confronted by the incarnate Jesus who speaks, unity is established in which Jesus ceases to be a "him" and becomes "thou," and the interpreter is translated from a dialectic of distance to a compassionate openness:

> The being whom I love can hardly be a third person for me at all; yet he allows me to discover myself; my outer defenses fall at the same

5. *Ibid*., p. 33.
6. *Ibid*.

time as the walls separating me from the other person fall. He moves more and more into the circle with reference to which and outside of which there exist third persons who are the "others."[7]

Marcel maintains that only when I so communicate with other persons do I truly communicate with myself and discover transformation through inward relaxation, as well as escape that retraction into myself that mutilates relationships. Accordingly, an openness to Jesus as incarnate "thou" in turn opens up a region of fruitful relationships transcending the closed system of objectification and abdication. It is "a kind of vital milieu for the soul."[8] In the attitude of openness I expose myself to Jesus' claims and invitation instead of protecting myself from him by closed and distant systems of third-person language. I become penetrable to him and he to me. If I detach myself from his invitation to relationship and insist on examining him from without through the methodology of doubt, the relationship is destroyed. A decisive conversion in attitude is required for the interpreter to enter into this radical hermeneutic of persons, for it asks that the critic relinquish his demand to control the situation from a position of distant doubt and objectification.[9] This is consistent with the intrinsic claims of Jesus in the Gospels. A hermeneutic designed to discover him as he is will somewhere have to discover him as "thou" in a conversion that follows the path to "we."

Responsiveness Leads to Accurate Interpretation

Exploring what "we" means in the context of love and creative fidelity, Marcel turns to a phenomenological analysis of the words "belonging and disposability,"[10] describing them as a personal act in which I evoke a situation of welcoming another person as a participant in my work and in the undertaking to which I have given myself. It is the opposite of claiming selfishly that I belong to myself, which in the end is a self-defeating assertion because the unrelated "I" negates the possibility of any specifiable context. Belonging to others and being at their disposal, however, is characteristic of Jesus' self-understanding as he

7. *Ibid.*, pp. 33–34.
8. *Ibid.*, p. 36.
9. *Ibid.*, p. 37.
10. *Ibid.*, pp. 38–57. See especially p. 40.

lives out the role of servant on behalf of others. Similarly his call to his disciples is that they also be servants to others. He also invokes in them a deep sense of admiration, which tears them away from their inner inertia and selfishness. Admiration for Jesus promises an irruption of generosity in those who are not closed to something wonderfully new, as were the scribes and Pharisees.[11]

"More precisely," Marcel writes, ". . . I shall say that admiration is related to the fact that something is revealed. Indeed, the ideas of admiration and revelation are correlative. . . ."[12] The refusal to admire and the inability to admire, he observes, are characteristic of our age with its "tendency to view with suspicion any acknowledged mark of superiority." Underlying this suspicion is a burning preoccupation with the self, an attitude of "but what about me, what becomes of me in that case?"[13] The refusal to admire need not always be based on jealousy or resentment, however; admiration or enthusiasm may be suspect by the critical intelligence on the ground that they abolish self-control. But critical intelligence can only help us to understand and to discriminate the facts we subsequently appraise: it cannot *appreciate* or help us decide whether a work or a person is worthy of admiration. The ability to admire is a deeper spiritual response to another, the "affirmation of a superiority which is not relative but absolute; absolute, I repeat; the word *incomparable* has a clearly distinct meaning in this context."[14]

Applying this motif to gospel criticism, I would say that an authentic appraisal of Jesus requires on the part of the interpreter an attitude of admiration; he judges there to be here an incomparable superiority. One cannot walk with heavy boots over such art and expect to understand it. It is required of the appreciative interpreter that he be responsive, not that he scrutinize the Gospels with the goal of having or possessing them by means of an impersonal critical key, as though he were a file clerk filing facts in drawers and having them at his command. Such a model proves false, for neither Jesus nor the Gospels nor any other works of art yield their secrets to the record-file approach. As long as one refuses to be open and responsive to the personal claims of Jesus, he is, to use Marcel's expression, "captive of the category of causality," with its illusory claim to objective neutrality:

11. See Marcel's remarks on admiration, *ibid.*, pp. 47–48.
12. *Ibid.*, p. 48.
13. *Ibid.*
14. *Ibid.* His italics.

However, it may also turn out that submerging oneself suddenly in the life of another person and being forced to see things through his eyes, is the only way of eliminating the self-obsession from which one has sought to free oneself. Alone, one cannot succeed in this, but the presence of the other person accomplishes this miracle, provided one gives one's consent to it and does not treat it as a simple intrusion — but as a reality. Nothing is more free in the true sense of this term, than this acceptance and consent; and there is nothing which is less compatible with the sort of antecedent deliberation which an obsolescent psychology holds as the necessary condition of the free act. The truth is that as long as one is captive to the category of causality, so difficult to apply to the spiritual life, one will not be able to distinguish between coercion and appeal, or between the distinctive modalities of response each of these evokes from us. In my opinion, the word "response" should be reserved for the holy inner reaction evoked by an appeal.[15]

Jesus invites our acceptance of and consent to his personal claims and further invites us to see reality through his eyes, as one who is speaking and acting with the authority of God, and preeminently at our disposal. Only by a sympathetic and imaginative openness to Jesus' claims can we free gospel criticism from contaminating the future with mechanical theories that limit him to mere causal events of the past. Such theories claim objectivity but paralyze the image of Jesus for the present as well as for the future. Marcel reacts against this fatal immobilization of the past:

Contrary to a popular belief which finds its support in what we may call the current philosophy, it is not true to say that the past is immutable; for we cannot legitimately distinguish material events which are fixed, and an elimination which varies according to its source, a source which is the experienced present itself. The sort of past I am criticizing is not to be identified with the past it is or becomes when I reconcile myself to it.[16]

An unwillingness to respond to the appeal of Jesus on the personal level of meeting results in an inner inertia and indisposability. One's interest should not even be constricted to the form of the finished work, says Marcel, lest it be transformed into a having on which my thought

15. *Ibid.*, p. 51.
16. *Ibid.*, p. 52.

anxiously dotes, like something clutched in a dead hand. This is what Pharisaic Judaism had become for Jesus' opponents, and what theories of gospel origin become in the hands of New Testament critics where Jesus in the Gospels is not allowed to make his appeal because he is already assumed to be inaccessible as a self-conscious and self-understanding person. Such doctrines lead to a radical indisposability to Jesus as incarnate "thou."

Creative disposability, on the other hand, characterizes the work Jesus brings to fruition as it is embodied in his vocation to others. That is why the Gospels cannot be seen as isolatable stories apart from the self-conscious vision of Jesus as person. Indeed, his very works and words are indwelled by his personal "I" and disclose his intentionality. Hence we cannot discover the authentic Jesus of the Gospels by inserting him into a web of objective relations that contain him as a mere and distant "him." Jesus becomes manageable and exhaustible, without remainder insofar as we construe his life as something wholly quantifiable.

The paradox of Jesus' disposability toward the interpreter and the interpreter's disposability toward him is the major problem of gospel interpretation[17] and finds its solution, not in purely objective terms which denature the text and detach the interpreter as mere spectator, but in personal openness to his offer of forgiveness of sins and his invitation to join the open table-fellowship that characterizes the inaugurated kingdom of God in his ministry.

Actions Disclose Self

Marcel next considers the phenomenon of acts, contrasted with mere gestures, as indicative of one's self-revealing. Once again we gain valuable insight into Jesus' "I" as it is disclosed in action: "An act, I shall maintain, is more an act to the degree that it is impossible to repudiate it without completely denying oneself. . . ."[18] Two truths need to be appreciated in this phenomenology of personal act: the first is that an act is inconceivable without a personal reference, a reference to an "it

17. Marcel refers to this general hermeneutical problem as "the metaproblematic of mystery, which I continue to regard as fundamental, and which if improperly construed, will give rise to the most harmful interpretations. There is always a danger of interpreting a mystery as a shallow agnosticism of the end of the nineteenth century." *Ibid.*, p. 56.

18. *Ibid.*, p. 109.

is I who . . ."; thus a description of Jesus' acts is tantamount to his saying, "It is I who am doing this and in so doing I disclose who I am." Secondly, in Marcel's words, "the act only presents its character of act to the agent or to whoever mentally adopts, through sympathy, the point of the agent."[19] Hence, there are two vectors, one proceeding from the actor, in this case Jesus, whose "I" is demonstrated somatically in his action; the other a receiving vector, as the gospel interpreter sympathetically adopts the point of view of Jesus the agent. In this meeting there is an ever-present danger that one may want to objectify Jesus' act by considering it a nonact and removing Jesus' creative "I" which stands behind and within it. Marcel warns that our modern tendency to objectify is so strong that we inevitably want to represent an act to ourselves as an effect of some other cause, and to ask who or what caused it — for example, the critic wants to attribute a number of Jesus' acts to the apologetic concerns of the evangelist, but has little grasp of the ways in which Jesus' acts specify who he is and what he envisages as his horizon of intention. As a unique and creative person Jesus specifies concretely who he is when he envisages, appraises, and confronts a situation with courage, exposes himself to determinate action, and assumes responsibility for that action.[20] By his acts and words Jesus makes certain claims and disclosures about himself.

What we are dealing with here in gospel criticism is the need to allow Jesus to appear as he intentionally claims to be. When radical criticism assumes the law of causality in the creation of sayings and acts of Jesus by the early church, it reveals its own intentionality of doubt regarding the reliability of the evangelists as faithful witnesses to what Jesus has said and done. Much modern gospel criticism no longer evinces faith in the validity and inspiration of the text, but addresses only opinions regarding the causal development and relative worth of those texts. Marcel distinguishes between opinion and faith, defining opinion as detachment and nonparticipation, and faith as its opposite. "It should be noted at once that we do not have an opinion, strictly speaking, of those beings with whom we are intimately acquainted. . . . : The more a state of affairs concerns me, the less I can say in the strict sense of the term that I have an opinion of it."[21] It would not be amiss to suggest that evangelicals, and especially those

19. *Ibid.*, p. 108.
20. *Ibid.*, pp. 114, 117.
21. *Ibid.*, pp. 122, 129.

(like me) converted from liberal theology, feel a certain sadness and incredulity toward those who express mere opinions about Jesus' words and acts, as though they could casually examine the words and acts of their wives and children without commitment! Such a depersonalized claim entails "that I have an opinion about the universe only to the extent that I disengage myself from it (where I withdraw from the venture without loss)."[22] In critical objectivism without faith one is tied to nonparticipation. The open interpreter, on the other hand, may or may not be sophisticated in analyzing the detailed paraphrastic activity of the gospel evangelists, but he or she has that essential quality of openness and faith in the story that allows the authentic voice of the intentional Jesus to come through with primary authority. The more concerned one is for the message of the Gospels and the primary speaker who is Jesus, the less one has a theoretical opinion of the material, and the more he passes from the sphere of opinion to the sphere of faith.[23] The sphere of faith or belief is interpreted by Marcel to mean that one opens a credit account to someone; that is, one says, "I freely put myself in your hands . . . ; it is as though I freely substituted your freedom for my own; or, paradoxically, it is by that substitution that I realize my freedom." Or, "I welcome you as a participant in my work, in the undertaking to which I have given myself."[24]

This giving or lending or rallying oneself to another is an essentially mysterious act that is personal. The "I" is believing in a "thou," not a thing; for "one can only trust a 'thou'."[25] Thing-language is impersonal and distant and is essentially problem-oriented. But as Marcel observes, "As long as we think in terms of a problem we will see nothing, understand nothing."[26] The drama and mystery of the gospel story, however, focus on Jesus as the personal embodiment of God's saving reign, and accordingly in reading and interpreting the story one is compelled to make certain commitments to him who meets us in the drama. This paradox of participation is a striking phenomenon in the Gospels, for the one who meets us on the gospel pages is the very one who places himself at *our* disposal, has as it were faith in *us*, gives and rallies and extends his credit to us, and thus is eminently qualified to call us to

22. *Ibid*., p. 129.
23. *Ibid*., p. 130.
24. *Ibid*., p. 40; compare p. 134.
25. *Ibid*., p. 135.
26. *Ibid*.

place ourselves at *his* disposal, give and rally and extend our credit to *him*.

As long as we stand distantly aloof from the text, however, and think of it in terms of a problem, we will see nothing, understand nothing. But in the openness of love, which is faith itself, the interpreter is confronted by the incarnate Jesus and discovers God's unconditional love of the creature, a gift that will not be revoked.[27] Jesus becomes vulnerable love, which is placed at my disposal. My appropriate response is one of obedience to the text in the sense of obedience to the one who becomes incarnate through the text, so that the deep meaning of the gospel comes alive when I reciprocally place myself at Jesus' disposal in loving belief.

Of course this is what in other forms C. S. Lewis, J. R. R. Tolkien, I. T. Ramsey, and Michael Polanyi are saying. But Marcel makes his own creative passage to the hermeneutic I am suggesting for gospel interpretation. Perhaps his most imaginative and appropriable insight is his description of the phenomenon of creative fidelity, which is bound up in the act of faith and is inseparable from a sound New Testament hermeneutic. It is, writes Marcel, in the plenitude of mystery that creative fidelity plays its role, where the loved one is present as the "thou": "Fidelity truly exists only where it defies absence, when it triumphs over absence, and in particular, over that absence which we hold to be — mistakenly no doubt — absolute, and which we call death."[28] It seems to me that the real hermeneutical struggle in gospel interpretation is to keep the personally indwelled text from falling continually into the state of a problem that is essentially third-person abstraction, where the person of the text is essentially absent, causing the story to die and the figure of Jesus to recede to a "he" or "it," rather than appear as "I am" and "thou."

Characteristics of Creative Fidelity

Creative fidelity is characterized first of all by a constancy that must be affirmed ceaselessly by the will in opposition to whatever would threaten it.[29] Second, creative fidelity reveals a mysterious kind of presence that dissipates any feeling of staleness that might arise from mere

27. *Ibid.*, p. 136.
28. *Ibid.*, p. 152.
29. *Ibid.*, p. 153.

constancy. Presence is the sense that another is with me as a friend who is faithful.[30] Third, it offers an essential element of spontaneity, which is truly an imaginative love not born of sheer duty or constancy.[31] This spontaneity always operates on the fundamental commitment to the other, for "the fact is that when I commit myself, I grant in principle that the commitment will not again be put in question."[32] This bars a certain number of possibilities which are demoted to the rank of temptation. Fourth, creative fidelity presupposes a radical humility in the subject, which is both compelling commitment and an expectation that finds its source in God. It is an essential consecration:

> It cannot be a matter of counting on oneself, or on one's own resources, to cope with this unbounded commitment; but in the act in which I commit myself, I at the same time extend an infinite credit to Him to whom I did so; Hope means nothing more than this.[33]

The posture of "I believe" for gospel interpretation entails a radical redirection of critical methodology. Creative fidelity as a hermeneutical attitude

> is always belief in a *thou*, i.e. in a reality, whether personal or suprapersonal, which is able to be invoked, and which is as it were, situated beyond any judgment referring to an objective datum. As soon as we represent belief to our minds, however, it becomes the belief of a certain person and a certain other person, in a *him*; we then envisage it as the idea or opinion A forms of B. It must also be said that I can at any time become a stranger to myself, and I can to that extent lose contact with my belief in its being as belief.[34]

The problem of the credibility of objectivist New Testament criticism today is that it has followed the path of doubt to the point where Christian faith, from which the gospel story has arisen, has itself appeared as a problem. The real problem is that the New Testament critic does not know what he believes. Jesus becomes problematic for the modern mind, which has voided the personal and the supranormal.

30. *Ibid.*, pp. 153f.
31. *Ibid.*, pp. 155ff.
32. *Ibid.*, p. 162.
33. *Ibid.*, p. 167.
34. *Ibid.*, p. 169.

Jesus makes claims that are tantamount to claiming the prerogatives of God. Hence the redactional refuge of referring such claims to the belief of the early church is symptomatic of a radical doubt that has been raised against the supranormal vision of Jesus. But "because of the very fact that we raise it, that it is a problem, we tend to intellectualize it, i.e. to falsify it; hence to see in belief an imperfect and even impure mode of knowing. . . ."[35]

The problem lies in the modern attitude of incredulity, another term for the critical intelligence that analyzes even personal language and acts according to a prior commitment to the objectivism of profane inquiry. From a religious point of view this doubt arises from a certain pride in one's reason, which may be considered sinful, since it coincides with a fundamental infidelity to the gospel story.[36] The story itself, and supremely the one who tells it and embodies it as incarnate "thou," is like a light that requires the interpreter or critic to be transparent and reflecting. The incredulous critic is opaque, the believing interpreter is translucent. Marcel observes that "insofar as I am not transparent, I do not believe," for belief is expressed in terms of translucent love and charity.[37] Modern radical criticism betrays overconfidence that autonomous reason can sort out answers to problems in abstraction; yet along with this positivism there is a negativism of radical doubt which questions all claims to truth and puts them to the test of some "objective" criterion that is assumed to be neutral and free of personal prejudice. Marcel trenchantly criticizes this malaise of Western post-Enlightenment intellectualism:

> Rationalism has introduced an abstract element into human relations which depersonalizes beings; and the democratic, secular philosophy which is a degraded aspect of rationalism, is also a distortion and complete perversion of that evangelical thought to which the temper of abstraction is wholly alien.[38]

Marcel proposes a hermeneutic that is phenomenological and reflectively empirical and that encompasses the wider scope of decisive personal experiences in disclosure and participation. The importance of immediate personal experience and participation in other persons is

35. *Ibid.*, p. 170.
36. *Ibid.*
37. *Ibid.*, p. 172.
38. *Ibid.*, pp. 8–9.

central to Marcel's hermeneutic of recuperation and plentitude. The meaning of personal existence — here, the meaning of Jesus as incarnate person — is discovered in Marcellian phenomenology through an analysis of the dialogue of Jesus. This descriptive analysis reveals Jesus' aspiration to engage himself in a project to restore the present brokenness of personal participation in the world. The phenomenological analysis describes his spoken and acted language which he indwells and which embodies him as he inaugurates the kingdom of recuperation and participation. Further, the analysis describes the presence of vertical transcendence which characterizes his claim to offer divine forgiveness in terms of open table-fellowship.

Jesus accordingly appears in the Gospels as incarnate being, whose empirical "I" discloses an inner awareness of a special messiahship; his "I" becomes a subject of disclosure and appears as "thou" in the arena of public address. While Jesus has a privileged access to his own consciousness and cannot be known exhaustively in his own subjective immediacy, it is nonetheless true that his awareness of himself as person-with-a-mission is experienced in terms of his embodiment in the world of persons, as being-there-for-others. Hence Jesus' self-understanding is "manifestory," and has civil status.[39] Through his incarnate being, which comprises spoken and acted bodily language, we glimpse his self-understanding, his vision, horizon, "existential orbit," in short, his personal pronoun *I*. Jesus' "I" is made known through his openness, disposability (*disponibilité*), and permeability to other persons. Reading backward from his spiritual availability in love and fidelity and in interpersonal communion, we confront the intentionality of Jesus who is related to his body as he is related to those who comprise his Body. The relationship he bears to others is analogous to the relationship he bears to himself; indeed, there is a functional or psychological relation between them, so that to read one is to read the other. Thus sympathy, feeling with Jesus, or putting myself in his position makes me copresent and "at home" with him in an intersubjective relationship that is entered by indwelling his personally indwelled language.

The centrifugal tendency of Jesus' language extends a sensation of receptivity and hospitality to the hearer-reader-believer and invites a resonant response of love and fidelity on his or her part. No authentic interpretation or representation of Jesus' language can be attained from

---

39. I am indebted to Robert Rosthal's summary introduction, *ibid*., pp. ix–xxvi, especially on this point, pp. xvi f.

the position of the mere spectator or from the posture of distant detachment. This model, which arises in radical criticism's attempt to be "scientific," is accompanied by emotions of distrust ("when in doubt, discard"), disbelief, impermeability, and egocentrism. This is not to say that the scientific method does not have its role to play in the analysis of Jesus' embodied language, but it must come as a secondary function of the intellect that has first acknowledged that knowing is primarily *personal* knowing, since it is persons who are being known and who are doing the knowing in whatever knowledge humans possess and pursue. The scientific habit can be abused and can lead to depersonalizing and dehumanizing, as Marcel is all too aware. As it has been applied in extreme gospel criticism, objectivism has followed the problematic approach (the Gospels are a "problem," Jesus is a "problem"), and in so doing has eliminated mystery, excluded revelation as a source for truth, and denigrated the supranormal. Only by allowing these components their proper role in Jesus' "I"-embodied language can the interpreter make proper response to Jesus' claims and to his appeal.

In sum, my study of Marcel implies that good gospel interpretation will require the interpreter to be open and responsive to the presence of Jesus, who is incarnate in his words and acts. Accordingly, the interpreter (I have avoided calling him a critic) must undergo a repentance in the sphere of his intellect. Anything less leads to a serious misrepresentation of the Speaker who embodies his "I" and "thou" in the folds of his spoken and acted story.[40]

40. See *ibid.*, pp. xxvi, 173.

10

Jesus As Author of the Evangelium
J. R. R. Tolkien and the Spell of the Great Story

One of the most impressive statements I have ever read on the deep meaning of language is J. R. R. Tolkien's essay "On Fairy-Stories."[1] This essay has influenced my own attitude toward biblical hermeneutics and exegesis and offers a promising new approach to gospel interpretation. Tolkien is a worthy mentor for understanding the nature of story because of his commitment to Christian faith and his belief, along with C. S. Lewis, that imaginative story-writing by a Christian only rings the changes on the basic theme that the original author of the gospel story has composed. Hence all who write imaginative stories out of Christian faith (or undertake any creative work) are considered subcreators in the image of God, the highest calling of a created human being.

The reader of this chapter must not, therefore, assume mistakenly that I am about to make the radical suggestion that the Gospels are fairy stories and ought to be interpreted as such, for that would miss the point of my hermeneutic altogether. Quite the contrary, I am interested in seeing how Tolkien uses fundamental Christian themes from the gospel story and applies them to imaginative stories of a second order. It is primarily this higher order I am interested in expositing. Accordingly, I will take his insights on writing Christian fairy stories on a secondary level and apply those insights directly to the Gospels, for it is from this higher level that the themes arise in the first instance. As we proceed, the reader will begin to see, I hope, the rich store of hermeneutical possibilities for interpreting the Gospels in the context of Tolkien's essay, and come to appreciate the similarity of this approach not only to that of Lewis, as one would expect, but also to those of Ludwig Wittgenstein, I. T. Ramsey, Michael Polanyi, and Gabriel Marcel. I will follow the same line of exposition here as in the previous

1. In the section "Tree and Leaf," in *The Tolkien Reader* (New York: Ballantine Books, 1966), pp. 2–84.

chapters, freely adapting germinal thoughts and applying them to the interpretation of the Gospels.

The Spell of the Evangelium

First, the Gospels portray a realm that is wide and deep and high, filled with all manner of wondrous things (on a level far more profound and real than any imaginative realm of faërie); they are full of beauty and an ever-present peril of "both joy and sorrow as sharp as swords." They evoke in the attentive reader a sense of awe and reverence:

> In that realm a man may, perhaps, count himself fortunate to have wandered, but its very richness and strangeness tie the tongue of a traveller who would report them. And while he is there it is dangerous for him to ask too many questions, lest the gates should be shut and the keys lost.[2]

This marvelous realm of the Gospels contains the whole world of seas, sun, moon, and sky, and the things that are in the earth: "tree and bird, water and stone, wine and bread, and ourselves, mortal men, when we are enchanted."[3] It is an enchanted mood that one must have if he is to read the Gospels aright, for as Tolkien reminds us later in his essay, the word *spell* means both a story told and a formula of power over the living.[4] Hence the words *God's spell*, or gospel, mean a story told and a strange and redeeming power over human beings. When the story is entered and received with attentiveness and obedience, one falls into a state of divine enchantment, comes under the "spell" of the evangelium. As I remarked in the chapter about Lewis, the first role of hermeneutics ought to be to prepare the reader to be receptive to the story of the Gospels, and to enter into its language so obediently that one becomes virtually enchanted and spellbound. That is the first mark of the good reader. It is also the mark of a great work that it can have this power over us. What we must avoid at all costs is a critical attitude that approaches the Gospels with preconceived notions and an arrogant sense of superiority and control. Critical and analytical studies can be made of the text as a secondary interest but must never be given pride of place; otherwise the story will become

2. *Ibid.*, p. 3.
3. *Ibid.*, p. 9.
4. *Ibid.*, p. 31.

merely our story, and we will be shut out from the wonder and awe
that are evoked in us only when we allow the "spell" to have its way
over us.

In the Gospels, after all, we are entering the perilous realm,

> which cannot be caught in a net of words; for it is one of its qualities
> to be indescribable, though not imperceptible. It has many ingredients,
> but analysis will not necessarily discover the secret of the whole.[5]

There is a kind of "magic" in the Gospels, which we might translate as
the presence of the supernatural, the "deep magic" of heaven, that produces the mood of enchantment when belief is present. The art of the
Gospels invites belief and leads to enchantment, and this introduces us
to what Tolkien calls the secondary world, which produces an alteration
in the primary world of ordinary everyday experience,[6] what Ramsey
would call the "straightforward" logical world, devoid of the odd. It is
the magic "of a peculiar mood and power, at the furthest pole from the
vulgar devices of the laborious, scientific magician." But a note of warning: "if there is any satire present in the tale, one thing must not be
made fun of, the magic itself. That must in that story be taken seriously,
neither laughed at nor explained away."[7] This warning ought to be
heeded by contemporary gospel criticism, which generally performs
according to straightforward logic and makes no allowance for the mag-
ically miraculous or supernatural. It is in fact functionally atheistic in
its operation when it disallows the supernatural element in the Gospels,
assigns it to the mythological framework of the times, and demytholo-
gizes it for our own. Tolkien is substantially in agreement with Ramsey, but approaches the question in a literary rather than a philosophical
style.

The Intent and Origin of Story

Next in Tolkien's exposition we come to two essential operations of
story which, when applied to the Gospels, might be said to satisfy
certain primordial human desires. One is to survey the depths of space
and time, and another is to hold communion with other living things.[8]

5. *Ibid.*, p. 10.
6. *Ibid.*, pp. 10, 52–53.
7. *Ibid.*, p. 10.
8. *Ibid.*, p. 13.

The gospel story aims at reconciling the fallen created realm to the author of the story, to bring it and all its creatures into covenant with him in the final eschatological day, and withal to explore the depths of God's redemptive space and time. Two attitudes evoked by the gospel story complement its two essential operations: a primal desire of imagined wonder and a belief in the story as true, since it is presented as true and is intended to elicit a sense of imagined wonder from the reader.[9]

Tolkien now turns a critical eye to the question of the origin of story. His reflections, when applied to the Gospels, confirm the approach already represented by Lewis and Ramsey. "Scientific" studies of certain aspects of story intend to be objective, but they do not really address the whole intent of the story:

> Such studies . . . are the pursuit of folklorists or anthropologists: that is of people using the stories not as they were meant to be used, but as a quarry from which to dig evidence, or information, about matters in which they are interested. A perfectly legitimate procedure in itself — but ignorance or forgetfulness of the nature of a story (as a thing in its entirety) has often led such inquirers into strange judgments.[10]

Tolkien's criticism could not be more apt in describing the motivation behind much criticism of the Gospels, where — as Lewis also would have it — the stories are not allowed to be what they are but are used for some other purpose than what they were originally intended, namely, for analytical questions regarding origin, style, authorship, and the like. This is all right, Tolkien allows, if in the process the intent of the story as a whole is not lost, as it often is in gospel criticism where the intent of the evangelist to introduce the "odd" grammar of the supernatural is not allowed to play its role, to be what it is. A truly phenomenological approach in the style of Tolkien's hermeneutic would allow the Gospels to say what they are intending to say, and not focus primarily on what the critic is interested in saying about them.

The gospel must be heard in its entirety as a story told; otherwise its intention will be lost. But this requires a desire of imagined wonder and expectancy on the part of the hearer or reader, along with a belief in its truth, or at the very least a suspension of disbelief. There are,

9. *Ibid.*, p. 14.
10. *Ibid.*, p. 18.

accordingly, two competing approaches to story and to the gospel story which afford different levels of truth: the concrete, which approaches the story as a whole just as it is; and the abstract, which deals only with partial aspects of the story. For Tolkien, as for all the interpreters in this study in their own particular ways, a proper interpretation of a Gospel must give first place to the whole phenomenon of its "form of life" in order for it to be itself; else it will be skewed by the predispositions of the interpreter. Analysis of the structure and the parts must proceed from the internal intention of the work as a whole, not the other way around.

In allowing the gospel to divulge its whole meaning, Tolkien would advise the interpreter to focus less on the development of its linear history (a fascination with the diachronic) than on the "alchemic" values of the living monument, on what it is in itself and what it has become for us. We should be more intent upon the "soup that is set before us" than upon the bones of the ox it is made of.[11] Like the history of other ancient stories, that of the Gospels is undoubtedly very complex, which is the other side of the matter and one of the legitimate concerns of the New Testament interpreter. He recognizes in each of the Gospels the "independent invention" by Jesus of strikingly new concepts of revelation and redemption, he observes the presence of significant strains of thought that indicate an inheritance from a common Old Testament ancestry, and in his study of the settings of the Gospels he comes to appreciate their diffusion from one or more centers in the early church.[12] But of these three — invention, inheritance, and diffusion — the most important and fundamental is invention or creativity, which focuses on the "odd" language of Jesus in terms of his own person and redemptive role. A concentration on inheritance, which is simply borrowing in time, takes us back only to the imagined ancestral inventor. While Jesus is indebted to the ancestral "inventions" or divine disclosures of the prophets, he goes far beyond them in the novelty of his own "invention"; thus his personal pronoun *I* cannot be exhausted by a historical explanation of ancestral origins. Similarly, if the New Testament critic concentrates almost exclusively on the diffusion of the essential gospel in the early church, on "borrowing in space" as inheritance is "borrowing in time," he only refers the problem of origin elsewhere.[13]

11. *Ibid.*, p. 19.
12. *Ibid.*, p. 20.
13. *Ibid.*, p. 21.

Contemporary gospel studies are for the most part taken up with inheritance and diffusion, and even redaction criticism, which might seem to be more inclined toward invention, is really a variant of diffusion, especially as it is practiced by the more extreme critics who would explain the gospel material not so much in reference to Jesus' inventive "I say to you" as to the evangelists' diffusion of tradition through the invention of the gospel genre. Only in regard to the language of the parables, as I have noted, does there seem to be a great deal of interest in the inventiveness of Jesus, though there are signs that the pendulum is beginning to swing back to Jesus as originator of the gospel tradition.

Of the tendency in radical gospel criticism to miss the intent of the whole, especially the intent of the principal inventor, Jesus, Tolkien makes a perceptive observation:

> It is indeed easier to unravel a single *thread* — an incident, a name, a motive — than to trace the history of any *picture* defined by many threads. For with the picture in the tapestry a new element has come in: the picture is greater than, and not explained by, the sum of the component threads. Therein lies the inherent weakness of the analytic (or "scientific") method: it finds out much about things that occur in stories, but little or nothing about their effect in any given story.[14]

Accordingly, the inventiveness of Jesus and the "oddness" of the supernatural presence in his speech and acts are two essential elements in each of the Gospels that give the overall picture its meaning. As for the presence of the supernatural, it is not a "disease of language," as Max Müller considered all mythology to be, but is so fundamental to the gospel that neither can be understood without the other.

Indeed, it is in the imaginative use of story that Jesus introduces obliquely the presence of the supernatural and becomes the cocreator (with the Father and the Spirit) and subcreator (as incarnate)[15] of the essential themes of salvation, which he develops inventively in the spoken and acted story of the Gospels. The "higher" is genuinely glimpsed in the Gospels — "Divinity, the right to power (as distinct from its possession), the due of worship."[16]

14. *Ibid.*, p. 21, n. 15. His italics.
15. *Ibid.*, pp. 22–23.
16. *Ibid.*, p. 25.

The Three Faces of Faërie

Tolkien now introduces the three faces of faërie, which can be prof-itably used to describe the Gospels: the mystical, which faces toward the supernatural; the magical, toward nature; and the mirror of scorn and pity, toward man.[17] The essential face of faërie is the middle face of the magical; similar, in the Gospels, is the presence of the miraculous, with its healings, exorcisms, nature miracles, and resurrections. But much more than in faërie, than in even the Christian faërie of Tolkien and Lewis, the other two are always strongly present in the Gospels: the face of the supernatural, reflected in the presence of Jesus, and the face of man reflected in the mirror of the good news, first with scorn as the sinner's real face is viewed through the scorn of the law, then with pity as the grace of Jesus heals the repentant sinner. The theme of the three faces lends considerable aid in understanding the purpose of the Gospels and the intention of Jesus and compels the interpreter to appreciate the supernatural, the miraculous, and the salvational ele-ments in the makeup of each Gospel.

Thus the strongly antisupernatural bias of radical gospel criticism invariably misses the point of the story, when the only face that is seen in the mirror is the reflected face of the critic himself. Or, to change the metaphor and return, as Tolkien himself does, to the metaphor of the boiling pot, it is the cauldron of story that is the secret of the story's meaning, not a preoccupation with what is in the stew. The cauldron casts a spell, as it were, where spell means both a story that is told and its formula of power over human beings. Only the attentive and obedient allow the story to have its total (and finally unanalyzable) effect, quite independent of the findings of the gospel folklorists; only they come under its spell and its power to open a door on other time— "and if we pass through, though only for a moment, we stand outside our own time, outside Time itself, maybe."[18]

Such elements, then, as the supernatural, the miraculous, and the salvational are not to be relegated to the world of children, as fairy tales to the nursery. They are meant for adults, as well as for children, as Jesus' own attitude toward adults and children attests. What he does in his inventive way is to create a secondary world of special grace within the primary world of common grace and everydayness. The evangelist himself is caught up in this secondary world and performs

17. *Ibid*., p. 26.
18. *Ibid*., p. 32.

as subcreator as he arranges the words and acts of Jesus (under inspiration of the Holy Spirit) to convey his spellbound view of the story to his readers where they are, locked into the fallen primary world and without hope apart from the good news of the story. As we in our turn read each Gospel it is imperative, if the hermeneutic of spell is to have its effect, that we also be caught up in the enchanted state of secondary belief.

Jesus the original inventor (along with the Father and the Spirit), as well as subcreator of the story, followed by the evangelist subcreators who compose the finished Gospels,

> makes a Secondary World which your mind can enter. Inside it, what he relates is "true": it accords with the laws of that world. You therefore believe it, while you are, as it were, inside. The moment disbelief arises, the spell is broken; the magic, or rather art, has failed. You are then out in the Primary World again, looking at the little abortive Secondary World from outside. If you are obliged by kindliness or circumstance, to stay, then disbelief must be suspended (or stifled), otherwise listening or looking would become intolerable. But this suspension of disbelief is a substitute for the genuine thing, a subterfuge we use when condescending to games or make-believe, or when trying (more or less willingly) to find what virtue we can in the work of an art that has for us failed.[19]

This passage is a key to each of the approaches to Jesus and the Gospels we have been considering in this book. Analysis of the parts is a legitimate enterprise for the scholarly interpreter, but analysis can be done from either the inside or the outside of the story. If it is done from the outside it may say something that is of relative importance; but it is only when interpretation is done from within the story that it will have any bearing on ultimate themes and be free of the language-game of make-believe, which is only a substitute for the real thing.

The gospel interpreter who reaches the heart of the story is in the "enchanted state" of belief; that is, he is really inside the "spell" as a believer who is both attentive and obedient to the text, not stifling disbelief while actually supported by some other commitment. If the interpreter enjoys the story for itself he will not have to suspend disbelief: he will believe.[20] In this state of belief he will then be able to analyze the planes of his own belief as well as those of Jesus and the

19. *Ibid.*, p. 37.
20. *Ibid.*, pp. 37–38.

evangelists. The heart of the story is arrived at not so much by asking "Is it true?" (its truth has already been assumed by one who is spell-bound and in the enchanted state), but by identifying the good and bad characters in the story, which is, after all, what it is about. It is far more important, Tolkien insists, that the interpreter get the "right side" and the "wrong side" clear.[21] This is especially true of the Gospels, where it is of utmost importance.

This approach to the gospel story and Jesus as person opens yet another important door to correct interpretation: like other enchanting stories, but on a consummately important level because of its uniquely redemptive character, the gospel does not have to do primarily with *possibility* (can we believe this or believe that — the preoccupation of demythologizing hermeneuts), but with *desirability*. The good inter-preter of the Gospels will not be concerned only with defending truth statements but with exploring and explicating how the Gospels awaken *desire* and are successful in "satisfying it while often whetting it un-bearably."[22] It is the abetting and satisfaction of longing or desire on the highest spiritual level (*Sehnsucht*, as Lewis calls it in *Pilgrim's Regress*) — the exploration of the supernaturally "strange" with "glimpses of an archaic and primordial mode of life" — that is the principal reason for a Gospel's being at all. That is the essence of its genre.

It is, then, in the spirit of humility and innocence like that of a child that one begs to enter the gospel story and divine its innermost secrets; but as Tolkien hastens to add, these virtues of entry do not necessarily imply an uncritical wonder, nor indeed an uncritical tenderness.[23] It needs to be noted that children are often more critically astute on es-sential matters than adults: "For children," as G. K. Chesterton once remarked, "are innocent and love justice; while most of us are wicked and naturally prefer mercy."[24] This is not to say that children are all good and adults all bad, for we were meant to grow up. But in growing up (and interpreting the Gospels, among other things) we must not lose innocence and wonder as we "proceed on the appointed journey." If the innocence and wonder are not lost along the way, then the adult can put more into and get more out of the Gospels than the child can. It all

21. *Ibid.*, p. 38, n. 23.
22. *Ibid.*, p. 40.
23. *Ibid.*, p. 43.
24. *Ibid.*, p. 44.

has to do with whether we can hold on to the wonder and innocence, to belief and primary naïveté.

Four Modes of Faërie

This brings Tolkien to consider the peculiar genre of faërie in the modes of the fantastic, recovery, escape, and consolation, which are eminently applicable to the gospel genre. First, as regards the fantastic, it is obvious to the believer that while the ordinary use of the term does not apply to the Gospels (they claim to be true in the primary world and the evangelists intend them to be true), the semantic connotation of the word *fantastic* is appropriate. The Gospels do have a fantastic quality of strangeness and wonder in their expression and, being of the secondary world transposed upon the primary world, allow the reader a "freedom from the domination of observed 'fact,' " and thus are "not a lower but a higher form of Art, indeed the most nearly pure form, and so . . . the most potent."[25]

There is in the "fantastic" Gospels an "arresting strangeness" (Ramsey's "logically odd"). Here the gospel critic who is used to being in charge by assuming an "objective" emotional distance will run into trouble with the arresting strangeness of the fantastic. "Many people," says Tolkien, "dislike being 'arrested'. They dislike any meddling with the Primary World, or such small glimpses of it as are familiar to them."[26] However, once the interpreter enters the fantastic world of the gospel with its supernatural and miraculous modes of discourse and disclosure, he begins to appreciate its "inner consistency of reality" which bespeaks a special skill, "a kind of elvish craft" (the inspiration of the evangelist in the formation of his Gospel). Few undertake to write a Gospel; few indeed are called to do so. But when a Gospel is undertaken and completed, "then we have a rare achievement of Art: indeed narrative art, story-making in its primary and most potent mode."[27]

The "fantastic" Gospels are not to be thought of as drama, for the supernatural and the miraculous, the logically odd of the higher world, cannot be fitted into the straightforward ordinariness of the primary world and re-enacted on a stage; the effect of the strong potion will be

25. *Ibid.*, p. 47.
26. *Ibid.*, p. 48.
27. *Ibid.*, p. 49.

lost and the story will fall back in the beholder's eye into the dullness
of the primary world with irreparable loss. The unique and odd quality
of enchantment is a necessary state of mind for the reader of the gospel
if he is to enter its secondary world; and when he does enter it together
with its designer, the senses of both are satisfied by the purity of its
artistic desire and purpose (one assumes this to be true of Jesus, who
delighted in happy response to his spoken and acted story; and we
would assume it to be true of the evangelists on their secondary level
of subcreativity). The gospel story does not seek to dominate by some
magical power over things as do demonic magic and self-centered greed:
"Uncorrupted, it does not seek delusion nor bewitchment and domination; it seeks shared enrichment, partners in making and delight, not
slaves."[28]

While the disbelieving critic (under the spell of the Enlightenment)
may find the supernatural oddness of the Gospels' subcreative art suspect and even illegitimate, Tolkien replies that the fantastic is a necessary human activity that does not destroy or insult reason and scientific
verity, but saves one from slavery to it. If it is at times and in some
hands abused, what in this fallen world is not carried to excess and
put to evil use?

> Men have conceived not only of elves, but they have imagined gods,
> and worshipped them, even worshipped those most deformed by their
> authors' own evil. But they have made false gods out of other materials:
> their notions, their banners, their monies; even their economic theories
> have demanded human sacrifice.[29]

Because of our derivative mode and because we are made in the image
and likeness of our Maker, we also make, and make creatively if we
allow that we are only subcreators when we fashion and mold a work
of art. Thus the evangelist recognizes implicitly that his Gospel is a
derivative art that depends for its very existence upon the original art
of the incarnate inventor himself, who in his words and works manifests the oddly fantastic and wholly original art of divine grace. The
specialist in gospel interpretation, far down the road as regards subcreativity and originality, is a genuine interpreter when he is faithful to
the fantastic work of art that is a Gospel, and essays the pleasant (but

28. *Ibid.*, p. 53.
29. *Ibid.*, p. 55.

not always easy) task of interpreting and analyzing its story and grammar, and especially the One who speaks and acts it. The issue at hand is that the fantastic cannot be demythologized if the gospel is to be what it intends to be and what Jesus intends to be. Otherwise the whole point of Jesus' incarnate ministry and his personal embodiment of the redemptive story will be lost, and only the face of the critic reflected in the mirror of research.

After treating the fantastic, Tolkien moves to recovery, which is the return and renewal of health, the regaining of a clear view, of seeing things as we were meant to see them — as things apart from ourselves, not held on to by some trite or familiar possessiveness. We see colors again and are startled anew (but not blinded) by green, blue, yellow, and red as they are in themselves, even though we have seen them countless times before. Recovery is a flight from the danger of boredom or the anxiety to be original, which may lead to a distaste for the delicate color or pattern, or to the "mere manipulation and over-elaboration of old material, clever and heartless."[30] Warning words, these, when we become "clever and heartless" critics! For who can design a new leaf? asks Tolkien. To let Jesus be what he says he is and the Gospels to be what they are is not a lower calling for the interpreter than to create imaginative theories with an anxiety to be original. Familiarity need not breed contempt, for springtime is not less beautiful because we have experienced other springs or because springs have returned since the world's beginning:

> Each leaf, of oak and ash and thorn, is a unique embodiment of the pattern, and for some the very year may be *the* embodiment, the first ever seen and recognized, though oaks have put forth leaves for countless generations of men.[31]

We should not therefore despair of waiting attentively upon the Gospels in the expectation of interpreting them with insight simply because we cannot be original, or because (for the artist) all lines must be curved or straight, or because (for the painter) there are only three primary colors. Only Jesus can create the novel and the new as with the Father he co-authors the plan of salvation and with the Holy Spirit energizes it with powerful effect. The evangelists are subcreators in ringing the

30. *Ibid.*, p. 57.
31. *Ibid.*, p. 56. His italics.

changes on the basic theme, as are the apostles when they write their letters to the churches — all of them directly and divinely inspired, so that their subcreations become for us the canonical material with which we ourselves work on a less than plenarily inspired level, as distant subcreators in an interpretative sense.

It is all an inheritance of wealth that we go over again and again because it never grows old and because it affords a continually new vision of things as we were meant to see them. The gospel interpreter is faithful to his task when he helps "to clear our windows, so that the things seen clearly may be freed from the drab blur of triteness or familiarity — from possessiveness."[32] It is the penalty of appropriation that the things we have appropriated either legally or mentally we think we know when we really do not, for we have ceased to look at them once we have laid hands on them and have locked them in our hoard.

Thus the Jesus of the Gospels has been lost to a skeptical criticism that has confidently claimed that the early church mythologically redacted Jesus into the fantastic Christ. The recovery of the Jesus of the Gospels will not come easily to the modern critic until, following Tolkien's program for recovery, he discovers humility before the text. Tolkien's agenda of recovery through the fantastic allows us to see Jesus from a new angle (new only for the modern, but really a very old and effective angle that is shared by the evangelists). From this new post-critical (that is, postskeptical) perspective one suddenly sees the queerness of things where before they were only ordinary and trite. Then comes a recovery and freshness of vision; but it is only a beginning.

Humility leads one to recover the deep sense that the fantastic is forged out of our created world, and that the Jesus of the Gospels, like a good craftsman, "loves his material, and has a knowledge and feeling for clay, stone and wood which only the art of making can give."[33] Jesus takes the simple and fundamental things of life, which by their very simplicity are made all the more luminous by their setting, and freely invests them with the deep meanings of the archetypal world. He can be nature's lover, not her slave, because he is the master and redeemer of nature. Hence in the fantastic story of his ministry we recover "the potency of the words, and the wonder of the things, such as stone, and wood and iron; tree and grass; house and fire; bread and wine."[34]

32. *Ibid.*, p. 57.
33. *Ibid.*, p. 59.
34. *Ibid.*

Next on Tolkien's agenda comes escape, which is one of the main functions of the fantastic Gospels. Escape is not a running away from reality but a discovery of freedom in what is real: "Why should a man be scorned if finding himself in prison, he tries to get out and go home? Or if, when he cannot do so, he thinks and talks about other topics than jailers and prison-walls?"[35] Jesus calls repeatedly for a commitment that is an escape to freedom through discipleship: "Follow me" (and I will make you fishers of men), and "lose your life for my sake" (and you will find it) have the ring of radical escape from triviality and unreality and, at great cost, of going home again. Escape from the ultimately unreal to the ultimately real is accomplished in terms of obedience to Jesus' own person, because he assumes in his own self-disclosure and commitment the status of ultimate freedom.

Real escape evidences not only love for the imprisoned and release for the captive but also opposition to oppression through "Disgust, Anger, Condemnation, and Revolt,"[36] all of which are characteristic of Jesus' mission as he faces demonic opposition and revolts against it with divine condemnation and anger. Jesus rebels against the transitory allegiances that have no ultimate substantiality, and speaks of things that are fundamental and permanent. Tolkien makes much of this theme and contrasts the "always new" of the modern scientific age (which tomorrow becomes obsolete) with the lasting and abiding story. "Real life" does not have to do with smokestacks and robots and their transitory products, but with the abiding qualities of life. "How real, how startlingly alive is a factory chimney compared with an elm tree?" might be applied with equal effect to transitory theories in gospel criticism, which Jesus always seems to outlast in spite of his "odd" supernatural behavior on behalf of recovery and escape. Tolkien felt very strongly that much of what the modern world called "serious" literature is "no more than play under a glass roof by the side of a municipal swimming bath," whose authors employ "improved means to deteriorated ends."[37]

True escape, in the sense in which Jesus embodies and proclaims it, is not an escape from life but from our present time and self-made misery, so that while we become conscious of the ugly side of our works and of their evil, we also recover an ancient delight with the works of our hands when they are dedicated to One who worked with wood and

35. *Ibid.*, p. 60.
36. *Ibid.*
37. *Ibid.*, pp. 63–64.

spoke of bread and wine. Jesus' recovery and fulfillment of the primordial desire to converse with other living things sets in motion an eschatology that provides an escape from entropy, death, and estrangement,
and recovers what was lost in the fall, indeed, enhancing that communion.[38] The final escape is from death, the threat of ultimate sepa-
ration from communion, and this escape is the oldest and deepest
desire, the desire for the great escape. Jesus' use of the authoritative
"I" points ineluctably to this final resolution, and in this sense Jesus'
story in the Gospels is genuinely escapist and represents in the highest
sense the fugitive spirit.[39]

There is one last dimension of consolation that is characteristic of
Jesus in the Gospels, and this concerns the happy ending, the eucatastrophe. As tragedy is the true form of drama, so the highest function
of the fantastic story — consummately the gospel story — is the joy of
the happy ending. It is a sudden and miraculous grace that does not
deny the temporary sorrow and failure of dyscatastrophe, but denies
universal final defeat. The good news of the evangelium gives "a fleeting
glimpse of Joy, Joy beyond the walls of the world, poignant as grief."[40]
The Gospels provide this happy upturn to the otherwise tragic down-
turn of nature and humanity. It is the mark of the good story of the
higher or more complete kind, like the original Gospels themselves,

> that however wild its events, however fantastic or terrible the adven-
> tures, it can give to child or man that hears it, when the "turn" comes,
> a catch of the breath and lifting of the heart, near to (or accompanied
> by) tears, as keen as that given by any form of literary art and having
> a peculiar quality.[41]

This is not an easy thing to do, and in the case of God's spell, which
is Jesus' story,

> it depends on the whole story which is the setting of the turn, and yet
> it reflects a glory backwards. . . . In such stories when the sudden
> "turn" comes we get a piercing glimpse of joy, and heart's desire, that
> for a moment passes outside the frame, rends indeed the very web of
> story, and lets a gleam come through.[42]

38. *Ibid.*, p. 66.
39. *Ibid.*, pp. 66–67.
40. *Ibid.*, p. 68.
41. *Ibid.*, pp. 68–69.
42. *Ibid.*, pp. 69–70.

The Function of Joy

Tolkien concludes his masterful hermeneutic with an epilogue on Christian joy, which is the mark or seal upon the true fairy story. Joy is a sudden glimpse of the underlying reality or truth that offers consolation for the sorrow of this world and the satisfaction of truth. In the eucatastrophe we have a brief vision, a far-off gleam or echo of the Gospel within the primary world. By grace an incalulably rich facet of truth shines into our otherwise gray world. Tolkien reveals the underlying Christian hermeneutic that informs all his writing. The concluding passage of his essay is a classic and should count as valuable currency in our attempt to understand the role of Jesus in the Gospels. I think it is one of the most important and perceptive passages I have ever read on the deep grammar of the Gospels.

> I will venture to say that approaching the Christian Story from this direction, it has long been my feeling (a joyous feeling) that God redeemed the corrupt making-creatures, men, in a way fitting to this aspect, as to others, of their strange nature. The Gospels contain a fairy-story, or a story of a larger kind which embraces all the essence of fairy-stories. They contain many marvels — peculiarly artistic [here Tolkien drops a footnote: "The Art is here in the story itself rather than the telling; for the Author of the story was not the evangelists"], beautiful and moving: "mythical" in their perfect, self-contained significance; and among the marvels is the greatest and most complete conceivable eucatastrophe. But this story has entered History and the primary world; the desire and aspiration of sub-creation has been raised to the fulfillment of Creation. The Birth of Christ is the eucatastrophe of Man's history. The Resurrection is the eucatastrophe of the story of the Incarnation. This story begins and ends in joy. It has pre-eminently the "inner consistency of reality." There is no tale ever told that men would rather find was true, and none which so many sceptical men have accepted as true on its own merits. For the Art of it has the supremely convincing tone of Primary Art, that is, of Creation. To reject it leads either to sadness or to wrath.[43]

Jesus' story, accordingly, is the source of all other good stories, because as the divine-human "I am" and "I say" he is the primary author of the evangelium. Jesus is the incarnate story, which he embodies in his own person as Son of man and Son of God, Messiah, Christ, Savior,

43. *Ibid.*, pp. 71–72.

and Lord. The reason for his coming is to do battle with the darkness of evil, rebellion, and death that wars against the divine "I am" who alone is capable of creation and primary art, and to offer to the darkness of the human heart the gracious light of salvation. The joy of the great eucatastrophe hallows the "happy ending," and in it the Christian finds that all his faculties have a purpose which can be redeemed. Acknowledging at last that he is *made* in the image of God and cannot rightfully claim originality of the fundamental themes, yet as redeemed subcreator "he may actually assist in the effoliation and multiple enrichment of creation."[44]

All this has been made possible by the Logos, the expression of God, who became flesh and personally authored the great story. Here is a hermeneutic of Jesus and the Gospels that has imagination, is attentive and obedient to the text, appreciates the logically odd, and acknowledges the authoritative intention of Jesus who indwells his words and acts as he personally authors the story of stories.

44. *Ibid.*, p. 73.

11

Jesus As Self-authenticating Authority
Presuppositions and Authorial Intent
in Cornelius Van Til's Hermeneutic

As I have tried to make clear in my use of contemporary hermeneuts such as Ludwig Wittgenstein, I. T. Ramsey, Michael Polanyi, Gabriel Marcel, C. S. Lewis, and J. R. R. Tolkien, their deployment for the cause of a better methodology by which to understand Jesus' intention (and thus to redirect gospel exegesis) does not commit me to subscribe to everything they have to say on every subject. A phenomenology of persons is often informed by their striking insights into the use of language in ordinary and theological conversation; hence this study has been considerably advanced and New Testament exegesis informed by their contextual models of discourse. But to repeat an important point, I do not feel compelled to underwrite their theological perspectives in toto; I have used them selectively in search of germinal ideas and, I hope, with discernment. I find myself closer theologically to some than to others.

This is important to bear in mind as I introduce a seventh figure who in many ways is closer to my theological orientation than any of the others, with the possible exception of Lewis, who has influenced me in a different way with his imaginative literary turns of phrase and generically unique Christian apologetic. Cornelius Van Til is a more formidable figure in that he represents a more strictly philosophical-theological and uncompromising apologetical approach to hermeneutics than do the others. Yet what they all express so well in their own ways, namely, that one's presuppositions govern one's whole language-game, Van Til articulates with such a relentless and overpowering consistency as an orthodox Christian that I find him quite compelling.

Though Van Til has often been at the center of controversy and has been criticized from theological right and left, his insistence on the sovereign and self-contained Trinity, the all-sufficient Christ, the inspiration of Scripture, and common grace as the ground of analogical language about God is fundamentally correct. It is fitting, therefore, that I conclude the search for a more adequate hermeneutic for gospel exegesis and New Testament Christology with an evangelical thinker of Van Til's stature and creativity. I do not agree with him on every point, but I think on essentials he is correct.

Analogical Knowledge

Working first of all from an epistemological and phenomenological point of view in confronting the spoken language of Scripture, we ask how God can address us in the person of Jesus, since his form of life is restricted by his embodiment in time and space and limited by the conventions of human language. What point of contact is there between God's truth and Jesus' intention, words, and works? Ramsey views the process of moving from ordinary human models to the language of God as a heightening of those ordinary models to infinite proportions so that they are appropriate of God. As an epistemologist in the tradition of the Reformers, Van Til also describes how the realm of nature is capable of providing these analogies. The reason, Van Til argues from Scripture, is that God has already invested creation with his own meaning. Creation is already interpreted by God; hence the finite person is a re-interpreter of facts that have their meaning in God who has created and sustains them. Our knowledge is therefore analogical of God's knowledge.[1] In keeping with Lewis and Abraham Kuyper, Van Til refers to God's knowledge as archetypal or original, and our knowledge as ectypal or derivative.[2] This is what Tolkien means when he writes of our subcreating God's original creation — we think his thoughts after him and ring changes in harmony with his original theme.[3]

There lie everywhere around us analogies of God's original creative power and deity (Rom. 1:20); and though these are widely miscon-strued by fallen finite creatures, the believer is enabled by faith in Christ and the enlightening ministry of the Holy Spirit through inspired Scripture to recapture something of God's original creative presence in common grace. Christ is our "ultimate reference point of predication,"

1. Cornelius Van Til, *A Survey of Christian Epistemology* (Philadelphia: den Dulk Christian Foundation, 1969), pp. 203ff.
2. *An Introduction to Systematic Theology* (Unpublished syllabus, 1971²), p. 203.
3. J. R. R. Tolkien, "On Fairy-Stories," in *The Tolkien Reader* (New York: Ballan-tine Books, 1966), p. 47; Cornelius Van Til, *A Christian Theory of Knowledge* (Nutley, NJ: Presbyterian and Reformed, 1969), p. 16.

our absolute source of truth, meaning, and possibility.[4] This enabling gifts us with the grace to be submissive and obedient to God's authoritative interpretation, as we become self-consciously faithful to God's own interpretation of the facts of creation.[5]

This fundamental hermeneutic involves two corollaries. First, it assumes that all exegesis for the evangelical Christian is fiduciary; that is, it is guided by the presupposition that all interpretative work is the appropriation or subinterpretation of God's archetypal interpretation of "the facts" by Scripture. Conversely, exegesis that tries neutrally to approach the data of Scripture as purely natural in its development is not obedient because it assumes, in Kantian fashion, that the human mind rather than the Holy Spirit is the original interpreter of the "text" of nature or Scripture. A second corollary of faithfulness to God's original interpretation in Scripture is that analogical reasoning will recognize not only continuity between God's meaning and ours, but also discontinuity. Van Til wants to emphasize the discontinuity as well as the continuity, since human fallenness is all too ready to identify its reinterpretation with God's own truth about himself, which in any exhaustive sense remains ontologically inaccessible to the human mind. It is precisely at this point that the greatest care needs to be taken to understand Van Til's hermeneutic. It is correct to say that there is discontinuity between our knowledge of God and God's being, for God is incomprehensible in the sense that no finite person can have exhaustive knowledge of his ontological being and experience. It is also correct to say that our human meaning does not exhaust God's original creative meaning about the created world. God is absolutely and self-sufficiently autonomous; he is the ultimate creative power and authority who has a privileged access to his own mind which we do not and cannot share. Van Til is always careful, and correctly so, to give glory to God's sovereign self-sufficiency. He is, I believe, correct to insist that at this point a genuine biblical theology parts company with all speculative theologies and philosophies that insist on preserving for the finite creature some right, independent of God, to human freedom and autonomy. This is the fundamental issue that has to be addressed if one is to understand the crucial importance of hermeneutics and how one's hermeneutic controls one's exegesis of the biblical text. This brings

4. Van Til, *An Introduction to Systematic Theology*, p. 101.
5. Cornelius Van Til, *The Doctrine of Scripture* (Philadelphia: den Dulk Christian Foundation, 1967), p. 15.

us to a closer study of Van Til's desire to underscore the role of presuppositions in the human quest to interpret the world.

The Function of Presuppositions

For some time I have felt that Van Til is correct biblically, theologically, philosophically, phenomenologically, and historiographically to
insist that no fallen human being — and that includes all of us — can
correctly interpret the data of nature and history without the aid of
divine revelation as it is mediated through Scripture by the Holy Spirit.
General revelation and special revelation are intimately related in an
organic and supplemental sense, and have been even from the first
moment of Adam's creation. It is not only that fallen persons since the
fall require redemptive revelation to interpret the data of creation properly, but also Adam and Eve themselves required special revelation in
order to know how to interpret the data of creation. God spoke the
word of interpretation to Adam and Eve in Eden and disclosed to them
in word-revelation the meaning of the fact-revelation (Gen. 1:28–30;
2:15–17). The two forms of revelation are correlative and inseparable.
Never, even before the fall, is fact-revelation sufficient unto itself, even
though nature is full of God's self-disclosure and bears his signature,
so that all are without excuse (Rom. 1:19–20; Ps. 19:1–6).[6]

This correlativity between general and special revelation, and the
necessity of the latter even under the optimum conditions of Eden, lies
at the center of Van Til's presuppositional hermeneutic. It is soundly
biblical and is the theme of part 2 of this study on Jesus as self-
conscious Messiah. Each of the selected authors has said something
similar and has been adapted to the thesis of this study, namely, that
Jesus as the phenomenon of God's special disclosure and redemption
cannot be understood except from *inside* the story, from the presupposition of belief. Attempts to exhaust the meaning of Jesus by reducing
him to the data or experience of historical interpretation inevitably distort him by removing the offense of his claim to correlativity with God,
a scandal to the natural mind, and force him into the presuppositions
of autonomous criticism and a naturalistic hermeneutic.

Accordingly, the Christian interpreter of the Gospels, who takes the
biblical revelation seriously when it says that the human mind is fallen

6. See Van Til, *An Introduction to Systematic Theology*, p. 133; *The Doctrine of
Scripture*, p. 65.

and will always interpret creation sinfully, is going to press his opponent's position hard as to the proper interpretation of "the facts" about
Jesus. He will point out inconsistencies in his opponent's methodology,
believing he has truth and reason on his side; but he will not be content
with that, knowing that only from within the presupposition of faith in
Jesus Christ as Savior and Lord can the facts about Jesus be seen as
they really are. Otherwise, a fundamentally autonomous and naturalistic hermeneutic remains unchallenged. Like Tertullian, Van Til presses
the argument relentlessly to the level of presuppositional commitment.[7]
Like Polanyi, but much more vigorously and biblically, Van Til impresses us with the importance of the fiduciary mode which underlies
all interpretative work and renders neutral and valueless exegesis
impossible.

Here an important distinction needs to be made between the circu-
larities of evangelical and nonevangelical hermeneutics, for both employ — unavoidably — the hermeneutical circle. Naturalistic circularity
attempts to interpret the phenomenological data about Jesus independ-
ently of the authority of Scripture and of faith in Jesus Christ, and in
that leap of faith accords the autonomous human mind an ultimate
authority of judgment that belongs only to God. Christian circularity,
on the other hand, enters the field of biblical interpretation in a spirit
of trust, acknowledging faith in Jesus Christ as Savior and Lord and
recognizing the ultimate authority of God and his inspired Word.[8] There
can be no neutrality hermeneutically or exegetically regarding the interpretation of the facts of Jesus. Logic, reason, exegetical method, indeed
the whole enterprise of learning and knowing are guided by fundamental commitments.

What does make it possible for evangelicals and nonevangelicals to
communicate and to appear to agree up to a point is the common ground
of a common world that is kept in orbit and in symmetry by the common
grace of God. In this sense, we share many common experiences with
nonevangelicals and nonbelievers. On a deeper level, everything in God's
creation cries out with his presence, even the submerged image of God
that the bent human heart tries unsuccessfully to repress, yet senses

7. See especially *A Christian Theory of Knowledge*, pp. 83–109, for an appreciative yet critical exposition of Tertullian.
8. For a clear and simple presentation of Van Til's essential apologetic method,
especially written for young people, see Richard L. Pratt, Jr., *Every Thought Captive*
(Phillipsburg, NJ: Presbyterian and Reformed, 1979). On circularity, see especially
pp. 51–60.

as guilt, anxiety, anguish, restlessness, and fear. There is also the Holy Spirit who makes communication possible and opens the heart to faith in Christ. But until that decision to return to God in faith is made by the unbeliever, his interpretation of "the facts" and that of the believer will be fundamentally at odds. There is no neutrality. Every fact and every exegetical attempt assumes a hermeneutic and a particular view of the world.

The point to be made here according to Van Til's hermeneutic is that an authentic exegesis of the fact and facts of Jesus Christ in the Gospels does not mean the imposing of a set of dogmatic assumptions upon brute and unknowable "facts," in Kantian fashion. Rather, it means that God has already interpreted the facts of nature and history through common grace by sustaining a world that is the proper vehicle for the incarnation of Christ and special revelation. Jesus Christ does not come into alien territory — occupied territory, yes, but not alien. Hence the physical laws of creation, wheat and wine, eating and fellowshiping, the language of persons and the movements of nations all become the materials Jesus uses to proclaim the inauguration of the kingdom of God and the time of salvation. Common grace and special grace find their union in him. This is the presupposition of proper exegesis.

The penetration of Van Til's analysis of presuppositions in contemporary hermeneutical thought is especially impressive in *The New Hermeneutic*.[9] As in his earlier works, Van Til relentlessly moves the reader to the bare line of assumptions underlying the new hermeneutic as it is represented principally by Ernst Fuchs and Gerhard Ebeling, who are deeply in debt to Martin Heidegger's epistemology, as he is in turn to Immanuel Kant, the modern father of autonomy in the realm of ideas. It would be well for us to see how Van Til critiques the new hermeneutic from a biblical point of view and reveals its essentially non-Christian presuppositions.

The goal of the new hermeneutic is to attempt to present Christianity in such a way that it will make more sense in the modern setting. With a focus on human receptivity, Fuchs and Ebeling carry on the previous work of Karl Barth, Emil Brunner, and Rudolf Bultmann, and further back the impulse of post-Enlightenment theology via Kant. The problem that remains unresolved concerns the place of the historical Jesus in the proclamation of the gospel. Why are the evangelists interested in him at all? In answering this question, modern phenomenalism and existen-

9. (Nutley, NJ: Presbyterian and Reformed, 1974).

tialism as Heidegger develops them are applied by Fuchs and Ebeling beyond the limitations of Bultmann's hermeneutic. If only (the new hermeneutic says) we pay more attention to the facts in the Gospels and demythologize them more consistently than Bultmann did we will see that they reveal in their narratives the sovereign grace of God — not in supernatural terms but in the existential exhortation to listen to Jesus, who makes God present for us. Jesus' words present the hearer with the possibility of new and authentic existence. Jesus moves in the sphere of words and becomes God's "verb," God's "time-word,"[10] of- fering an exchange of life for death through God's love. The New Tes- tament — and not only Paul and John, but the synoptic evangelists as well — becomes itself a textbook in hermeneutic by teaching the her- meneutic of faith in response to God's speech-event in Jesus.

Van Til now goes back to examine Fuchs's 1954 study on *Herme- neutik*, finding there the basis of his new quest of the historical Jesus in terms of language-event that speaks its yes of love. Jesus is not seen as an objective factuality — or, as I have earlier pointed out, he is not seen as person — but as "word of address," which can be translated into existential language that speaks today. Jesus is the material point of departure that makes it possible for us to recover a valid hermeneutic. We see directly at this point the influence of the later Heidegger on Fuchs, where the earlier Heidegger influenced Bultmann. Heidegger moved more in his later years to the poet's corner where he listened to the silent toll of being, seeking some sound or vision from that nou- menal and nouminous wholly other in which the authentic self partici- pates and becomes truly the free self. This is the true home of the self, the purely transcendent being which speaks to us of the possibility of future authentic being in faith, love, and hope. This purpose always remains hidden and can never be conceptualized in the empirical "I-it" terminology of science, metaphysics, or theology, nor of course is it possible for the written Bible to contain it. One can only stand in the truth of being and participate supraconceptually in it, aware somehow that one is the loudspeaker of its silent toll.

For Fuchs this being of the later Heidegger that addresses us is none other than the God of Christianity, and proper response to Jesus' ad-

10. See Ernst Fuchs, "The New Testament and the New Hermeneutical Problem," in *New Frontiers in Theology*, vol. 2, *The New Hermeneutic*, ed. James M. Robinson and John B. Cobb, Jr. (New York: Harper & Row, 1964), p. 136; Van Til, *The New Hermeneutic*, p. 6.

dress brings true self-understanding. But Jesus cannot be known as objective historical person with his own messianic self-consciousness; he can be known only in terms of his historic (*geschichtlich*) significance through the new hermeneutic as his language mediates the possibility of authentic existence "for me."[11] The same is true of Ebeling, who, though he sees Jesus as indispensable to Christian faith in terms similar to those of Fuchs, denies that Jesus, in the Synoptics, ever links the concept of faith with his own person or ever speaks of faith in himself. Rather, Jesus participates in the faith of which he speaks and points his language to the ground of faith and to participation in the essence of God.[12]

Van Til cogently points out that such knowledge of God reduces theology to anthropology, the implication being (as I would draw it out) that there is no interest in the new hermeneutic for Jesus' language as revelatory of *himself* and as indicating his own correlativity with God. Instead, Jesus is important only as he speaks *to us*; he can be experienced only as he poses a question in an "I-thou" encounter. Jesus is located, accordingly, as is God, only in the conscience of the self when one is addressed in the language-event existentially in the present moment of decision. Jesus as historical person is not objectifiable; if he is objectified, then he is falsified and becomes an "I-it" manipulable being. Only in the historic, not historical, nature of reality does God address me through the language of Jesus. Subject (I) and object (Jesus) are correlative; Jesus is known only as his language addresses *me*.[13]

The problem with this hermeneutic is that it substitutes the language of the self for God's own objective self-disclosure in the person of Jesus. The hidden presupposition of the new hermeneutic is that the final authority of what is authentic disclosure is the autonomous self. The interpreter is always in control, even when he claims to be addressed by God or by the language of Jesus. We can therefore appreciate the effect this sort of hermeneutic is going to have on one's exegetical method. There is no neutral exegesis, and the sooner the evangelical realizes that fact the wiser he will be in dialogue with nonevangelical exegetes. There will appear to be overlapping of exegetical methodology up to a point; but only when the biblical interpreter knows his liberal

11. See Van Til's discussion, *The New Hermeneutic*, pp. 8–12.

12. Gerhard Ebeling, *Word and Faith*, trans. James W. Leitch (Philadelphia: Fortress, 1963), pp. 202–245; Van Til, *The New Hermeneutic*, pp. 12–14.

13. *The New Hermeneutic*, p. 18.

colleagues' biases will he be aware of hidden agendas that predetermine the eventual interpretation of the data, since it will always be the case in liberal exegesis that the Scripture as inspired and infallible objective revelation from God will be rejected in favor of the right of the autonomous interpreter to determine what, if any, and when, if ever, the Bible is the Word of God. Van Til is very strong-minded on the issue and has often won much disfavor, as well as acclaim, for relentlessly digging down and exposing controlling presuppositions. If at times he has seemed a bit harsh, he at least asks (in a little, privately published monograph, *Toward a Reformed Apologetics*) for more grace to be *suaviter in modo* (gentler in style). But in matters so fundamental, it is not always possible to press an issue all the way home and remain eminently collegial, for a good deal of glossing over of vital differences goes on among most of us in order to preserve the collegial amenities of the guild of scholarship.

Another prominent representative of the new hermeneutic, and Van Til's critique of him, needs to be considered in order to point up a present danger in present-day hermeneutical scholarship. Since he continues to be the leading theoretician of the post-Bultmannian hermeneutic and exercises considerable influence in both liberal and evangelical circles, Hans-Georg Gadamer invites careful attention. In *Truth and Method*,[14] Gadamer carries on the Bultmannian legacy that the horizon of New Testament Christianity must be fused with our contemporary horizon, but in a radically critical sense. Both Kant and Wilhelm Dilthey, while basically correct in their assessment of the self, did not press the autonomy of the critical mind far enough. They did not see that the truly critical mind must reinterpret dogma itself in order to be free from it. Only in Heidegger, Gadamer argues, do we see the radical rejection of the notion of substance and its replacement by the absolute historicity of understanding.[15] A text that comes down to us from tradition puts a question to us as interpreters. The interpreter understands the text only as he understands the question and attains the hermeneu-

14. Trans. Garrett Barden and John Cumming (New York: Seabury, 1975) from *Wahrheit und Methode* (Tübingen: J. C. B. Mohr [Paul Siebeck], 1965). See also Anthony C. Thiselton, *The Two Horizons: New Testament Hermeneutics and Philosophical Description with Special Reference to Heidegger, Bultmann, Gadamer, and Wittgenstein* (Grand Rapids: Eerdmans, 1980), especially chapter 5.

15. See Van Til, *The New Hermeneutic*, pp. 82–88 for a critique of Gadamer's historicism. References in Van Til are to *Wahrheit und Methode*, especially pp. 206–257, 351f.

tical horizon of questions (*Fragehorizont*) within which the direction of meaning of the text is determined. This penetration by the interpreter of what the text says opens up the horizon of questioning and necessarily invites a diversity of answers. Gadamer allows at this point that he is indebted to R. G. Collingwood's "logic of question and answering" as developed in *An Autobiography*[16] and in the *Idea of History*. In the latter, Collingwood writes, "The fabric of human society is created by man out of nothing, and every detail of this fabric is a human factum, eminently knowable to the human mind as such."[17]

Van Til spends several pages exploring this brash but widespread historicist hermeneutic, which Gadamer shares along with many contemporary theologians and New Testament scholars. It is radically Kantian and Heideggerian and focuses epistemology not on isolated particulars or abstract universals but on historical experience, which can be defined only in terms of the life of the autonomous mind. The historical past exists nowhere else than in the world of ideas as the interpreter moves in his or her critical re-creation of an imagined past. The historical past is therefore the present because it deals with the expression of thoughts that are lived through in the mind of the historian. Van Til quotes Collingwood's statement, which attempts a Copernican revolution in modern historiography and hermeneutic: "So far from relying on an authority other than himself, to whose statements his thoughts must conform, the historian is his own authority and his thought autonomous, self-authoring, possessed of a criterion to which his so-called authorities must conform and by reference to which they are criticized."[18] Perhaps the most widely quoted passage from Collingwood, one to which I warmly subscribed during my liberal years, is the following:

> Freed from its dependence on fixed points supplied from without, the historian's picture of the past is thus in every detail an imaginary picture, and its necessity is at every point the necessity of the apriori imagination. Whatever goes into it, goes into it not because his imagination passively accepts it, but because it actively demands it.[19]

16. (London: Oxford University Press, 1939), pp. 30–31.

17. (London: Oxford University Press, 1946), p. 65.

18. Collingwood, *The Idea of History*, p. 236; Van Til, *The New Hermeneutic*, p. 85.

19. Collingwood, *The Idea of History*, p. 245; Van Til, *The New Hermeneutic*, p. 86.

This imaginative reconstruction of history by the historian does not give him license to create whatever he wants, for there is evidence to be taken into account, and this must be fitted into a coherent picture. However, the historian never addresses whether the "evidence" is true or false in and of itself, but instead concentrates on its meaning for the historian as he or she reconstructs the historical event. Van Til observes how the hermeneutic of Collingwood and Gadamer controls the exegetical work of modern liberal scholarship on the question of the Jesus of the gospels:

> This historic Jesus is constructed by the hermeneutical principles of the internally self-sufficient man. Jesus *must* be that which aids him in his attempt to find authentic self-existence. Reality must be of such a nature as to furnish Jesus with an infinite supply of grace with which man can develop his authentic self.[20]

True interpretation of the historical Jesus must be existential, that is, in terms of my needs and questions; hence the historical Jesus becomes the historic Jesus, or the contemporaneous Jesus *for me*. There is for Gadamer no objective revelation from outside history.[21] All historical data meet us only within present history and are therefore subject to continual reconstruction in the dialectic of question and answer. The Word that is Jesus is pure speech-event which is discerned by the listener-interpreter from the normative viewpoint of his own horizon. A historical fact is not past but present; and what is historical is contemporaneous as we fuse the horizon of the present with the horizon of the past (*Horizontverschmelzung*).[22]

Summing up his case, Van Til remarks that "Gadamer in German-language thinking and Collingwood in English-language thinking stand together in assuring the ultimate self-sufficiency of man as his own final source and criterion for meaningful linguistic expression."[23] In this connection one should read E. D. Hirsch's excursus on "Gadamer's Theory of Interpretation"[24] for a trenchant critique of the epistemological problems inherent in this interpreter-centered approach. His percep-

20. Van Til, *The New Hermeneutic*, pp. 87–88. His italics.
21. *Wahrheit und Methode*, p. 357.
22. *Ibid.*, pp. 356–396.
23. *The New Hermeneutic*, p. 87.
24. In *Validity in Interpretation* (New Haven: Yale University Press, 1967), pp. 245–264.

tive — and I believe correct — indictment of the Heidegger-Bultmann-Gadamer legacy confirms Van Til's analysis that this school represents a deep and destructive skepticism about the very possibility of ever rehabilitating a text's (or a person's) original intentions. Gadamer directly attacks the premise that textual meaning is the same as the author's meaning. Accordingly, the historical Jesus as the objective incarnation of the preexistent Son who speaks and acts intentionally and authoritatively as the voice of God for our time is rejected by Gadamer and his school.

Here lies the central issue between an evangelical hermeneutic and a liberal hermeneutic. With Van Til the evangelical exegete and theologian work from the presupposition that God not only is able to speak but also has spoken authoritatively for all time in his inspired and infallible Scriptures, supremely in Jesus Christ the incarnate Son. By the ministry of the Holy Spirit the objective truth of Scripture and the continuing validity of the intention of Jesus which is embodied in his words and works confronts the interpreter with authoritative truth-claims.

The Relationship Between Faith and Interpretation

Van Til is sometimes faulted for overkill, of which his linking of Gadamer with the extreme idealism of Collingwood may be an instance. For Gadamer wants to insist that the interpretation of a text is not totally at the mercy of the interpreter's horizon, but has a horizon of its own, a tradition, which must be fused with that of the interpreter. He is aware of the danger of subjectivity. But then so is Collingwood, who reacts against any suggestion that his idealist historiography is identical to the craft of the novelist. After all, there are data that have to be interpreted. Van Til's rejoinder to both men is valid, however, for there is no way they can make good on the claim that there are objective data from past history whose horizons of meaning can be known by the interpreter, without the interpreter's hermeneutical horizon reconstructing those data. Gadamer may sense the problem, but he cannot resolve it. Indeed, the way in which he has set up the interpretation of historical texts through a dialectic of question and answer virtually determines the autonomy of the interpreter in deciphering the text, for both problems and answers are constantly changing and require a continuing reconstruction. The horizon of the critic must always remain normative. Hence, Jesus' own understanding of his mission is unrecoverable; I can only try to find his understanding of authentic existence as it addresses my existential needs and questions.

Van Til's presuppositional approach to hermeneutics only points up the epistemological dilemma of the modern exegetical task. One might even say that Van Til, as a representative of orthodox Christian faith, and having demonstrated the irrationalism of an autonomous hermeneutic, shows the way to solve Gadamer's dilemma. The only way is to become an orthodox Christian and enter the authoritative horizon of the Scriptures by faith. Only by working from within the believing Christian community and by accepting the canonical authority of its biblical texts can the interpreter be addressed by the authentic Word of God. The authoritative self-disclosure of God in the Bible constitutes the special revelation that correctly interprets the historical data about Jesus of Nazareth and the church's proclamation of him. Without this presuppositional posture within the canonical revelation of God, there is no check on subjectivity and relativity in the interpretation of Scripture.

Van Til's presuppositional approach to hermeneutics offers an important correction to Hirsch, who also criticizes Gadamer for his subjectivity and plumps instead for the right of the author of a text to posit a normative meaning or horizon for posterity. The *meaning* remains stable, while its *significance* for the individual interpreter may vary.[25] This is all well and good, and I agree with Hirsch (and expect Van Til would as well). But how can one be sure what the real meaning of a text is (Hirsch suggests the analysis of genres as clues to the meaning), and that the author has really intended that meaning? It is all very well to counter Gadamer's subjectivity with an appeal to authorial intent — if one can establish the genuineness of the text, and then fathom its meaning. If these two operations can be carried out successfully, then the text does indeed bear the signature of the author's intent, as I have argued in analyzing Jesus' language by employing a phenomenology of persons. The problem with Hirsch's hermeneutic is that, impressive as it sounds, it does not assure us that we have analyzed the text properly so as to have arrived at the author's intended meaning. We may only be committing the intentional fallacy in thinking we have captured, or been captured by, the author's intended meaning, when actually we may have reinterpreted the text according to our own intended meaning and subtly, if unconsciously, missed the original meaning altogether. This happens regularly in literary and historical criticism.

25. *Ibid.*

The problem is a serious one and is, from a secular point of view, insoluble. It underscores the Kantian question of how I can know the thing in itself — in this case, the author's intended meaning — without passing it through the sieve of my own experience and understanding. In that case the original meaning has been melded with my meaning, so that only the fused phenomenon can be known, not the author's original meaning. Or at least I cannot be certain that I have recovered the author's intended meaning. There must always be a gnawing doubt that I have not got hold of the real thing. That, from Van Til's perspective, is the problem the finite interpreter faces in every realm. Without special revelation, God's revelation in nature cannot be properly interpreted. The fall aggravates the problem, but even Adam, prior to sinning, required God's special interpretation of nature to help him understand God's disclosure in nature. This means that Hirsch's critique of Gadamer is on the right track, but fails because of the presence of ambiguity in all human interpretation, whether literary, historical, sociological, or scientific.

The only possible way out of this maze of criticism and subjectivism is to enter by faith into God's own interpretation of his own created data. This requires the autonomous critic to relinquish his rights to have the first and final word, and comes by his humbly confessing his creatureliness and sinfulness and experiencing a rebirth of his heart and mind by faith in Jesus Christ as Savior and Lord. The gift of God's Spirit then imparts a new wisdom which comes through the power of the cross — it is the mind of Christ (I Cor. 1:18 — 2:16) through which all things are seen no longer from a human point of view (*kata sarka*, II Cor. 5:16-17). Such is the presupposition of every believing Christian; it is the hermeneutic by which the Christian stands within the believing community and accepts the canonical Scriptures of that long-standing body of believers as normative and infallible. This was true for nearly two thousand years until the rise of autonomous criticism in the modern age. It is also the testimony of the faithful evangelists and apostles to whom were imparted the oracles of God. The recipients of divine revelation put in writing their authorial intent — correlative with the divine intent — that Scripture is authoritative. Jesus uses the address of the authoritative "I say to you" (e.g., Matt. 5:21-48), and is faithfully recorded in the Gospels as speaking the oracles of God; Luke claims reliable testimony (Luke 1:1-4; 24:25-27), as does Paul (I Cor. 15:1-20; II Cor. 4:2; Gal. 1:12, 15-16; II Tim. 3:16), Peter (I Peter 1:10-11; II Peter 1:16, 20-21), and the author of Hebrews

(1:1-2). The genre of the New Testament faith is clear: the believing community lives within the redemptive story of Jesus Christ and accordingly has high regard for the written testimony of Scripture to Christ.

With this presupposition of the all-sufficient Christ and the authority of Scripture, the believing Christian is supplied with the heuristic vision and commitment, to use Polanyi's terminology, to investigate the meaning of Jesus Christ and the story of Scripture. There is no possibility of finding neutral ground where the real meaning of the Scripture texts can be discerned with scientific tools apart from some commitment to or against the supernatural. A descriptive phenomenology of the language of Jesus is at best only a scratching of the surface grammar and does not get at the depth grammar of Jesus, which comes only through faith in him. Moreover, "neutral" exegesis is not purely descriptive, for the intention of the interpreter to approach the Gospels without presuppositions already discloses a tacit component of commitment to critical agnosticism in its desire to get at the *real* meaning of the text apart from sharing the faith of the New Testament community.

Discovering Authorial Intent

But the meaning of the Gospels can not be so easily discovered from the outside. Presuppositionless exegesis is simply not possible, and it is naïve to think that it is. This would be my criticism of Krister Stendahl's definition of the exegetical task. Stendahl had argued in his famous and widely influential article on biblical theology that the historicocritical method underlies proper exegesis and aims to get at what the text *meant* by a purely descriptive methodology.[26] What the text means today is the task of hermeneutics. This is fundamentally wrong for two reasons. The first is that the historian's task involves hermeneutical assumptions in the very method it uses to get at what a text *meant*. To use Polanyi's term, there is a tacit component in the historicocritical approach, namely, that it is possible to recover the *Ding an sich* or meaning of a past text, and that the meaning is recoverable through the objective tools of critical research. Few evangelicals will deny that textual, historical, linguistic, literary, and sociological analysis will shed light on the setting and uses of language in the Gospels

---

26. "Biblical Theology, Contemporary," in *IDB*, vol. 1 (New York: Abingdon, 1962), pp. 419, 424.

and their tradition. But when the most preliminary stage of critical research, text criticism, is acknowledged by one of its foremost exponents, Bruce M. Metzger, to be an art as well as a science and dependent on the judgment of the text critic as he weighs probabilities,[27] we are wise to acknowledge the role of the interpreter's grid in framing the questions and designing the tools to answer them in light of a given text.

Van Til, were he doing a critique of Stendahl, would probably point to the many interpretations Stendahl infers from the Scripture texts that reveal he is not performing the purely descriptive task he has set for the New Testament scholar, but is in fact interpreting what he thinks the texts actually *meant* by what he believes they really *mean*. For example, in discussing Christology in the article, Stendahl makes it clear that the writers of the New Testament are seen, in light of a critical historical approach, to have positions that "come miles apart from one another as contradictory," and that as far as Jesus' messianic consciousness is concerned — "yes-or-no," did he think of himself of Messiah — the evidence descriptively would appear to be no:

> Those who claim a straight messianic consciousness in Jesus overlook the evidence that the messiahship in Jesus' earthly ministry has a strong futuristic note.[28]

But of course Jesus looks forward to the fulfillment of his messianic work. If, however, Stendahl is really doing descriptive exegesis, he will see, as we have seen in part 1 of my exegesis, that Jesus does claim by his very words and acts that he is consciously the Messiah. There must be something that is holding Stendahl back from the evidence, some hidden agenda that predetermines how he will describe what he thinks the text really meant, historically — not what the church thought it meant, but what it *really* meant, what the *real* Jesus, the *Ding an sich*, actually thought about himself. And when it comes to that, Ernst Käsemann is to be preferred, for he at least admits that he is giving only his personal opinion when he denies Jesus' messianic consciousness, in spite of evidence to the contrary. Stendahl's exegesis is more dangerous, however, for he actually thinks that he is scientifically and objectively

27. *A Textual Commentary on the Greek New Testament* (New York: United Bible Societies, 1975), pp. xxiv, xxviii, xxxi.

28. "Biblical Theology, Contemporary," in *IDB*, vol. 1, p. 426.

describing the actual historical "meaning" of Jesus. From my point of view as a practicing historian and exegete, I see Stendahl's description of Jesus and New Testament Christology as a contemporary redaction in terms of what Jesus Christ means to him, given his hermeneutical horizon. This is the sort of thing to which Van Til makes us sensitive. Our presuppositions *do* play a determinative role in interpreting a textual tradition like that of the Gospels. The very questions we ask of the text and the tools we devise in going about that task betray our own attitudes toward the text and the kinds of answers we will find. The hermeneutical circle is clearly operative here. Where the exegete goes in is where he comes out — unless in the process he accepts the evangelists' witness to Jesus as self-proclaimed Messiah and therefore historical as to what Jesus meant. But then the interpreter goes in a different door.

Accordingly, any attempt to avoid Gadamer's Kantian dilemma is bound to fail, apart from an orthodox view of inspired Scripture. For Stendahl, the preacher may fuse the horizons of "means" and "meant," but

> it is once more clear that we cannot pursue the study of biblical theology adequately if the two tenses are not kept apart. For the descriptive biblical theologian this is a necessity implied in his own discipline; and whether he is a believer or an agnostic, he demands respect for the descriptive task as an enterprise valid in its own right and for its own sake. For the life of the church such a consistent descriptive approach is a great and promising asset which enables the church, its teaching and preaching ministry, to be exposed to the Bible in its original intention and intensity, as an ever new challenge to thought, faith, and response.[29]

Certainly, the serious exegete is going to do his homework in biblical languages and backgrounds, which is the reason the theological seminary where I teach is one of the few which requires both Hebrew and Greek and careful exegetical preparation of all those working for the master of divinity degree. But the assumption that the descriptive biblical theologian not only can but also must keep his discipline separate from Christian faith reflects in its very framing of the task a contemporary prejudice, and militates against such a biblical critic ever really getting at the original meaning of the texts — or more accurately, the

29. *Ibid.*, p. 431.

authorial intent of the original speaker, Jesus, and the intent of the evangelists. Indeed, such a neutral and descriptive approach is impossible apart from just the opposite of Stendahl's hermeneutic; for a truly descriptive exegesis of the original meaning of a text is possible only if the exegete enters into a personal relationship with Jesus Christ and enters the story from inside, and accepts the authoritative witness of the evangelists who are also part of the hermeneutical community of faith. Only through the common faith engendered by the Holy Spirit can the exegete bridge the gap between then and now, and describe the reality of Jesus and the story about him at the level of their depth grammar.

This is precisely Van Til's point and the awesome challenge of his hermeneutic. Only in humble acceptance of God's own special interpretation of history in Jesus Christ can one properly use the tools of historical research; and then the tools that arise from the common grace of God's general revelation help elucidate the texts of the special revelation in respect to their linguistic, historical, and sociological setting. The interaction of common and special revelation is important, and is faithful to a biblical and Reformation view of Scripture. The point of entry into the hermeneutical circle, however, is special revelation through a personal relationship with Jesus Christ and a humble obedience to the inspired text of Scripture. In this way, and only in this way, can the original authorial intent of Jesus and the evangelists be discovered. The dualistic approach of Stendahl's hermeneutic will lead not to the depth grammar of the Gospels but only to the imaging of the interpreter's own face in the well of history.

This criticism of Stendahl's hermeneutic is all the more ironic in view of the fact that he sees the work of the Spirit in the formation of the canon, and indeed in the gift of prophetic and inspired teaching down to our own day.[30] But that openness of the canon also endangers its validity in interpretation, since subjectivity and relativity may now be more the rule than the exception. It is perhaps this problem of hermeneutical relativism that forces Stendahl to limit the Spirit's inspiration to the realm of theological interpretation rather than to ensure the infallibility of the evangelists' witness. Whatever has prompted him to adapt his hermeneutic of "meant" and "means," he has laid out an unrealizable task for the exegete; for not only is it impossible to get at the deep meaning of Jesus Christ neutrally by critical tools of the human

30. *Ibid.*, p. 429.

mind, but also, because of the notion of an open canon, it is impossible to get at the normative interpretation of the New Testament canon itself, since it is not really normative if subject to continual revision. Hence, it would be fair to say that Stendahl's belief that we can get at the original meaning of a text is valid, but not in the way that he thinks. The search for the real meaning of facts in the created world of nature and history can be achieved only by the aid of God's own "canonical" interpretation of those facts. That requires the exegete to defer to the authoritative witness of Scripture. Otherwise, the autonomous critic will demand the right to give an authoritative statement on what the text actually meant; but it will really be only what the text means to him. For without the Holy Spirit as guarantor of past meaning there can be no sure knowledge of the past. There can be only a present subjective meaning of the "past" that is subject to change. And that, of course, is the state of contemporary liberal theology; it is constantly shifting ground. Kant was right if the critic rejects the authoritative canonical Scripture. He can never know the meaning of anything as it is in itself, not even contemporary persons or events, let alone persons and events of the past. But if canonical Scripture is accepted as authoritative, then Van Til is correct: God's self-disclosure in inspired Scripture and in Jesus Christ is his own interpretation of the deep grammar of nature, history, and of human existence. By the common grace of God's general revelation in creation, there are many overlappings of knowledge on the level of surface grammar (Ps. 19:1–6; Matt. 5:45; Rom. 1:19–20) which allow believer and agnostic to agree on a considerable body of scientific, linguistic, social, and even religious data, for we share a common created world. But though we may agree on surface meanings, the deep and ultimate meanings are spiritually discerned (I Cor. 2:6–16). Here it is crucial to get our presuppositions out in the open, for these have to do with the ultimate meaning of the phenomena.

A similar but less severe critique of the Stendahl hermeneutic comes from the hand of Brevard S. Childs, whose *Biblical Theology in Crisis* regrets the demise of biblical theology and criticizes the Uppsala University school, which interpreted the exegetical task as primarily historical and descriptive and distinct from later theological reflections.[31] Childs maintains that this approach, widely disseminated by Anton

31. (Philadelphia: Westminster, 1970), pp. 26, 79, 82, 141.

Fridrichsen et al. in *The Root of the Vine: Essays in Biblical Theology* (1953), and by Stendahl's article, has abetted the growing polarity between biblical studies and dogmatic theology. He calls for a new wedding of the two areas, acknowledging that the overemphasis on the critical approach has eclipsed the theological, but that the heart of the interpretative task is theological:

> The historical method is an inadequate method for studying the Bible as the Scriptures of the church because it does not work from the needed context. It is not capable of raising or addressing the full range of questions which must be asked.[32]

With this criticism I would certainly agree, as would Van Til. But observe what Childs proceeds to do to rectify the situation with his canon criticism:

> Surely some will object to this line of argument by asserting that the exegete's only task is to understand what the Biblical text meant, and that the critical methodology is alone capable of doing this correctly. The historical reading is exegesis: everything else is "eisegesis." Our response to this type of objection is by now familiar. First, what the text "meant" is determined in large measure by its relation to the one to whom it is directed. While it remains an essential part of Biblical exegesis to establish a text's function in its original context(s), the usual corollary that the original function is alone normative does not follow. Secondly, the question of what the text now means cannot be dismissed as a purely subjective enterprise suitable only to private devotion and homiletics. When seen from the context of the canon both the question of what the text meant and what it means are inseparably linked and both belong to the Bible as Scripture. To the extent that the use of the critical method sets up an iron curtain between the past and the present, it is an inadequate method for studying the Bible as the church's Scripture.[33]

Certainly I would agree with Childs that a new look at biblical theology is necessary and that the exegete has a responsibility to interpret the Bible as the Scripture of the church and to develop rigorous exegetical skills that are commensurate to this task.[34] But what he pro-

---

32. *Biblical Theology in Crisis*, p. 141.
33. *Ibid.*, pp. 141–142.
34. *Ibid.*, p. 143.

poses is really Barthian, as was observed by a liberal Old Testament scholar in conversation with me several years ago. Childs continues to do typical form criticism of the text, then moves to canon criticism.[35] He is still moving in the realm of two compartments, for he tries to determine what the text originally meant by traditional critical methodology, and then downplays that original function as alone being normative. Subsequent functions of meaning play an equally important role along with the original function. So what one finds here hermeneutically is a pluralistic functionalism in terms of the church's ongoing interpretation of biblical meaning. Childs's emphasis on the importance of canon is commendable, but he has not addressed two serious questions. First, he has not really allowed the authoritative witness of the original biblical writers to inform his use of form-critical methodology. And second, a corollary, he has not allowed the authorial intent of the original speaker or writer to set the definitive meaning of a text. That is why he places considerable emphasis on the history of interpretation: "There is a sense in which the text is in as much movement as the reader." Thus the interpreter gains a better understanding of what each person brings to his interpretation, and thereby sees the variety of possibilities within a text.[36]

The problem with this hermeneutic is that it brings theology and exegesis together at the wrong point. I like Childs's insistence that the two go together and are indeed inseparable. However, he does not identify the canonical authority of Scripture with the inerrant truth-claims of its writers, but with the functional process of the Spirit in the ongoing church. The doctrine of inerrancy is rejected because, in his view, it defines the medium apart from the canonical context.[37] But what does this mean, except that canonical formation is located in a process of changing contexts? For Childs, neither Jesus nor the evangelists nor the apostolic witnesses give us an authoritative and reliable body of factual truth about God, creation, and salvation. Rather, the process of critical reinterpretation by such differing witnesses as Paul, Luke, or John provides a warrant for later development, down to our own time.

35. See *The Book of Exodus: A Critical, Theological Commentary*, Old Testament Library (Philadelphia: Westminster, 1974); *Introduction to the Old Testament As Scripture* (Philadelphia: Fortress, 1979).

36. *Biblical Theology in Crisis*, p. 145.

37. *Ibid.*, p. 104.

Now the appeal to the canon does not restrict the interpreter to any one particular exegetical method. Obviously, the tools of interpretation will change and vary according to each age. Certainly the historicocritical approach has become a hallmark of the modern period, and is an impressive contribution, above all, of modern Protestant scholarship. But the issue at stake is the context for doing one's exegesis. By taking seriously the canon, one confesses along with the church the unique function that these writings have had in its life and faith as Sacred Scripture. Then each new generation of interpreters seeks to be faithful in searching these Scriptures for renewed illumination while exploiting to the fullest the best tools available for opening the texts. Ultimately, to stand within the tradition of the church is a stance not made in the spirit of dogmatic restriction of the revelation of God, but in joyful wonder and even surprise as the Scripture becomes the bread of life for another generation.[38]

This summary statement sounds good on the surface, but I am sure Van Til would find it, as I do, a fuzzy definition of canon and exegesis, for it qualifies the authority of the original meaning of Jesus and his witnesses by appeal to subsequent reinterpretation in the church. The final court of appeal for the meaning of Scripture is the autonomous interpreter; there is no dogmatic or authoritative restriction of the revelation of God, which continues into the present as each new generation offers up its different interpretative tools and insights.

In what sense can this pluralistic and processive hermeneutic be faithful to the authorial intent of the original authors of Scripture? This is left undefined. But I might suggest that the attempt to renew a basically neoorthodox view of Scripture will be no more successful than the earlier short-lived biblical theology of the post-World-War-II period. The movement is unclear about its convictions: it wants to use orthodox theological language while carrying on exegetical tasks that reflect a nineteenth-century confidence in historical criticism. Only an orthodox approach to Scripture's own claims to authority and a radical renovation of historicocritical assumptions in light of scriptural presuppositions will give the interpreter a sure foundation for exegesis that is not relativistic.

On this essential matter Carl F. H. Henry would agree with Van Til when he observes that what the writers of Scriptures say about them-

38. *Ibid.*, pp. 106ff.

selves and their work is an important aspect of the phenomena of Scripture, and that historical criticism shows a deep-seated prejudice when it rejects the self-acclaimed authority of the scriptural canon. Scripture claims the normative authority of God's mighty acts and revealed Word in Jesus as attested by his chosen evangelists and apostles. Hence, "why should not the Bible itself be the presupposition of historical criticism of its content? On what basis will a biblical scholar choose alternative presuppositions?"[39] Affirming the commitment of evangelical theology to a proper historical criticism (for historical criticism is never neutral), Henry appeals to the presupposition of the Scriptures themselves: "Biblical events acquire their meaning from the divinely inspired Scriptures; since there could be no meaning of events without the events, the inspired record carries its own intrinsic testimony to the factuality of those events."[40]

This is essentially a Van Tilian position on the impossibility of a presuppositionless biblical criticism, and it is what lies at the heart of evangelical exegesis, whether an individual evangelical exegete is aware of it or not. What distinguishes this kind of biblical interpretation is its realism, in squarely facing the fact that no exegesis — indeed, no interpretation of any datum — is without its tacit component of belief in a controlling methodology; and that the controlling methodology — the heuristic — is a fidelity to the intrinsic claims of Scripture itself, not an autonomous heuristic that is alien to biblical faith. Only in this way is Jesus' gracious ministry to a fallen world discovered anew in each generation and proclaimed with saving power.

---

39. Carl F. H. Henry, *God, Revelation and Authority: God Who Speaks and Shows*, vol. 4 (Waco: Word, 1979), p. 401.

40. *Ibid.*, p. 403.

Appendix

Observations on *Matthew*

A Commentary on His Literary and Theological Art[1]

The enthusiastic recommendation of this volume by F. F. Bruce as a courageous and fresh presentation of the story of Jesus is sufficient notice that evangelical readers will need to take the study seriously. "It is indeed," Bruce writes, "an epoch-making book in the evangelical study of the New Testament" (from the dust jacket). Perhaps no recent large-scale work on the Gospels illustrates so dramatically the penalties of uncontrolled redactionalism as does this volume of 652 pages. It is not an expository commentary in the traditional sense, designed for homiletical purposes, but a "close reading" of Matthew's diction that attempts to highlight the literary and theological creativity of Matthew as he weaves historical data together with his own imagination and creates a historical novel about the meaning of Jesus Christ.

Something on the order of this monumental study was bound to come sooner or later, considering the fact that a number of New Testament scholars of evangelical confession have hinted at going all the way with redaction criticism, convinced that a doctrine of inspiration covers the canonical finished product and indeed encourages complete honesty and integrity in describing the phenomena of the text. One can only gasp, however, at how deeply Gundry has cut as he performs a painful surgical operation on the first Gospel.

Gundry is correct about a number of things. As I have indicated in the previous pages, there are hard data in the Gospels that suggest a freedom on the part of the evangelists in quoting Old Testament texts and in describing and adapting Jesus' words and works. These I have called the hard facts with which the New Testament exegete has to deal (pp. 127–128). As I shall point out, however, Gundry runs into serious problems when he tries to interpret those hard facts, and especially when, with a confidence I cannot share, he assigns the soft facts to Matthew's inspired imagination. But at the very least his book is valuable for its exhaustive delineation of Matthew's distinctive diction in comparison with that of Mark and Luke. Gundry is also correct, I am convinced and as I have already suggested (pp. 93, 100), in dating Matthew, along with Mark and Luke, in the early sixties and assigning the first

1. By Robert H. Gundry (Grand Rapids: Eerdmans, 1982).

Gospel to Matthew the disciple and apostle, an eyewitness of Jesus' ministry.[2] So far the agreements.

It is Gundry's methodology that appears to me to be lacking scientific control as he sets out to negotiate his way around the hard and soft facts of Matthew's distinctive style. Nowhere in the entire volume does he indicate any sense of the importance of Jesus' role as the original creator of Matthew's story line. As I have insisted in my own study, redaction criticism has so far demonstrated little sensitivity to the fact that the spoken and acted language of a person discloses his intentionality in ordinary discourse, and that this is crucial in establishing the range of Jesus' diction and its generative effect on the evangelists before we can begin to talk about their creativity. Otherwise there are no controls on the extent to which redactional trajectories can be assigned to the minds of the evangelists. Only occasionally does Gundry hint that behind Matthew's free-swinging redaction as a historical novelist there is a dominical tradition originating from Jesus, but he never reveals what this tradition is in any systematic fashion, nor does he delineate the criteria by which the supposedly authentic dominical words of Jesus might be separated from Matthew's imaginative story line. This is a crucial and fatal flaw in his methodology, for there is no control that I can see being exercised over the application of redactional theory. The only criterion seems to be that wherever Matthew varies from Mark (or occasionally Luke) there is occasion to assert that Matthew has adapted, radically modified, or created out of whole cloth a saying or an episode in Jesus' ministry. With little sense of the difference between hard facts and soft facts (between the obvious and not so obvious), the commentary is like a skiier racing out of control down a rock-strewn mountainside. The irony of this is that a neo-Bultmannian such as Norman Perrin, whom I have critiqued at length for his failure to follow through consistently with his phenomenology, appears to be a defender of orthodoxy in contrast to the total absence in this study of solid criteria by which to identify the authentic diction of Jesus and the created diction of Matthew, other than that Matthew happens to vary in his account from Mark and Luke.

Surely this sort of analysis of gospel language must be taken to task. It is another example of how a modern fascination with language has apotheosized diction and contracted Jesus as speaker out of the story. Gundry is not really interested in what Jesus said and did, but in what he believes Matthew has made him say and do in light of the supposed theological viewpoint of Matthew and the needs of his audience. The commentary is really a psychohistorical study of Matthew rather than an attempt to see how Matthew was concerned (as I am sure he was concerned) to present a deeply accurate portrayal of the Messiah who had discipled him. In Gundry's study, however, Jesus appears as little more (if the reader will excuse the expression from

2. *Ibid.,* pp. 599–622.

analytic philosophy) than the ghost in the machine. The Gospel of Matthew is no longer about Jesus; it is about Matthew. It is not a Gospel transparent to Jesus, but a text the critic does something with.

These general remarks prompt me to make a further critique of the commentary along the lines of my own study.

First, in order for redactional studies of the Gospels to have integrity they must first establish what Jesus himself proclaimed about himself. There must be guidelines. Perrin does this carefully with his inherited criterion of dissimilarity, which at least gives us a minimal core of authentic sayings that defines in barest terms the dominical tradition Jesus establishes. Gundry has given us no systematic clues as to what he believes the dominical tradition is. Now as soon as the critic does establish what he thinks Jesus' authentic sayings are, I want to analyze them carefully as to what sort of person would use such language. As the reader has noted if he or she has worked through my study, Perrin and his school run into trouble when the core sayings are scrutinized according to the analytical questions of a phenomenology of persons, for the core sayings turn out to be so radical that they can only imply an intentional Jesus who could also have uttered the discarded explicit christological sayings. I suspect, in reading Gundry, that he would reject some of the sayings Perrin accepts as authentic. But then I want to know by what scientific criteria he would arrive at a dominical core. He must have this core in hand if he is going to be certain that a "soft-fact" passage has been created by Matthew. Surely the only criterion cannot be simply Matthew's variations from Mark and Luke, for he cannot assume that Jesus spoke only once on each subject in only one form of diction. It is more likely the case that many if not all of the soft facts with their variations in diction were generated by Jesus' own original and creative mind. How does one know that they were not? And why would one assume that they were not?

If Gundry replies (as he does) that conservative Protestants have bent over backward to harmonize and to attribute differences in accounts to alternative translations from Hebrew or Aramaic, to paraphrastic activity by the evangelists, complementary reports, Jesus' own repetition of sayings and deeds, and to topical rather than chronological arrangements, but that these must be used with discretion,[3] my rejoinder would be that one must also use the redactional method with discretion. If one were to count up the total number of deliberate changes Gundry ascribes to the creative mind of Matthew, the sum would be shocking even to some nonevangelicals. From the birth narratives to those about the death and resurrection of Jesus, the story line has been so thoroughly edited and recast that quite simply the reader does not know what is going on; he has no idea as to what really happened and what is the creation of Matthew's own mind. But this emotional reaction aside for the moment, I want to know how Gundry can make good on his confident

3. *Ibid*., p. 626.

assertion that all the soft facts are edited facts? The criteria for deciding are simply not stated in any systematic or scientific fashion.

My first criticism of his study, then, is that, like James Dunn in his *Christology in the Making*, Gundry has started too far down the line, with Matthew rather than with Jesus. Redactional studies have got to be clear and convincing about what is actually redacted, and one cannot be clear and convincing unless there is a point of reference: What did Jesus himself say and do? What is the standard by which the critic can be sure he is describing legitimate redaction and not just expressing his own imagination? If it is objected that my desire to establish Jesus' dominical tradition sets up a canon within the canon while the redactionist takes the finished Gospel "as it is," I would ask, "How then is it? Is it faithful to Jesus' ministry, historically speaking, or is it largely semihistorical redaction?" One cannot beg the question by appealing to the Gospel as it is. The question is how the phenomenon of the Gospel came to be and what role its principal figure, Jesus, played in its appearance. On the basis of my own study, I honestly feel that Gundry's commentary is largely in error because it essentially contracts Jesus out of the story and shifts the focus of attention to Matthew as creative genius rather than Jesus. This was not, as I read his Gospel, the intention of Matthew.

Second, I find the commentary's persistent contrast of Matthew and Mark a questionable methodology on which to build such a thoroughgoing redactional program. The project is based on a series of assumptions: that Matthew the apostle actually wrote the Gospel (with which I concur); that the Gospel is to be dated prior to A.D. 63 (again, a reasonable guess); that Papias' remarks about Mark and Matthew (interpreted by Eusebius, *H. E.* 3:39.1–16) are earlier than usually thought and reflect an even earlier tradition going back to the apostle John;[4] that this affords us apostolic evidence that Matthew wrote his Gospel for the precise purpose of bringing order out of the chaos of Mark (and is therefore early evidence that Mark wrote his Gospel first). This is certainly a questionable interpretation of a difficult passage, but it does serve Gundry's hypothesis that Matthew's primary intention was radically to redo Mark.

Gundry anticipates two rejoinders.[5] Would Matthew, an apostle and eyewitness, have used the Gospel of a nonapostle, Mark? Yes, he says, since according to Papias (Eusebius 3:39.15) Mark wrote down Peter's reminiscences. But would Matthew have borrowed so extensively? Gundry replies that our modern antipathy toward plagiarism was not shared by antiquity. But I would observe that this argument cuts both ways. Perhaps moderns (especially professors) are so suspicious when they see verbal similarities that they automatically suspect borrowing. It is alternatively possible, however, that all four Gospels were written concurrently from common as well as complemen-

4. *Ibid.*, pp. 609–620.
5. *Ibid.*, pp. 621–622.

tary apostolic perspectives and that this may account for agreements and varieties in style. The point is that hypotheses about the origins of the Gospels are very speculative, and the critic must be careful not to stake too much on their comparison. Gundry's heavy reliance on the hypothesis that Mark must be first and that Matthew necessarily modifies Mark makes me even more suspicious that the last word has not yet been spoken on the so-called synoptic problem.

In replying to the second rejoinder (would Matthew, an apostolic eyewitness, have edited Mark and other sources so extensively?), Gundry asks us to widen our horizons and appreciate the fact that Plato and Hellenistic culture generally were fond of writing semihistorically, as were the Jewish authors of midrashic and haggidic literature.[6] But surely this sociological argument, so popular today in New Testament circles, could be used to explain away everything distinctive in the New Testament, including the Christian belief in the divine inspiration of Scripture, to which Gundry also holds. Plato also believed in the divine state of *mania* in which philosophy, song, epic, and verse were inspired by the Muses. Are the Gospels, then, simply variations on themes common to comparative religions? The evangelical exegete has to be very careful that a fascination with sociological backgrounds does not set the agenda for the interpretation of the New Testament. As I know well, this is a current attraction in christological studies. Few scholars are interested in starting their Christology with Jesus. Most want to work from Jewish and Hellenistic backgrounds, perhaps because the study of backgrounds affords a limitless, relatively safe, and academically respectable field for doing history, objectively free from doctrinal commitments.

Accordingly, I find Gundry's heuristic for justifying his interpretation of Matthew as a historical novelist less than convincing and based on a set of risky commitments. I think his own questions are utimately damaging to the project. Assuming (I think correctly) that Matthew the apostolic eyewitness wrote the Gospel bearing his name, it is inconceivable to me that he would have relied so extensively on Mark's account, and would so radically have altered his Gospel. The question is a serious one and concerns Matthew's own authorial intent. Has Gundry read it properly, as he thinks,[7] or has he committed the intentional fallacy, the fallacy of misplaced concreteness? I think there can be little doubt on further study and reflection that the latter is the case, for any interpreter of a Gospel who excludes a primary focus on the protagonist of the story line — Jesus himself — is bound to miss the point of the story.

This leads to a third observation that a wide spectrum of evangelical believers will understand in this debate, including those with very little formal education who nonetheless have a deep and mature experience of Jesus as

6. *Ibid*.
7. *Ibid*., pp. 129ff.

Savior and Lord. It is the issue C. S. Lewis and J. R. R. Tolkien bring into focus when they consider how one reads a great piece of work like the first Gospel. How good a reader is the critic? How powerfully is he grasped by the spell of the story? Does he taste the soup, or does he only analyze its ingredients? I suspect that a clue to the improper reading that lies behind this commentary lies in the introductory section entitled "The Theology of Matthew,"[8] where Gundry gives pride of place to the problem of the mixed church to which Matthew is writing. This mixture of true and false disciples in the church determines Matthew's entire approach, Gundry feels, and explains the evangelist's creation of a Jesus whose law and authority are awe-inspiring. In other words, the historical setting of the early church conditions what Matthew pragmatically creates to meet a historical need. The first Gospel is, accordingly, an instance of apostolic opportunism, or if that is too strong a word, adaptation, not an authentic presentation of the words and works of the incarnate Jesus. Nowhere in this programmatic section on the theology of Matthew is it even hinted that Jesus himself anticipated the problem of a mixed church and spoke authoritatively and prophetically on the subject. Indeed, nowhere is it stated that Jesus the incarnate Messiah is of central importance of Matthew. Rather, at the very beginning of the commentary the a priori assumption is made that Jesus will not be given the benefit of a doubt as the original and creative speaker behind Matthew's diction. The spell is broken (it was for me) and the power of the first Gospel lost in a reading that does not really listen to the story, for the story is about Jesus, not Matthew and the problems of the early church retrojected upon the life setting of Jesus. Matthew, I think, would be aghast that he had got himself in the way of the central figure in the story.

This brings me to a fourth critique and the warnings of I. T. Ramsey, Michael Polanyi, and Cornelius Van Til. Gundry wants to explain every jot and tittle of Matthew's peculiar diction and assign it to the creative imagination of the evangelist. Ramsey reminds us of the importance of accepting the logically odd in religious discourse without trying to reduce it to something else, while Polanyi points out that we know more than we can tell and ought not to venture on projects that try to tell everything. The tacit component of faith in Jesus Christ who confronts and addresses the believer in the story line of the text is vitally important and must be preserved within the conviviality of the believing community. The reason that evangelical readers of this commentary are warmly exercised by its tendentious ascription of every peculiar dictional phrase to Matthew's editing is that it blurs the mind of Matthew with the distinctive Christian belief in the incarnation, that here in Jesus, embodied in human flesh, God is speaking and acting. One simply does not have a sense of the story line, of who the real Jesus is as contrasted

8. *Ibid.*, pp. 5–11.

with the redacted Jesus. The spell is broken. As Van Til would observe, a peculiar set of presuppositions is at work here.

But it really does not matter, Gundry informs us, because whether the historical Jesus made a particular statement or Matthew did, it is all authoritative and canonical because "the Spirit of Christ directed the editing."[9] Indeed, all evangelicals believe that the Spirit of Christ directed the writing of the Gospels and the formation of the canon. It is part of our fiduciary commitment to trust God's Word. But the issue before us (my fifth and last point) is not whether Matthew is wholly inspired but whether his Gospel is inspired as the commentary has described that inspiration. Is there not here a docetic tendency[10] like the neo-Gnosticism in Bultmannianism that downplays the uniqueness of the diction of God incarnate in Jesus in favor of Christ incarnate in the evangelist? But can Gundry really sustain the integrity of biblical inerrancy by such an appeal to the final canonical composition? If the whole text, including the editing, is inspired by the risen Christ, what would possibly compel the critic to go to the trouble of trying to distinguish Matthew's peculiar diction from that of Jesus? If, as Gundry seems to believe, the early church made no distinction between the words of the historical Jesus and the risen Christ, why should we? Indeed, how could we?

Of course, if Gundry and other redactionists could make a convincing case that the evangelists (functioning as early Christian prophets) were actually inspired to utter new sayings of Jesus and to create new episodes in his earthly ministry, then we could accept this situation as the way the Holy Spirit worked, though we could never be certain of the historical basis of our faith. But as I have argued in my study, there is little scientific evidence for so radical a hermeneutic. It is legitimate to talk about the authorial intent of the evangelists and to be reasonably confident that they are exercising their inspired paraphrastic prerogatives in regard to the obvious hard facts of the Gospels. But the soft facts — Jesus' explicitly Christological words and works — do not lend themselves to a simple "when in doubt, redact." As I said in my preface, we need to go back to the christological drawing board and to the intentionality of Jesus before we can even begin to think about readaction criticism on such a scale.

9. *Ibid.*, p. 640.
10. Cf. *ibid.*, p. 638.

Subject Index

Author Index

Scripture Index

259